A
SOLDIER
AGAINST ALL
ODDS

A Memoir
by
LT. COL. JASON PIKE

First published in 2022
Published by **jasonpike.org**

Dedicated to
Dennis Earl Pike
With special dedication to
Nancy Carol Pike
and
Beverly and *Chantel Pike*

TESTIMONIAL

I was raised up by a man with the heart of a Viking but the simple faith of a child. The larger-than-life, number-one influence on me in my life is Dennis Earl Pike, my dad.

WRITING THIS MEMOIR DAMN NEAR KILLED ME! In February 2021, I was admitted to intensive care at the Stone Oak Methodist Hospital in San Antonio, Texas, suffering from blood clots in my lungs and legs. An off-duty physician's assistant told me privately, probably outside the boundaries of formal rules, that I would likely die, and he advised me to sign a DNR or "do not resuscitate", since the death that I was facing would likely not be a comfortable one. The clots were formed as a consequence of sitting behind a computer for long hours and the stress caused by stirring the sediment of so many mixed recollections. Besides that, a bout of pneumonia further complicated the situation. Floods of memories were returning, of past issues with the law, of myself breaking many established rules, protocols and the many failures that characterized my journey, the consequences of which I faced, but also simply escaping death, just as I did more than once, most recently with that hospital visit. As the reader will come to appreciate, carrying this project to it's conclusion was a Herculean task for me. I have cried, got drunk, laughed, and gnawed my fingernails as this memoir slowly came to fruition. My feeling about it all was, if this damn book kills me then so be it, I nearly died and returned a few times during my thirty-one years in the service.

— LT. COL. JASON PIKE

ADDITIONAL REMARKS

I FIRST MET JASON PIKE in 1996 at Aberdeen Proving Ground, Maryland. At the time, Jason was a young Army captain, and he's since grown into a decorated veteran with a remarkable capacity for reflection, connection, and storytelling.

As Jason's former supervisor, we've kept in touch over the years. Jason has always invited others into his life, openly sharing the *snafus* and successes that define each season. These seasons have shaped his relationships, his vocation, and his decidedly purposeful approach toward life. In view of his academic challenges and momentous career, Jason is a soldier who continues to persevere in all areas of his life.

I was impressed, but not surprised when Jason informed me about his upcoming memoir. This book is a compelling account of persistence, tenacity, and resolve in the face of adversity. It weaves Jason's earliest moments with fast-paced tales of survival, secrets, and hard-fought successes. Collectively, the book paints the picture of a man who is both proactive and reflective: one who pushes through tough times, yet looks back so that others might learn from his most vulnerable moments.

In these moments, failure is never a consideration. Instead, Jason derives meaning from every situation, whether he's recounting a minor decision or a near-death experience. With this mindset, Jason accomplished thirty-one years of military service, beginning as a seventeen-year-old Army National Guard Private and retiring as an Army Lieutenant Colonel.

Led by Jason's humorous, action-packed narration, readers will race through thirty-one years in a matter of hours. When they close the book, they'll have a lasting understanding of what it means to become our best selves – and to do so against all odds.

— DOCTOR EDWARD EVANS

J ASON PIKE IS MANY THINGS, but I know him best as a friend – and one of the most honest, industrious people in my life. I served alongside Jason in the Army for more than 10 years; since retiring, we've traveled, grown, and navigated life together. Wherever Jason goes, and whatever he's doing, he's consistently himself: a man who grew up in Georgia and South Carolina, and managed to land in Korea, El Salvador, Afghanistan, and several other countries as a member of the U.S. Army.

As both a friend and supervisor, I've walked alongside Jason through some of his greatest challenges. I'm consistently in awe of his willingness to share his story – failures and fiascos included – for the benefit of others. In each place and season of his life, Jason approaches his work, family, and personal projects with the utmost care and focus. His memoir is an amusing, fast-paced testament to his integrity as a human, his talent as a storyteller, and his commitment as a father, husband, and friend.

— COLONEL MITCHELL MEYERS, U.S Army

FROM HUMBLE BEGINNINGS to an esteemed military career, the story of Lieutenant Colonel Jason Pike is as awe-inspiring as the man himself. In his powerful memoir, the decorated combat veteran shares tales of adventure, success, and failure – the totality of which could fill several lifetimes.

It is rare to meet an officer as candid as Lt. Col. Pike, who fearlessly reflects on his life and career in uniform. On every page, he selflessly places his life on display so that others might learn from his experiences, ranging from the greatest highs to unimaginable setbacks. In the face of significant learning challenges, Pike defies the odds and graduates from Clemson University. As an officer, he receives countless military awards and decorations, and is invited to join the 10th Special Forces Group in 1992.

Pike's journey is equally defined by success and struggle. Amid army investigations, arrests, infighting, and near-death experiences, Pike pushes onward with a stunning refusal to quit. His grit, resilience, and remarkable vulnerability shine through every sentence, providing light and hope to readers in any season of life.

— **Col. JACK WEDAM**, USA, Retired

I AM FORTUNATE TO KNOW TWO SIDES of the Pike family: Lieutenant Colonel Jason Pike and his father, Dennis Pike. I worked alongside Dennis Pike in Spartanburg, South Carolina at Univar Chemicals, and later supervised his son, Jason, when he was a young lieutenant in the South Carolina National Guard. Jason's father could roll up his sleeves and make chemical sales against all expectations, which earned him the nickname "Used Car Pike." When I later supervised Jason, I quickly realized that both Pikes share an unusual capacity for persevering – and ultimately, succeeding – against all odds. In many ways, Jason's memoir is a conversation with his father. Throughout Jason's recollections of success, failure, and adventure, Dennis' influence is pervasive: in both words and actions, Jason pays tribute to his father's diligent, unflappable spirit. As someone who knew both men, I know that Jason has accomplished an extraordinary task by condensing the lessons of father and son in one, powerful book. This book is not merely a compilation of extraordinary events, but a reflection on the people that make us, shape us, and move us to share the story of our lives.

— MAJOR GENERAL RETIRED DARWIN SIMPSON, USA, Retired

AS A SECTION LEADER in the Army National Guard, I led Private Pike in the early days of his military career. At times, he was difficult to reach, but I believed in his potential and worked him hard. Pike accepted challenges quietly, never disclosing any personal struggles or a hint of resistance.

Years later, in the process of reconnecting with Pike and learning more about his book, I've discovered two things: first that he's faced enough adversity to fill two memoirs, and second that he's a soldier in all areas of his life, despite living with a learning disability and facing the setbacks that now fill his memoir. With this book in my hands, I have a much clearer vision of Jason Pike: a remarkable man who worked his way through college, earned two master's degrees, and retired from the Army with illustrious honors. Through unfailing belief in himself, Pike has acquired the belief and esteem of others. It's an adventure and an honor to read his story.

— SGT. FIRST CLASS MARK STEVENSON, Army National Guard, Retired

FOREWORD

I FIRST MET JASON PIKE THROUGH A PROGRAM conceived by both my colleague Kirk Hansen and me in 2017 through Spartanburg Methodist College, where we continue to teach history. We began collecting oral histories from veterans associated with Spartanburg County in the summer of that year. The Herald Journal and WSPA Channel 7 graciously disseminated a call for volunteers who might share their stories so we could honor the experiences and sacrifices of the local men and women who served in the military. It was through this program that I met Lieutenant Colonel Jason Pike, who emailed us to participate about a week after the news regarding the Hub City Veterans Project launched. Little did I realize that Jason would become not only a key to the project's success but also a close friend and inspiration in my own life.

When Jason's message hit my inbox, I read over the enclosed note, then opened the email's attachments. There, I found a series of pictures from Jason's career. Two stood out. In the first he stood with a group of Special Forces soldiers dressed in cold-weather gear, the photo taken, maybe, somewhere in Canada on an operation. There's little he is allowed to say about that particular op, and its mystery confounds me. I remember saying out loud, "This man has seen some serious stuff." The second photo depicted a closeup in his officer uniform, rows of medals gleaming in the light. He sported no hair on his face or head as both were shaven smooth. He had piercing blue eyes that reminded me of a Tom Clancy character, and his hardline jaw asserted strength and power. I was looking at one of the Army's finest. I thought that this man was immune to failure, and the chiseled seriousness on his face portrayed a similar immunity to humor. After meeting him, I realized that looks can be deceiving. Jason exuded humility and lived to serve others. His humor engaged gut-wrenching laughter, but more importantly his story was one of unwavering courage and overcoming immense adversity.

Traveling from his residence in San Antonio, Texas, where Jason now calls home, he arrived in shorts, a tee-shirt, and sneakers. South Carolina's summer gave us brutal heat and humidity, but the college had given us a working air conditioning system. He brought with him a series of notes that organized his life into a timeline to make sure we covered specific topics. We sat at a small, round table in the faculty lounge of Walker Hall. Despite a small break for a quick lunch, we talked for over six hours. Luckily, the interview occurred pre-COVID, and masks were not required. I imagine the expressions of shock and awe from Kirk and myself were quite funny for Jason. His story is powerful, which is easy to say, but experiencing it is not. While this book encapsulates his experiences, excellently written by Jason and assisted by Peter Baxter, I often feel words cannot capture what he has accomplished considering the adversity he has faced. Much of it is unbelievable. Some of it is strange. All of it is encouraging.

His story began in grade school at the age of 7, when he and his parents learned of his severe learning disability. They were told Jason never would succeed. According to his teachers, he was doomed to fail. I like to think that if most of us heard a guarantee of a detrimental future from those who are supposed to inspire us to greatness, we immediately would quit and relegate ourselves to whatever terrible prospects might occur. Not Jason. Instead, he used that moment to change his life. He worked incredibly hard, determined to give those teachers the proverbial (and literal) middle finger.

Jason later enrolled at Spartanburg Methodist College in 1984 and joined its ROTC program. He secretly wanted a commission to join the military as a career and become an officer. He began to develop strategies to succeed in college, and he realized that he would, as the old military adage goes, "improvise, adapt, and overcome." I once heard a friend state that a person does not understand how to succeed once without failing at a least a dozen times. Often, through no fault of his own—although I will admit Jason has done some fairly crazy and adventurous things in his life—he faced brutal failures growing up, academically, and especially in the military. Each time, he developed personal strategies and tactics to succeed but also did so with exceptionalism. His teachers told him he was doomed to failure, yet he achieved a bachelor's degree and two master's degrees. Drill sergeants claimed he would fail in the military, yet he reached the rank of Lieutenant Colonel. People told him he would lack accomplishments in his life, but Jason has become one of the most financially successful individuals I have met through sheer determination, self-learning, and an iron will to succeed. Further, he received the Bronze Star, Legion of Merit, and Expert Field Medical Badge, all three notoriously difficult earn in the military.

Despite these facts, Jason refuses to brag, refuses to portray any sort of pretentiousness, and refuses to call himself a hero. "The heroes are the ones, who didn't come home," he told us. "Now, let me tell you about another time I managed not to die by doing something stupid." Indeed, the mental image of Jason attempting to escape from a hole filled with animal feces in South Korea, his electrocution in the doorway of an airplane, running from police helicopter after burning trash illegally, nearly breaking his legs after a faulty parachute jump, and being stabbed in ROTC are just a few Pike stories that will endure for me.

Jason's story is one of overcoming adversity, a tale of an average person who overcame and enjoyed great success. It comes with glowing achievement but balances with numerous wounds suffered through a hard life and long military service. He walks this path with great strides, a smile on his face and beer in hand. Regardless of what he has experienced for good or ill, Jason's jovial sense of humor and desire to teach others to believe in oneself persists. This is the ship Jason sails, and his father Dennis Pike serves as its anchor.

Losing a parent represents one of hardest experiences a person will face in their lives. From youth, Jason's father became the capstone upon which he built his life. A Soldier Against All Odds is as much about Dennis as it is Jason. I find myself contemplating Jason's story and final moments with his father as they remind me of my own. I feel like our destinies crossed at an important moment for both of us. Jason was ready to tell his story, and I needed to hear it before my own father became ill and passed away at a time when I personally felt defeated by professional failures. When the moment came for me to face those adversities, Jason was there through it all, sending text messages each day and calling to talk. He had been through it before. He knew how to survive. For that, I am eternally grateful. It is in Jason's story that I learned, and you the reader should learn, more than a lesson about overcoming. Rather, Jason's story is about healing from loss, facing hopelessness, and emerging from the other side. Here lies perhaps the most intriguing and powerful lesson from Jason Pike. Jason does not argue that time heals wounds. Jason teaches us how to overcome while being proud of the scars we have. They stick with us as reminders of who we are, what we faced, and how we survived. Jason has received many scars. He is prouder of them than the accolades he has earned. Jason also refuses to let wounds fester. He is a man who constantly moves forward.

Today, Jason participates in amazing activities. He travels, spends time with family, and engages other veterans who have post traumatic stress. I am lucky to talk with Jason a lot. We discuss everything from pandemics to politics, crazy things he has done to ways we rear our daughters. Every few months I receive a picture of him surfing somewhere with a strange grin upon his face. Getting older has failed to slow him down. You will find early in the book that Jason nearly died from blood clots during 2021. Somehow, I believe he told death itself to go to Hell. That is the Jason Pike I know. I choose to have few friends, and I am fortunate to call Jason one of them. I hope you too will enjoy his tale about life and all it can throw at a person. Certainly, my life has become richer for knowing him and hearing his story, one of humor, sadness, and the strength. Like the phoenix of Greek mythology, when faced with insurmountable odds, Jason rose from ashes, stronger and more determined, time and time again, to surmount them.

— **DR. COLE CHEEK**, Professor of History and Anthropology, Spartanburg Methodist College, January 2022

ACKNOWLEDGEMENTS

To all my enlisted soldiers and noncommissioned officers, you know who you are…

Major General Darwin Simpson, Retired, National Guard leader and friend of the family

Fred Pike, for stories and history of my dad

Cora Pike, for stories of my dad

Sgt. First Class Mark Stevenson, Retired, for brutal honesty and leadership when I was enlisted in the National Guard

Diane Cole, for history on my dad and mom's death and family dynamics

Ralph and Mary McClain, on input on my dad's life

Sgt. Harry C. Moore, Retired for friendship, details of Basic Training, and my criminal correction story

Dr. Edward Evans, for excellent leadership in Maryland

Sgt. Maj. Sam Oak, USA, Retired, for being a great leader and helping me out

Col. Mitch Meyers, for friendship and excellent leadership in Korea

Sgt. Maj. Malisha Palmer, Retired, for being a great leader and helping me out

Specialist Troy Cadieu, for verification of me being in deep shit

Capt. Yira Rodriguez, USA Reserve for leadership in Afghanistan

Sammy Shaw, for verification of myself in a Criminal Correction Facility

Dianne Mailloux, for friendship in my early-adulthood rogue behavior

Col. Jack Wedam, USA Retired, for stellar leadership in Germany and consultation for writing this book

Col. William Corr, USA Retired, for excellent leadership in Korea

Dr. Cole Cheek, for getting the thought in my head to write a book and encouragement

Johnny Messer, Herman Whitaker and **Dean Cochran** for history on my father's life

Sgt. Maj. Sam Oak, USA, Retired, for being a great leader and helping me out

Peter Baxter and **Cody Rollins**, for technical assistance

TABLE OF CONTENTS

INTRODUCTION

I am not afraid to fail anymore; I done that already.
LT. COL. JASON PIKE

I AM A SOLDIER AGAINST ALL ODDS, and what follows is a genuine and frank account—the good, the very bad and the very ugly—of my thirty-one years in uniform. Diagnosed at age seven with an acute learning disability and failing first grade that year, I was sent back to repeat it. At age nine, I was diagnosed with *osteomyelitis*, a crippling bone disease, dissolving the bone of my knee, that added to my academic challenges a significant physical disadvantage. My military career began when I signed up with the National Guard at age seventeen and continued through more than three decades of both national guard and active service to retire at the rank of lieutenant colonel. I was told that none of it would be possible, and for that advice there was certainly very good grounds. I was not college bound, plain and simple. My story, therefore, is one of perseverance, and a refusal to quit, no matter what, a characteristic gifted to me by my father. Once I did it, everyone asked "how the hell did you do it?" And many times, I asked myself the same question. What follows is a brutally honest tale of an unorthodox life, a rogue career, and an often-maverick character not easily aligned with the military credo. It is the chronicle of a life that will inspire you to wince, cry, and laugh. It is my hope that the lessons I learned through the course of my life and my military career will be an inspiration to anyone confronting the future from a place of disadvantage. It is possible, through determination, careful application, and bold strategy, to overcome or compensate for personal humiliation, brought about mostly by my own mistakes, being haunted by investigations, academic difficulty, arrests, many ass-chewings and physical frailty. I did pay the price for being me. This is how I did it but most importantly how survived it. A reader will, I hope, find this story a unique account of how a high-ranking officer from Fingerville, South Carolina can fail and make many, many mistakes in life and yet still succeed. The moral of my story is never give up!

— **Lt. COL. JASON G PIKE,** January 2022

A THIRD CLASS OF
WHITE PEOPLE

*He makes me to lie down in green pastures; He leads me beside still
waters.*
PSALM 23

FOR AS LONG AS I CAN REMEMBER, on the wall of my parents' bedroom, there hung a small wooden frame containing a single military medal. I saw it every day, and although sometimes I paused to look at it, somehow I never got around to asking about it. I recall it had an eagle and anchor motif, a blue, gold, and red ribbon, and it was understood in some way to relate to my father's service in the US Navy. Beneath it was affixed a small brass plate with his name engraved on it: (PO2/E-5) Dennis Earl Pike. It was only much later, as he lay dying, that I discovered it was a Navy and Marine Corps Medal, the highest noncombat commendation for valor awarded by the Navy. My father was a Southern man, a natural storyteller, but he never did tell that story.

STORYTELLING IS EMBEDDED in the culture and psychology of the South. Although these days, there are storytelling festivals and folklorists who keep the tradition alive, entertaining tourists and breathing life into ancient yarns of the Appalachians, when I was a kid, it was just what folk did to keep in touch, to archive family history, and to entertain one another. When my father and his cousin Fred would meet up from time to time to drink, smoke cigarettes, and tell stories, I don't think they even noticed the kid sitting quietly in the shadows or on the stairs, listening to them. I got to know a whole lot about my dad that way, and then the time came when he and I would sit around, drink beer, and tell stories. By then I was active-duty Army, and there were stories aplenty. I told myself often that one day I would get to the bottom of that medal story, but I never did. Somehow it always slipped my mind. Time, when you are in the prime of your life, is never-ending.

Then one day, time ran out. It was early in December 2010, and I was in one of those "drinking from a firehose" situations that you get into sometimes in the Army. My unit was about to ship out to Afghanistan, and there were a million and one things to take care of. In the middle of it all, my brother called to tell me that Dad had been checked into the hospital that afternoon, back in Spartanburg, South Carolina, for tests and observation. Dad was seventy-five years old, and it did not sound too serious, so I put it to the back of my mind and got on with the job.

I was forty-five years old, holding the rank of lieutenant colonel, and standing at the threshold of the most important assignment of my career. At the end of a damaging three-year deployment to Korea, and with my professional reputation in tatters due to a federal investigation, I had been handed a last-minute opportunity to redeem myself. I understood that an Afghanistan deployment would probably be the climax of my career and my last chance before I retired to pick up a few credits and make up a little bit of lost ground. I was determined to make the very best of it, and more importantly, to make sure that not a damned thing went wrong. There is a truism in the military that getting a soldier into the field is about twice as hard as commanding him when he gets there. A few frenzied, detail-heavy months of training and preparation typically precede any deployment overseas, in particular into a war zone, and this one was no different.

It became clear over the course of the next few days that my father's condition was not improving, and the decision was made to transfer him into an intensive care unit. The family began to gather at his bedside, and my brother suggested it was time for me to join them. It happened that I was scheduled to visit Fort Jackson in South Carolina later that month, for a combined leadership meeting, so I took the opportunity to drive up to the Mary Black Hospital in Spartanburg to visit him.

"Jake!" he said as I walked through the door of his room. "Grab a beer. There's one in the closet."

Jake was a family nickname, and years of comradery and easy familiarity were folded into that friendly greeting. I knew there was no beer in that closet. His mind was dwelling on happier times. I didn't want to believe that he was dying, but he was. He was my father. His name was Dennis Earl Pike, and the remaining hours and minutes of an exceptional life were quickly slipping through his fingers.

THE STORY OF THE PIKE FAMILY in the United States can be traced to the very earliest settlement of the American colonies. The first of them was John Pike, a Wiltshireman who arrived in the Massachusetts Bay Colony in about 1635. He immigrated with his son, also named John, to join many others from his home county in the south of England who had settled the valley of Quascacunquen. From there the rest followed. At some point, probably during the Civil War, the first of them began appearing in the South, settling the southern foothills of the Appalachians, and it is from this remote branch that my family is derived. Part of that tree took home around Hendersonville, in the mountains of North Carolina, and there my father was raised. He was born in Inman, South Carolina, very close to Hendersonville. His branch of the family did not distinguish itself by judges or priests, high-ranking military officers nor minor politicians, but instead they passed through the phases of Appalachian history as anonymous and impoverished hill farmers, mill workers, and migrant laborers, sometimes referred to as a third class of white, or even white trash.

The story of my father's family is the story of a generation of men and women caught up in the poverty and depression of those times. I sometimes like to think of more innocent times, when the landscape was still clean and empty, and when those hill communities flourished on land that they occupied and owned. That was not my father's world. Poverty came into that world alongside of industrialization and labor. In Virginia and Kentucky, it was coal, the railway lines and land speculators, and in the Carolinas, it was cotton.

To the north of Spartanburg County, around the town of Fingerville, the place where I was raised, the ruins of old textile mills are everywhere. At one time, it was the only game in town. A wage-labor class took root around it, people they called "lint-heads", who owed body and soul to the company. At the end of WWII, military contracts dried up, and things began to get real tough. The fifties and sixties saw a deep social decline, as alcohol, drugs and government money replaced moonshine and wages. I remember when I was a kid, you'd sometimes see those real poor folk around, and we'd call them "white trash." People can be poor and live on welfare without being white trash. White trash is something different. It is almost a tribal

4

thing. A "third class" of whites. Everyone in the South is poor, but white trash is something different.

One of my earliest memories of childhood was driving up from Norcross in Georgia to Hendersonville with my brother and my dad to visit Aunt Mary. She was the youngest of my dad's siblings, and he, the oldest. I remember her as a gentle, soft-spoken woman of sweet nature and simple outlook, who was the matriarch of an extended family. As a young girl, she was raised in the same shack in Hendersonville where my father once lived. Two rooms and a dirt floor.

Mary married and moved down the hill into a house on the edge of town. There she passed her days with my Uncle Ralph and a sprawling tribe of children and grandchildren. By the time I met Ralph, he was an old-timer living on social security. He was a thoughtful man, tall and angular, who spoke almost in the pure dialect of Appalachian English. His stories and yarns flowed in melodic stanzas, almost like epic poems, in the old mountain tradition of storytelling. The house was pretty run down. Dad once told me that he gave them money to fix it, but it was never done. I think sometimes maybe he liked to show himself off, and let them see what he had become, and how far he had traveled, and show his sons the same thing.

The story, as he told it often, was that his parents paid two buckets of corn to a midwife for his delivery, after which his father moved on and was never seen again. No one is even really sure what his father's name was. His mother was Frances Pike, a dirt-poor, unmarried woman of the southern Piedmont, about whom there were few stories told. Dad loved her very much, but he was honest about it. My dad suggested that she was a lesbian and even a prostitute.

Fred Pike was his cousin, a half-cousin, actually, and besides Mary, he was the only person still living who knew my father well as a child. When I started to think seriously about putting pen to paper on this memoir, I tracked old Fred down, and found him living in a small suburban house in Alpharetta,

Georgia, north of Atlanta. He was reclining in a La-Z-Boy, aging, and surrounded by the memorabilia of a long life. Even then he was a square-jawed, rough-bearded man, fists fat and heavy, and scarred by a violent past.

"So what you want to know about ol' Picky boy?" he asked me. "I know he ate pencils."

"Did he ever eat pussy?" I asked.

He laughed. "Well, he say he didn't, but you know he lie a lot. They say in the Navy if you get too old to cut the mustard, you gotta lick the jar."

Fred Pike was an old-timer, a man of the mill towns around Inman, South Carolina.

"My grandaddy started working down there in the mill when he was eight years old. Daddy started when he was fourteen. They called us lint-heads in those days because we worked in the mills and had cotton lint in our hair. We was poor folk beholden to the company. That's the way it was in them days."

"But you were not as poor as Dennis, where ya?"

He smiled and shook his head.

"Nobody poorer than dirt, Jake," he said. "Zeke was poor as dirt when dirt was white. You know he had to shit back of the house, outside, up on the mountain, in the outside, on the ground, wipe his ass with leaves 'n' grass. People would say, when we grew up, we'd be white trash prob'ly, but we was workin' people. White trash is different. Those people on the mountain, they wouldn't get stable, just move all around the fuckin' place. You move all the time, you white trash. Fucker need to settle down, need to get a home."

"Anyone lower than white trash?" I asked him.

"At that time? Only niggers."

Until he was about twelve years old , Dennis Pike was raised in that shack up on Stoney Mountain Road. Old Nick Wright, his stepfather, was a depressed man, beaten down by poverty and missing a leg. He would tell the story sometimes that that leg was blown off in the fighting in Europe, but the truth is it came off under a train when he was hoboing during the Great Depression. The shoes the kids wore and the blankets they slept under were picked out of trash cans and dumpsters. Fred went on, he went on to say:

"Where Dennis grow up, back side of the mountain, it was only forest. Wasn't even a house, more like a lean-to or a shack. There was a creek on the side. They get their water outa that creek, a spring really. They didn't have an outhouse or nothin', just shit in the back. They went up on the mountain and shit, the wipe their asses with mountain laurel leaves. The reason he chewed pencils all his life is because he ate that damn tree bark, because he was so damn hungry, and one time they had to take him to a doctor to pull that shit out of his rectum. Eatin' the pine tar off the trees. He was eatin' it as food. What's inside of a child makes him want to do that?"

One day, when he was twelve years old, Dennis and ol' Nick Wright had a shit-storming fight, and Dennis picked up a chair and smashed it over Nick's head. Then he walked out of the shack in the clothes he was wearing and never came back.

"Well," said Fred, "if you got demons in your head, they elusive as hell. As the ol' preacher say, 'Get behind me, Satan!' Satan is always chasing you, always chasing you—at least 'cording to the Baptists. 'Get behind me, Satan.' That's why he was always fighting. It was in the ninth grade when I see him again. I done heard earlier about him breakin' that chair over ol' Nick Wright's head, knocked the shit outa ol' Nick."

Dennis attended Balfour Elementary School in Hendersonville, and for a while he was passed around various relatives until he ended up with Cora Pike. I asked Fred if he could recall much about Cora and how the whole crazy web of relationships worked.

"You start here," he said. "You got Jim and my grandfather. My grandfather and Jimbo, they were brothers, they were twins. Jimbo married Cora when she was fifteen years old

7

because he needed somebody to take care of his kids. Frances Pike was one of Jimbo's kids. She was a tiny woman. Some say she was a tomboy; some today maybe thought she would be gay. When Dennis came down the mountain, he went down to Fingerville, to Cora's sister or somebody, then came over there with Cora, and Jimbo and Betty and Louise, and Donald, who we called Abe."

It is all still a bit of a mystery to me, but either way, it was Cora Pike who ended up taking my dad in, in the ninth grade. When he left school, he joined the Navy, training in San Diego as a Navy radar man. I recall he felt no particular attraction to the military or the uniformed services, and his objective in signing up was the same as so many other young men from the South. He just wanted to escape poverty, and he wanted an education. From the Navy, he attended Wofford College in Spartanburg, South Carolina, graduating in three years. From college, he went to the corporate world and ground his way up to the summit by hard work, determination, and intelligence. His majors were mathematics and chemistry (he once told me he majored in chemistry because his second-grade teacher told him he would never amount to anything and ignored any questions that he had in class), and mt dad entered the corporate class as a sales executive with Univar Chemicals. That is the story of Dennis Pike in a nutshell.

I PULLED UP A CHAIR AND SAT DOWN at the edge of his bed. It was evening, and the wards were quiet. My mother did not care for me visiting him after hours, but it was a silent time, and mostly he was lucid and clear in mind.

"Grab a beer from the closet."

I pretended I had, and I said to him, "Hey Dad, you remember that day in Norcross, when we went to look at the house for the very first time?"

"How could I forget it, Jake?"

THE LESSONS OF
AN ORDINARY
CHILDHOOD

I will not be won by weaklings, subtle, suave and mild,
But by men with the hearts of Vikings, and the simple faith of a child.
ROBERT W. SERVICE

IN MY MIND'S EYE I CAN still recall the picture of a young boy, compact and sturdy, blonde-hair, blue-eyes, maybe three or four years old, squatting beside a flowing creek. The creek ran through a heavily shaded glade, so typical of the hill country of Georgia. A narrow pathway led up to the road, a few hundred feet back, and beyond that was the yard of a small, red-roofed suburban home. The shaded knolls and valleys were scattered with similar homes, and in the distance, past the open pastures, I could hear the soft hum of traffic.

More than once when I was growing up, my father would ask me my earliest memory of life, and it is this. I can clearly recall, there in Cobb Meadow, playing in the mud and water with his voice calling down to me from the top of the hill.

"C'mon, Jake! Let's get outa here!"

I remember I ignored him, and he called out again, and I went on ignoring him. After waiting for a few minutes, he strolled down to the creek-side and stood there behind me, telling me again that it was time to go. I looked up at him and began to cry, because I did not want to leave that place. As he told the story later, he stood there for a moment or two, scratching his chin, and figuring that this might be an omen. He made the decision then and there. This would be the property that he and Mama would buy. It would be our first family home, and it was here that my childhood started.

TO PAINT A PICTURE OF MY CHILDHOOD is to paint a picture of any upwardly mobile, suburban family living in the South of the 1970s. The town was Norcross, Georgia, located in Gwinnett County to the north of Atlanta, not far off of I-85. Although, in the last twenty years or so, it has all been sucked up into metropolitan Atlanta, in those days it was still a small town, set against a backdrop of neighborhoods, open fields and farmland. It was the kind of place where the focus of life was school and church, and the main business was the gas station, the neighborhood market, and the feed store. Cobb Meadow was then, and still is, a small neighborhood of Norcross, and in those days, Atlanta was just close enough that you could see its glow on the southern horizon at night. It was a comfortable, middle-class suburb, family orientated, and accessed only by a single, black-top road. The common sounds were always children playing, dogs barking, and roosters crowing. There was a market nearby, a drive-in theater, a few churches, and a school. As kids, we lived free and wild, uninhibited and unsupervised. There was enough space to grow, but it was also tight enough for a gang of boys of different ages to hang out together, drifting with ease and familiarity in and out of each other's lives. As I reflect on it, it seems to me that that style of living even then was beginning to fade into history, and mostly it is gone now. They were the years just on the edge of the computer age, when the fun was still mud-ball fights, hurling vegetables at cars at night, rattling roofs, and staging mock battles in the woods with BB guns and air rifles. We had a particular holler—something between Tarzan and a rebel yell—and if one of us wanted to call the others names out, we'd stand somewhere on high ground and cup our hands and just holler and find out who was about, and there was usually one holler in reply somewhere. This was our communication.

Dad took us on Saturdays to some local gas station where we got peanuts and Coke. We'd put the peanuts in the Coke and we drank the Coke and ate the peanuts kinda at the same time while my dad talked to people coming in and out of the store. After that we would drive down various dirt roads all lined with trash. At the time people just openly dumped stuff on the side of the road, like refrigerators, stoves and appliances. It was all just trash on the side of the road, and it was here that he would let my brother and me take turns driving the car. We were just young kids, and he watched with joy. "Do not tell your mama…!" This was always a constant instruction and we always abided by it. "Do not tell your mama!" And yes, we knew it, and we never did because we wanted to keep on having fun.

Sunday, I recall, was always the day of the week to be most feared. On a Sunday morning, all hell would break loose at home, just like regular clockwork. Get up, get ready, put on clean clothes, comb our hair, and brush our teeth. Everything had to be in order before we went to church, and usually it took spanking and a lot of yelling to make it happen. I remember looking up at Jesus in the Stations of the Cross and the old pictures and thinking to myself – "If he could look so beaten up, why do I have to come to church looking so fresh?" These days churches make me nervous. My mom was always active in the church and very conscious of appearances, and it pained on her to own up to being responsible for such an unruly and rough-

12

edged boy. Dad was kind of the same. He was in his early forties, in the prime of his life, and although he was well established on the executive floor, he was still at the root of it a Southern man. He and his sons were confederates. Each one, father and sons, was a naughty little boy on his best behavior.

Generally in the South and, in fact, countrywide, the 1970s was a time of growth and optimism, and as social barriers broke down, it became easier for men like my dad, if he had the right stuff, to get ahead. The Vietnam War was still a daily fact of life, and in the South the military culture flourished. No Southern man in uniform was ever called a baby killer, and the sons of the South flocked to the ranks. Like many Southern men, my dad one time looked to the military as his way out, and so did Fred, and in both cases, it was. It was understood that if a boy was too dumb to educate, then the military would gladly train and arm him, and if he happened to be smart and progressive, then they would educate him. People in the South were still poorer than most places, and wherever the white trash was to be found, the Army recruiter was never far away.

As a family, we were comfortable enough that my mother could quit work to raise the kids, and she did, and once she quit, she never went back. She was a tall type of woman, the kind that the old-timers like Fred used to call "handsome." She was very pretty, but she was an exacting woman, very particular in most things, conscious of appearances, demanding high, maybe impossible, standards. She was active in the community, on the school boards and the local church committee, and she ran a tight ship and kept a clean and well-ordered house. She was a formidable woman. Some might say that she ruled the roost, and maybe she did. There were very few people, man or woman, who held sway over my father quite the way that she did.

My siblings—Dennis Jr., or "Denny," my older brother, and Beth Ann, the youngest—grew up across the hall but in different parallel worlds that did not overlap. We were never really close as children, and we have tended to remain that way as adults. My mother and my sister shared one orbit and my father, my brother, and I another. Our worlds coincided from time to time, all the while circling around that great, warm and powerful center that kept the whole intact. My dad's own loveless, nomadic, bastard childhood bred in him a passionate commitment to the family, which was often manifested in strange ways. I recall, for example, that he did not care to ever see one of his children curled up in a bed. To him, a child curled up in a bed was a cold child, and if he ever saw me lying in my bed all curled up, he would ask in fright, "You cold Jake? You cold?"

He was also a rough and resilient man who bred the same stuff in his sons, and that also manifested in strange ways. Often, I recall, when he picked us up from football practice, he would make us ride in the trunk not to get mud all over the car. If he stopped at the 7–Eleven, he would buy us a couple of Gatorades and toss them in the trunk, and we would sit and drink them in the dark. You can't even do that to a dog these days, let alone a couple of kids. Those were the kind of life lessons that were unorthodox but they were practical, and I learned them from my father, and he loved us very, very much.

While he was a highly principled man, he was also pragmatic, a product of his own environment, and not a man too governed by convention or scruple. He grew up hungry, and if he needed to steal to eat, he would steal, if he needed to fight, he fought. I remember Fred Pike telling me once, "Y'know, Old Picky Boy and me, we played football together. I was a quarterback and running back, and he was a right guard, and he was one mean fucker.... Back in them days, he'd take a handful of sand and throw that shit in a man's eyes. He was a badass. I assaulted a lot of people in my life. I love to fight, but I was scared to fight Pick. I wouldn't take his ass on."

In his hiring practices, Dad would judge a man by that simple criterion. "You ever had a fight?" he would ask, and if the answer was no, he would close the book. If a man never fought with his fists, he had no passion, no aggression, and no drive. He never hired women. In those days, this required no explanation, and he never hired blacks. Women, in his eyes, were unreliable because they were emotional, and they had a habit of getting pregnant and leaving, and he had no patience for that. He liked a man who played football or baseball, because that meant he was a team player, and if making that touchdown required a fist to the balls or a handful of sand in the eyes, he had no problem with that. He never hired anyone who smoked a pipe because he felt that meant they were cerebral, thought too much, and were lazy.

He loved to tell stories, and although sometimes— often, in fact—those stories strayed from the facts, they all combined to create a narrative of life, love, and expectation. Here's an example. One of the stories he often used to tell was how Jake broke down the garage door to escape the babysitter. One evening, when Mom and Dad were out, he hired a neighborhood woman to come babysit. I think I was about ten years old, and it pissed me off because there was something going down with the kids in the neighborhood, and she locked me in. I went into the garage, looked around for some tools and broke out. I was pretty sure I would get a beating for the damage to the door and for disobeying the babysitter, but that's not what happened. He looked at the damage to the door, heard my story, and he was impressed. I kinda felt rewarded. There was no trouble. He appreciated my determination and resourcefulness, and with plenty of embellishment, that story hung around for a few years.

This unorthodox and sometimes unpredictable worldview had been drummed into my dad by his life and experience, and as a consequence, it influenced me and how I looked at the world. Keep in mind I was a kid who was actively pursuing and listening to his stories. While his fundamental integrity was never in question, his worldview was also uncluttered by pseudo morality and fair play. He had no place in his life for bullshit, and neither do I. If a boy is raised to eat dumpster food and pine resin, walking barefoot, and wiping his ass with mountain laurel leaves, he is by necessity conditioned to do what he can get away with, and the only man lower than dirt in those days was a black man.

I remember the tales of old one-legged Nick Wright collecting food from trash cans and dumpsters in the city and bringing it home for the kids to eat. My dad would tie rags on his feet for shoes. I'm sure Dad did the same thing, stealing food and things, and I know he stole a little bit wherever he could. One day we were driving up from Norcross to Inman, South Carolina, to visit Cora Pike. He happened to see a watermelon field, and he said to us, "Boys, I'm gonna teach you how to steal watermelons. The first thing you need is a knife."

The knife was required to cut the stalk, but before that could be done, it was necessary to know how to thump the watermelon to tell if it was ripe. We all three belly-crawled up a row of watermelons, thumping this one and that one, and staying low and keeping out of sight. We thumped until we found a good one, then we cut it. With two or three ripe watermelons under our arms, we all three belly-crawled back to the edge of the field. It seems to me a boy acquires skills like that just to eat, and I am pretty sure that he stole more than watermelons in those days. I was never hungry, but I like watermelons, and I became a pretty good thumper.

The child in him never died. Let me tell you. One time he showed me how to shoot bottle rockets at passing cars. When I was a kid, he taught me the word "trajectory." You got to set that bottle rocket in its seat, light the fuse when you see a car coming along, and then aim at the car, taking trajectory into account. You light the fuse with just enough time to launch it at a passing car and then laugh and whoop like crazy when it hits. Mostly the cars belonged to friends and neighbors, and they knew who was behind it. Dad was popular with the

16

neighborhood, with the older folks for sure, but even more among the kids. He liked kids, and he was good with them. He loved to stand around smoking cigarettes, maybe just drinking a beer, and watching healthy, well-fed, and unburdened kids having fun. He had a thing for kids. All the boys of the neighborhood were his boys. He treated them like his own.

One day he bet a kid down the road by the name of Jim Mansour that he could beat him in a running race. He bet him a dollar bill that he could lick him running five miles. Jim was a teenager, kind of a geeky kid, but he was a good runner, and he figured it was a safe bet. Dad told me, "Son, we're gonna beat this kid. We're gonna cheat, and this is how we're gonna do it."

Jim agreed to give Dad a short head-start because he was older. We had a go-kart, and Dad told me that as soon as he was out of sight to pick him up in the go-kart and take him home by a back way, and we'd wait there for Jim to come round. Jim never thought that Dad would cheat, so he could hardly believe it when he arrived back, sweating, out of breath, and confused, and there the old man was, fresh as a virgin.

"Hand it over!" Dad demanded with a grin on his face. "I won the race fair and square."

There's no fair fight. Whatever it takes to win in life is fair. Jim Mansour never did figure out how a smoking and drinking man of forty-one could beat him, and we never told.

Another time there was a particular odd kid down the road. No one lined him, that I was around with. He was just odd, just an odd guy growing up thereabouts. He only had his mother because his father had left. My dad took a particular interest in the kid saying, "this is the best kid in the neighborhood, you need to be good to him, you need to be friends with him." I found that odd. I was with another gang of boys and my dad, who I looked up to, was favoring the most odd kid in the neighborhood. He told the boy one time, "I am your friend, and I will always be your friend." He like the people who were the underdogs. Anyone who was an underdog, that's who he favored.

When it came to crime and punishment, he also had his own peculiar way. One time there was some kind of party at home, and we kids came up on the back yard and stole a whole bunch of beer and liquor and we hid out in the neighborhood and got drunk. All the kids were passed out in various people's yards, and Dad got a call from a neighbor telling him that his kids were drunk and passed out on the side of the road, and he better get out there and take care of the situation. He came out of the house and tracked me down and told me to breathe so he could smell my breath. I held my breath, and he said, "Get in the house, Jake." Years later, as the incident found its way among his repertoire of stories, he told me he wanted me to go home because if he did not, I'd pass out from holding my breath. I was never giving up even in that situation.

Later, when we were all sober again, he said to us, "You boys want to drink, you can drink in here with me. You want a beer? I've got beer. You want liquor? What do you want?"

We didn't drink, and his us asking was not to shame us or get us drunk and sick so that we regret drinking but to treat us like men if we wanted to behave like men. You want to drink, he said, drink out in the open; he had no problem with it. He had a problem with a neighbor calling him up and telling him his boys were all drunk out in the neighborhood, passed out, but if we wanted to drink, then be at home and drink with him.

When he was mad, we knew he was mad, and we only had to see him unbuckle his belt to change our ways. One time I was doing something bad at home, and Mama told me that when Dad gets home, I'm in for a whooping. Later, when he came home, he came into my bedroom and said, "Your mama tells me you need a whooping, so this is how we're gonna do it. You put the books there in your pants, turn around, and each time I whip your ass, you yell loud and clear. Make sure everyone in the house hears you."

Denny used to bitch to me about when we were whipped with a belt. "You get the strap side," he would say, "and I get the buckle."

A couple of our neighbors belonged to the Klaudt family, who were well known at one time in the old South. Old man Klaudt was a German immigrant and passionate believer who married a Native American woman of the Sioux-Mandan people. She was a descendent of a minor chief and notable leader of the Indian Wars, and a distant relative of Chief Sitting Bull. In those days, Native Americans were still openly called Indians, and old man Klaudt and his Indian wife, with a bunch of mixed-race kids, started what they called the Klaudt Indian Family Gospel Group. First, it was with their own kids, but later with quite a few of their grandkids. In the fifties and sixties, the ensemble became pretty famous, playing the Grand Ol' Gospel Opry a few times and making a good amount of money. By the seventies, they were not so popular anymore. The whole novelty of a band and chorus dressed up as Indians and singing old gospel tunes had sort of run its course by then. The band was still together, and still toured, but it was a side gig now, and Ken Klaudt, who was third generation, was in insurance and made a pretty good amount of money. I remember that the family had a swimming pool when not many folks did.

The younger son of the family was a kid named Kent, and he was the Indian when we played cowboys and Indians in the field back of the house. Somewhere we saw a movie of a ranger staked out on the plains or in the desert, left to die of thirst, and we got all hot and sweaty and laid out there in the sun pretending like we were cowboys and Indians dying of thirst. Sometimes, when the Klaudt family set off in their big old Star-Cruiser tour bus, my dad would let me go along, traveling in the back of the bus and seeing all the big cities with Kent. Sometimes we'd be on the road a few weeks, sometimes for months. Sometimes we would be out on the road a few weeks, sometimes a month. There was a CB radio in the bus they'd use to talk to the truckers and sometimes fool with them. They liked to see us boys pretend like we were women – we had higher voices back when we were younger – and ask a trucker to meet up somewhere for a good time. They were Christian men, but they thought that was pretty funny, and we did, too.

IN THE WEEK or so that my dad lay in the ICU, I divided my time between my work at Fort Jackson and evening visits to the hospital. As a uniformed officer of the US Army, I was shown greater respect and given unusual leeway in the times and circumstances of my visits. During regular visiting hours, the family was mostly present, and the conversation was general and impersonal. "How are you feeling? Are you comfortable? Is there anything that you need?" Things of that nature. To me visiting hours did not apply. He was my dad.

My mother and my sister worried about my dad's treatment and possible misdiagnoses, and to keep a handle on things, they hired a private nurse, a friend of the family, to monitor him and keep the regular medical staff engaged. Diane Cole looked at him and told us that she believed that he was suffering from a urinary tract infection, and as the days passed, this was confirmed, and she told us he was likely dying. His moments of lucidity stretched in and out a little bit in the evenings, and because she was with him all night, she had the best opportunity to jot down his thoughts and reflections as he, too, came around to the fact that he probably was dying.

Chantel, my daughter, looked in from time to time with her mother. Of all his grandchildren, each of whom he loved unreservedly, it was Chantel who intrigued him the most. She is half Asian and, is blessed with an exotic beauty that combines her mother's slight frame and elegance and her father's Nordic coloring and solid construction, and just a little bit of white trash. His face would light up when he talked about her. He was impressed with her natural intelligence and easy familiarity.

"You always surprised the hell out of me, Jake!" he said, something that he repeated often over the years. "I never thought you would go so far as you have, but she is brilliant. She'll never fail."

To Diane he confided his thoughts on all his children. Dennis Jr., or Denny, was the thinker, the restless spirit, and the committed one. Beth Ann he saw as embracing all the problems of the world, the teacher and the carer. In me, his youngest son, he saw a reflection of himself, a rock of a man, unhurried and thoughtful mind, who took the facts of life in slowly and deliberately, but mixed them up well and arrived at deeper conclusions. I was an underdog. As his sons approached puberty and adolescence, he began to examine them more critically, arriving at certain conclusions. In his eldest he identified the potential for academic excellence, and so Denny was groomed for that role. In me he saw less. He saw a boy with physical frailties and an intellectual disadvantage that provoked an instinct of protection. It was never spoken of directly, or ever addressed that I can remember, but there was no doubt that I was his favorite son, and I was given passes and let off the hook in ways that my brother never was.

When I was aged eight or nine years old, Fred Pike's family and ours went down to Florida for a holiday. One day, as I was jumping in and out of the hotel pool, I bumped my knee hard, which triggered some sort of an aggressive infection that was diagnosed a few weeks later as *osteomyelitis*. *Osteomyelitis* is a bone infection, its cause typically a bacterial infection, and its symptoms are inflammation and pain, and pain I certainly do recall. Mine was a particularly aggressive infection that almost completely dissolved the bone of my left knee, not once but twice. It was treated with a very painful series of antibiotic injections directly into the knee. Although this did eventually clear it up, and although an irregular cartilage did grow back

21

eventually, it was never quite the same, and for a long time I was forced to use crutches. It left me physically compromised, which came on top of other problems that were beginning to develop. It was something that we never spoke about in specific or direct terms when I was a child, and even when I was an adult, it was never directly referred to. My dad did not want to stigmatize me or burden what was already likely to be a difficult transition into adulthood. Now that I was a man of forty-five, with my career moving towards its climax, and as he was confronting his own mortality, he was inclined to admit that he had not been optimistic for my future in the beginning. My left knee is nine years younger than the rest of my body. The damn thing grew back.

"You always surprise the hell out of me, Jake," he said. "You're damn different, no doubt about that."

LESS THAN BEST

I DO NOT REMEMBER EXACTLY when I first got the hunch that I was different. I believe it was that day that I noticed my first-grade teacher looking at me differently, with an expression of inquiry on her face, and asking me strange and probing questions. Later I saw that same expression on the face of my father, also asking me the same kind of questions.

Then, as the children of the neighborhood began to enter their formative years, when learning commenced and when information was assimilated and knowledge accumulated, I felt myself beginning to fall further and further behind the pack. Information was being heaped on my plate at a crazy rate, and I struggled to cope, sensing all the while that as the other kids were easily devouring their platefuls of learning, progressing, and thriving in school, I was not. The difficulty seemed to lie in shapes and configurations, in the backward and forward facing, or upside-down alignment of letters, what they meant, how to create them. To me, simple instructions seemed abstract and unclear, while the basic principles of word formation, addition, subtraction, and multiplication, they seemed bizarre, and I couldn't understand. Reading was difficult, and writing almost impossible, and that has remained the case my entire life.

In the fall of 1972, I still have the letter, while I was in first grade at Rockbridge Elementary in Norcross, Georgia, I was referred on the recommendation of a school counselor to the Emory University Reading Center in Atlanta, Georgia, for an evaluation. There I was put through various standardized tests: the Peabody Picture Vocabulary Test, the Bender-Gestalt Test, the Wepman Auditory Discrimination Test, among many others. The results were summarized in a letter to my parents, and buried in four paragraphs of carefully chosen language were one or two key points.

"As we discussed," it ran, "there were several signs of a specific disability…All writing was a slow and painful business for him…Jason does not recognize enough words yet to score on word recognition tests.

"At the present time, Jason has difficulty reading at the beginning level. Orally he reads very slowly, word by word. Silently, he works very quickly, but with poor comprehension. It is recommended that you explore the possibility of enrolling him in a program set up for children who have good intelligence with difficulty in learning."

Ultimately, the conclusion was given that "Jason is not ready for second grade and will have to repeat first."

I feel—in general, philosophical terms—that I was capable of understanding much more than I was able to express. Somehow, the questions I was asked did not seem to connect with the answers that were expected. The tests were varied, and as I remember them, fairly straightforward, and the kindly way in which the whole assessment was administered, and in such rare surroundings as a university facility, caused me to feel that I really was special. On reflection, and with the benefit of hindsight, I understand that given the opportunity to move forward at my own pace, with time to think through every possibility related to a particular problem, I had the capability to mostly compensate for it.

"I never thought you were dumb, or stupid," my dad said to me. "You just took it all on board real slow, but real clear, and mixed it up well and came out with a good thought and a good understanding."

My mama was a meticulous planner. She always had a wall calendar overflowing with the times and dates of appointments. That impressed me very much, although I did make fun of it. Later I took to using one myself, and it was something I became very good at. On reflection, I guess what was going on was I was looking for and finding ways to compensate. My world was not dimly illuminated. Far from it. I had a specific linear method of thinking, without any particular ability to think laterally, or "outside of the box," but with a methodical, ruminating cognitive process that thrived in an unpressured environment. Eventually I was able to come out of that box. This did not, however, align with the expectations and teaching methods common in the schools at that time, and I was looked upon as being slow and intellectually challenged.

How my parents dealt with such a gloomy projection for my future was never communicated to me. I can guess that they were disappointed, but they were happy that I was healthy and alive. I cannot recall precisely how the news was broken to me that I would need to repeat first grade or even how much it meant at the time. I guess my disappointment was mainly at being left behind by my friends, most of whom were kids I knew from around the neighborhood. I would repeat first grade while they all moved on up to the second grade. It was then that I understood I definitely was different, but not in a good way. I guess the upside to it was that thanks to this, and my *osteomyelitis*, I learned very early on in life the reality of physical pain and failure. It taught me resilience, and it taught me the value of perseverance.

In the meantime, when I was about twelve years old and in the sixth grade, Dad asked me how I would think about leaving Georgia. I didn't like it. I had my friends in Norcross, and when he told me he was thinking of moving the family to Fingerville, South Carolina, I liked it even less. My Mom did not like it much more. She was a sophisticated woman, accustomed to the amenities and social opportunities of Georgia and Atlanta, and the idea of moving back to the hillbilly country of his kinfolk had no appeal to her at all. He framed it as a necessary move in the advancement of his career, which, although maybe not untrue, was also not the main reason. He was going home. He wanted to go back home and show himself and say, "Hey, look at me, look what I've done, and I'm back."

In the end, he did what he figured he had to do. In 1978, we left Norcross and moved to a house, a rental house, on Lake Bowen in Spartanburg County, close to Fingerville, and there we waited for the house to be built. The land was on the shore of the lake in the rolling hill country of South Carolina. Although it was in the poverty belt, it was nonetheless in a beautiful and richly appointed acre or two of land looking down on the water. My dad and I talked about this a lot. The hills of Piedmont commence just north of Inman and so we both wanted to push north the boundary north, to get out of the city, while Mama pulled south in the direction of Spartanburg. He and I both yearned for the wilder places.

He bought the land, and he built his house. It cost seventy-eight thousand dollars in 1978, easy to remember because there were two seventy-eights. We moved in at the end of the year, I was enrolled in Boiling Springs Junior High, seventh grade. It was maybe the most free, and uninhibited phase of my life. I talk about a Huck Finn childhood in Georgia, but really it was here, with lakes and woods and unlimited space. We built a raft and put it out on the water. We cut down trees and made a log cabin on people's land. I don' even know whose land it was. We had a lifestyle of complete freedom, on the edge

26

of a fish-stocked lake, with dogs and kids and time, space, freedom, and security. While my mother gritted her teeth and accepted the inevitable, he came home, and we kids discovered paradise.

AS A CHILD RAISED IN THE SOUTH I thrived on that old tradition of story-telling. I may not understand formal school instructions very well, but I understood the storytelling, and I still do. In a traditional sense, stories were, and sometimes still are, how family histories are kept alive, where life is breathed into the memories of the dead, and the cycle of life is nurtured and retained. Why it is that I know so much about my father's life and family is only because of those stories. And the reason I know so little about my mother and her side of the family is that her stories were never told. My Dad, like all men of the rural South, was a natural storyteller. He told stories all the time, often repeating them, embellishing them, or altering them to suit the needs of the moment.

Often when he talked about his life and experiences, the details were allegorical, blended into parables intended to impart a message and deliver a moral. Others were just yarns of a distant time and place, a world past and escaped, but remembered well and not regretted. When he drank, he would tell stories, and as the evening progressed, his voice would grow louder and his mood grew melancholic and sometimes quite intense. If he lost momentum, I would prod him with a question, and away he would go again. It was a pleasure for me, and I listened and learned and came to understand. I had a way to get him going in a good way. Oftentimes my mother or my sister would come out of the bedroom and tell us to shut up and go to bed.

At other times, if we were driving in the car together, he would divert round to a small settlement on the site of an old cotton mill on the outside of Fingerville. The place was pretty much a squatter camp, with shacks and old trailers, where a community of dirt-poor folk lived. He would park the car a distance up the road and he would crack a beer or two and just take it all in. He would yarn about poverty, what it is like, what it means, and how it degrades the body and the spirit. There is no good side to poverty, he would say, its all bad. He drove through Fingerville from time to time just to remind himself, and to remind me and my brother, where he came from. He told me that seeing it all made him want to work harder, to validate some point that continued to fester, remaining somehow unproven in his mind.

I was a little bit of a rebellious kid, and I told my dad, "Dad, when I grow up, I don't never want to put on a suit and tie!"

He looked at me, smiled for a while, and said something like, "There's a suit and tie, there are coveralls, and there are boots and fatigues. You decide, boy."

Stories were the bonding agent of Southern life. Old Fred Pike was another great storyteller, and he told me once that when men talk, there should be no subject forbidden other than sex with their wives. No dust was ever allowed to gather on old skeletons in long-forgotten cupboards.

"Jake," Dad once said to me. "Don't let me linger after my time. I don't want to be kept on some damned life machine. When my time comes, cut the cord."

There was never any reason to affirm our love and regard for one another. It was an understood fact. Ours was the tradition of porch swinging, of folk ruminating about this and that, about local gossip and the times of yore. That was, as it remains, a tradition of the South. It was a disarming, free-spirited narrative of life as it actually happened. Although he cleaned up his language when he entered the corporate world and began to mingle with different types of people, when he and Fred met over a six-pack or two to tell stories and reminisce, he lapsed back into character. That character was a drawling, profane Southern man raised in the rough, a storyteller of the old style South, with a frankness and honesty polished by generations empty of pretension. It was honest, and it was open and it was different.

"NOW SON," HE TOLD ME ONCE, as we drove into Inman to visit with Cora Pike, "there is something I need to tell ya. You're going to meet Betty and Louise. Now, Betty is a little slow, and they say she is the product of incest."

I told him that I ain't care about that.

Later, as Fred Pike and I were talking things over in preparation for this book, I put it to Fred Pike that Betty Pike may well have been the product of incest, which caused him to scratch his chin and consider the idea with some unease. Maybe there were things other than a man's relations with his wife that make awkward telling. There was a dark underbelly to life in the South in the old days, and in some places there still is.

"People used to say," he admitted, "because Betty was a little squirrelly, but I don't know."

"If she was," I asked him, "who would it have been?"

"If it was incest, that means somebody nailed her up, and that means it was Jimbo. Must a been ol' Jimbo. He married Cora when she was fifteen, and Betty come outa Cora, so— maybe they was related somehow, or maybe it goes back further. I reckon it was him. I reckon, I don't know. Nobody else to hit her up. They might have explained that just because she was a little squirrelly, but, you know, a lot a folk do incest in these parts—you know, in the South. They got an old saying down here, 'If it ain't good enough for your own family, then it ain't good enough for me.' Lotta crazy people, them Pikes."

When I was about thirteen or fourteen years old, I took a summer job working at the Gaines Packing House in Inman, South Carolina, just a half a mile or so from where Cora lived with Betty and Louise. The Gaines family were a big deal in Inman at the time, owning gas stations and stores and all kinds of dealerships, and the packing house was one of their businesses that employed quite a few kids from the surrounding neighborhoods. It was a summertime job because when those peaches started coming in they had to be cleaned and packed and shipped out quickly. For the first year, I worked loading the eighteen-wheelers before I moved up into the loft area making boxes with an automatic stapling machine. It was repetitive work over long hours, but the pay was good, and I guess my dad figured I might as well get used to manual work, since that was likely to be my future. I surely was never to be college bound.

Lunch times, I would walk the short distance to Cora's house on Bridger Street to pass the time and to eat lunch. Cora was in her mid-seventies then, a small woman, no taller than five foot two, but sinuous and strong. Her eyes were blue and bright behind heavy spectacles, and the years of struggle and hard living were etched deeply into her face. She was a kindly, intelligent woman, humble, unpretentious, and unimpressed by the airs and graces of those who looked down on the Carolina hill folk. She had moved into town some years earlier, into a small and simple home with indoor amenities, and there she lived with her two unmarried daughters.

Louise never did marry, but Betty had been married one time, just for a little while, some years back. Frances, my grandmother on my father's side, was also one of Cora's daughters, although she was long dead by then—in 1973, according to Fred—and not much spoken about anymore. The only time I ever saw my father cry was when he first heard of his mother dying. Each surviving daughter was probably close to sixty, maybe a little younger, because they were all conceived and born when Cora was still just a child herself.

There was a brother, too, whose name was Don Pike— we called him Abe—and although he came and went a lot, I remember seeing quite a bit of him. It was difficult to get into the head of Don Pike, who said little and mostly kept to himself. He chain-smoked cigarettes and owned a fifty-five Chevy. I remember once riding in that car, as a kid. It had no floorboard on the passenger side. It was just an open hole looking down on the road.

"Don't mind that," Don told me. "That's just my air conditioning."

No one knew much about Don Pike.

"He was a cheap fucker," Fred Pike remembered. "That's all I know. He was the cheapest fucker in the world. When it was time to buy his round of beers, he would leave to take a piss."

Betty was squirrelly for sure. She was a smiling and engaging soul, but she was slow, spoke like she had a mouthful of marbles, and was completely dependent on her mother and sister. I doubt if she would ever have been able to live alone, and I believe she died early after Cora passed. I remember that my lunchtime visits were a highlight of their day. They would welcome me in and feed me great Southern food like corn on the cob, green beans, ham, biscuits, and gravy. The biscuits were the best I have ever had. Then we would pass the time on the porch. Three old women living together, the remnants of another time. They were happy to pass the time in the company of a youth who was growing into manhood between their world, the old world, and the new world created by my father, and reinforced by my mother. Both of them, Mom and Dad, for their own reasons, sought to distance themselves from Dad's origins, but that did not mean disrespecting the old folks or looking down on them.

"You gotta make doctor or lawyer," Cora would say to me. "You need an education, child. Your daddy is a success only 'cause he got an education."

She did not care for me scratching my feet. I would take my shoes off on the porch and scratch my feet. I don't know why, but she did not like it. "You gotta change out your socks

31

sometimes, Jake!" she would say. "And you ain't got to scratch your feet."

She saw such similarities between my father and me that she often told me I had been misnamed. It should have been me and not the older son, she said, named Dennis. "You are Dennis and not Jason." She said.

I remember Cora did not care for my mother. The stories told on that porch in those days were family stories, and sometimes she would look at me from the corner of her eye and ask me about my mama. I think she thought I was being cagey when I did not tell her much, but the truth is, I did not know much.

My mother preferred to keep her contact with my father's family as distant and brief as possible. She welcomed visits from Cora, Mary, and Ralph only very occasionally, and with little sincere affection or warmth. I recall Mary telling me after Dad died that she did not feel comfortable attending the funeral, that she felt she would not be welcome. Fred came to the funeral—hell! nothing could keep him away—but he said the same thing. The warm and engaging presence of my father had passed away, and all that remained was a woman, my mother, who knew him through a marriage of fifty years, but did not care to know from where and among whom he originated.

On Mom's side of the family, there were no stories. That tradition did not exist among the new, industrial aristocracies. It seemed to me that they were trained to speak only in generalities and shared nothing of substance with one another, let alone with anyone from the outside. I can say that, while I knew as much as it is possible to know about my mother after her marriage, I knew almost nothing about her life before. It was not talked about, and I knew not to ask. I wondered about it sometimes, though. It seemed unnatural, but I knew not to ask. What I did know is that my mother was raised in Denver, Colorado, in the well-to-do home of Bill Geer and his wife Hattie, who we knew only as Nana. She had a brother and two sisters, who were Richard, or Dick, Betty, and Judy. Nana was a Hatfield, of lesser stock than her husband, but well married and securely positioned, and now with certain social affectations that she passed on to her daughters. Although his wife drank heavily and chain-smoked cigarettes, Bill Geer did neither.

About Dick, Judy, and Betty, I know nothing at all other than the essential and sanitized facts of their lives. They did not tell, and we did not inquire. Bill Geer was an executive engineer, well positioned in the higher administrative class, with both old and new money. I came to acknowledge a degree of superficiality with the Geer family and a sense of elitism without any of the ease of interaction and the funny stories. The way they communicated was always very strange to me. Instead of asking, "How are you doing?" they queried another member of the family, asking, "How is he or she doing?" Instead of talking to you, they seemed to talk around you. I found it odd. I once asked Fred Pike about it, and this is how he remembered it:

"Pick met Nancy in Dallas when she was an ex–United Airlines stewardess. He was in an apartment complex, which was where he met her. She worked out of Denver, Colorado, with United Airlines. How she got to Dallas I don't know. I think her family was originally from Denver. Her father was a nice guy. Her mother liked her damn booze about five o'clock every day—she drank Manhattans. Old Man Geer, your grandpa on your mother's side, he didn't drink. He didn't smoke. He was a nice-assed guy."

As my dad told the story, he saw an attractive woman one day struggling to open her apartment door, carrying an armful of shopping or such, and so he came down a level and offered to help. They got to talking and three months later, they were married. That's all. As a younger man, and in fact even as an older man, my dad had a way with women. Old Fred, with his unashamed profanity and knack of cutting through the bullshit, described Dennis as a "swordsman," which was a

33

colloquial term among the older men of the South to describe a man who was a womanizer.

"In the old ancient days," he recalled, "they would call ol' Dennis a 'swordsman.' He'd fuck anything that walks. He's a swordsman. Women loved his ass. He walked around slouched and get them to feeling sorry for him. Women want to mother him. And he'd take advantage of that shit and move right in."

Both my mother and father were chain-smokers. I recall Mom smoking so much in the morning she would cough up these old "lungers,", black lungers, almost like black tar. It was loud, and you could hear it across the house. As a kid, I remember the house being filled with smoke. Later in life, they both stopped smoking. Dad quit cold turkey when the doctor told him he would never see his children graduate high school, and mom quit sometime in the 1990s with the help of nicotine patches. She only did quit when it began to be socially unacceptable to smoke. She was not white trash, She was high-class. There was a cultural and social dynamic going on and she didn't want to be associated with people who smoke, who were at the time, and now maybe, white trash. She wasn't white trash. She was high-class.

Mom was very socially conscious and had private misgivings about involving herself with a Southern man of a family so rough, uncultured, and impoverished. A collection of letters existed, and maybe still exist somewhere, that were exchanged between Mom and her parents, telling them about him and wondering if she was doing the right thing. I guess she wanted their approval. It seems to me that they would not have encouraged such a marriage, and I am sure that because of her sense of herself and loyalty to her class, she had good reasons to be cautious. But she was a willful woman, of independent ideas and a strong backbone, and what was never in doubt is that they loved one another sincerely.

Fred knew the story better than anyone, and he had his ideas. "Nancy was never secure," he told me. "She was never secure, because—well, because he was a swordsman. Every town he traveled to, he had one. He had one in Memphis who was a millionaire—he used to tell me about her. He had a lot of them."

Dad also had a sharp sense of money and money management. He looked up to Bill Geer, and Bill Geer liked him. It was Bill, my grandaddy on my mama's side, who taught him about the stock market, about investments, and a philosophy of wealth and money management that stayed with him and that he passed on to us. He was a young executive in the 1970s when Bill Geer began to mentor him about stocks, mutual funds, blue-chip stocks, growth stocks, and all of that. I can recall the conversations, sitting and eavesdropping as I was accustomed to do, and a lot of that language rubbed off on me and sank in. I don't know exactly how much money Bill Geer made and how much he inherited, but I do also recall him talking sometimes about his trips to Cuba before the revolution to go big-game fishing, and that was not the kind of thing poor men did back them days. I recall my dad was just like a little kid himself, eating it all up.

My dad used to say to me that there were three men that he most admired in his life: Winston Churchill, Bill Geer, and Hamp Pike. I would be negligent if I was to write a memoir without finding somewhere to include a few words about Hamp Pike, even though he existed in my life in the stories my father told, and in the enigma of his finances. My dad used to say that if I reminded him of anyone it was old Hamp. Hamp Pike emerged from the many tales told about him as an old bum, a gambler, sloppy in dress, but who always had money somehow, and would almost always give my dad a few bucks when he came around. Hamp was the kind of guy who traveled around, living his life his way. You could never tell when he would be around, but whenever he was around, he would put his hand in his pocket and pull out a few notes, a few dollars, and give them away to whoever asked. He was never short of a little bit of money to give away. My dad always thought its kinda strange that a poor man like Hamp, a ragged, rundown drifter, always has a little money in his pocket to give. He died at a card table somewhere. He won a big game and as he was reaching across the table for his winnings he had a heart attack. They thought it proper to bury him with that cash in his coat pocket. It was his last winnings. Fred Pike and my dad always figured that there was a probably a million bucks buried somewhere, or stuffed into some old mattress, or maybe old Hamp Pike took all that he owned in life with him to his grave.

"Compound interest," my dad would tell my brother and me. What the hell is compound interest?

You put your money in the bank, or in some investment, and then you get interest and dividends. They give you money for nothing and then pay you interest on that interest. Compound interest. It builds wealth without you having to work for it. I heard this so many times!

I remember once I took a personal finance course and brought a book home, and he picked up the damn thing and read it from cover to cover. He read it more than I did. Nothing he did was rocket science, and nothing he drilled into us was revolutionary. Compound interest has been around since the beginning of time, but no one up on the mountain ever thought about it, because no one had any damn money, and most of them could hardly read. It was not about education or intelligence, but behavior. I recall one time in 1977, when he and Mama were planning a trip to Colorado, Dad told Denny and me, "Sons, if you want to visit Colorado, you're gonna need to buy your own airline tickets. Do your chores and find work and put it into your savings accounts. When the time comes, I'll take it out and buy your tickets. Need to start now. You've only got six months."

We knew him well enough to take this seriously, and for all that time, I recall running chores, doing stuff around the house and on the farms and smallholdings around the house.

Anything I could do. Every week, we went to the bank on a Saturday and put the money into our savings accounts. I really enjoyed our trips to Colorado. Later, as we sat in his hospital room and talked, I reminded him of that. He thought about it awhile and then shook his head with a smile.

"You certain about that, Jake? I sure have no memory of that."

A constant theme of our lives—in particular my brother's and mine—was financial responsibility, discipline, and independence. In 1973, when old Bill Geer died, he left a lot of money, and each of his grandchildren was given a stock. Mine was an IBM stock, which at the time was worth about four thousand dollars. Dad controlled it until I was eighteen. That was his rule. He had a sink-or-swim attitude. He would provide us with food, clothing, and shelter, but at age eighteen it was up to us. He would not even accept a collect call. I think, as the years passed, he was inclined to regret some of the abnormal pressures he placed on my brother and me, in particular my brother.

But the fact is that we did save up, and we did pay for our own airline tickets, because those trips to Colorado were a lot of fun. The Geers owned a vacation cabin outside Black Hawk, Colorado, where he and his boys hiked and fished. These were valuable life lessons. Dad admired Bill Geer as all the while Hattie Geer looked down on my dad. Nana loved her Manhattans, and when we visited, she would ask Dad to mix her a Manhattan. "I'm gonna try," he would say to me under his breath, "to mix Nana a Manhattan, but I can tell you now it ain't gonna be right."

Rarely did any of the Colorado side of family visit us either in Georgia or South Carolina. I recall on the occasion of such a visit that my mom would get very anxious. She began cleaning non-stop, way beyond her normal regimen of cleaning, which was pretty damn clean. I used to call it "cleaning over the clean." She cleaned the clean, and it was advisable to be careful around her because she could easily knock the shit out of you out with her elbows. I mostly remember that it was her parents who came, and she would grow more anxious and it became more hellish as the day approached. It was a big old anticlimax when they arrived, and then she was okay, and once they had gone, things got back to normal.

And that is how it was. Besides the necessary reunions, the Geers and the Pikes did not much overlap. Mom looked at the Pike family, and maybe even my Dad did too, and they saw the likes of Betty Pike. I don't know if the Geers ever knew about that part of my dad's life. Betty's condition was maybe born of incest, but also just as likely some throwback to a long and intermingled genetic line. Where else did that genetic heritage maybe come to the surface? When my Mama looked at her own son, his difficulties daily more manifest, I am sure that she, and perhaps even my father, wondered about it.

IN 1978 I ENTERED SEVENTH GRADE at Boiling Springs Junior High School in Spartanburg County. Although I did not fail another year, I could never score any higher than the middle averages. There were kids lower than me in average scores who passed, and I guess the truth is that South Carolina, just above Mississippi, has one of the lowest-performing school systems in the country, and it wouldn't make sense to fail everyone. I did not realize just how bad it was until I joined the military and had a daughter who passed through various school systems, including the Department of Defense school system. The South Carolina school system was geared in some ways to produce underachievers.

I was not categorized as college bound. There was no question about that. My school counselor, whose name was Mrs. Drake, with access to all my scores and assessments, specifically advised me against aspiring to enter college. My SAT scores were enough to confirm this, besides which it was just an understood fact that needed no explanation or further reinforcement. There were not too many kids in that world who were college bound anyway, and in general, the expectation was not encouraged. My brother Denny was a far more gifted student than I, and although not quite hitting the level of valedictorian, he consistently finished in the top two percent. My high school transcript put me at 122 out of 325, around thirty-seven percentile points, so it was Denny who came under pressure to carry the family flag forward into the next generation. My father's personal history left him with probably an exaggerated sense of the necessity of a college education, and he pressed my brother hard.

For me, that lack of expectation was kind of liberating. I was left to cruise through junior high on the understanding that I would probably take a trade or acquire some sort of technical skill. Dad suggested I get into agriculture or maybe start a small business—a bait and tackle shop or something of that nature. He could sense a streak of creativity in me and saw perhaps a future in the entrepreneurial field. I was very interested in agriculture, and I grew things at home. I had a compost pile where I bred worms, and generally I liked and understood nature and the cycle of life. At school, I took vocational agriculture and was a member of the Future Farmers of America. Spartanburg was a rural county, so I worked at the Gaines peach shed packing house, and farming and agriculture, they were everywhere.

The thing that sticks in my mind about that agriculture program was the teaching method of Mr. Haltiwanger. It was a fifty-five-minute class, but he gave only twenty-five minutes of instruction, concise, detailed, and to the point, and I found that very doable. That was a very valuable lesson for me. Take it all in in digestible portions. Shorter is better than longer, and I got into the habit of reviewing my notes no more than five minutes after the lesson. There was a library attached to the facility, and

I would often go in there to sit and revise my notes. I remember there was a soil-judging contest to assess the quality of particular soils for certain specific crops, and I studied that in just this way, and sure enough, pretty soon, I became an expert on dirt.

In the South of the 1980s, the old moonshiners were moving into marijuana. I picked up a few seeds from some of my friends from the old Norcross days and planted out a couple of fields. I also made a business of hanging around the liquor store and paying the old-timers to buy me beer and liquor. I sold the pot and the booze in the schoolyard and made a few dollars. One day my dad asked me where the hell I got all of that dammed liquor, and I told him, and he was impressed. He was less impressed by the pot.

"What the fuck is that?"

"It's a weed," I replied.

"I know it's a fucking weed, and I know what kinda weed it is. I want you to rip that shit up and put it on the compost. You got any more of that shit?"

I admitted that I did have another field in the woods back of the house.

"You smoking that shit?" he asked me.

"No way. I'm selling it."

"Mmm. You sure surprise the hell out of me, son."

He was also a risk taker. That's where I got it from. Coming down off the mountain with the idea of educating himself and breaking out of the cycle of poverty was a risk. He appreciated risk-taking and encouraged it. He also suggested that I think about joining the uniformed services. In the Southern states, a lot of boys plan their future in the military. For an average or below-average academic performer, it is often an obvious choice, hell, sometimes the only choice, because there were a whole lot of underperformers in the Southern school system at that time. If you could pass a simple multiple-choice test and had no diseases or physical infirmities and no felony convictions, you could get in. It was then, and still is today, a respectable institution with multiple avenues for advancement.

"You don't need to sign up full time," he told me, "just join the Reserves. Keep one foot in a normal job, and if you find that you like it, you can always join full time."

For me, the options were wide open. While I was only encouraged not to fail, Denny came under heavy pressure to succeed. Neither of us, however, was spared indoctrination into my father's fundamental philosophy of "No quitting!" To him, quitting was unacceptable on any level. If you don't understanding anything else that I'm talking about, you need to understand this shit.

My lesson came pretty early, when I signed up for seventh-grade football. There was some issue with my documentation—I believe it was my birth certificate, which had been lost in the move from Georgia. The coach was a disagreeable asshole who was called Mr. Smith. He also taught English, and although he let me practice, he would not allow me to play in any of the games until my documents were correctly submitted. My dad was sympathetic because it was a miserable situation, but he told me I was going to sit on that damn bench for a whole season, if that is what it took. My parents applied to the state for a duplicate copy of that birth certificate, and for the months it took for anything to happen, I sat on that goddamned bench in full kit and was never allowed to play. Even though I would never have asked to quit, he made it clear to me that I would not. When that certificate eventually came through, there was just one game left in the season, and I got to play, and we lost, and I broke my nose on the first play of the game and was put back on that damn bench. After that, I never cared to play football again. The lesson I learned, reinforced in so many other ways in my early years, was never quit. Never quit! That was the fundamental life lesson passed on to me by my father, who knew well enough the value of it.

In 1982, I was in the eleventh grade, seventeen years old, and a year behind because of repeating first grade. Under military statute, a kid can sign up at seventeen with his mother's signature. Although I was still in high school with one more year to complete, I was old enough to sign up, and that was the decision I made. A friend and I, a black kid called Willy Watson, drove one day to the Westgate Mall in Spartanburg County, where the recruiter's office was, and there we took the entrance test. I passed, and Willy did not. I don't know how the hell I passed! There were a lot of kids in the country who would have failed. When the Army asked me about previous injuries and operations, I lied and I told them, "I am good," and that was that. They never knew about my knee problems, and I never told them. I went down to the Reserves recruitment office, and there was no one in the entire building to take my application, so I drove away, and swung by the National Guard, and they said, "Sure, we'll take you." I raised my right hand and entered military service at the age of seventeen.

THE DUMBER YOU ARE

It's not that I'm so smart; it's just that I stay with problems longer.
ALBERT EINSTEIN

I ASKED MY DAD ONE TIME, "Did I ever tell you about the time I got locked up in the damned CCF at Fort Sill, Oklahoma?"

"Fort Sill?" He narrowed his eyes as he cast his mind back some forty years, to the day when he and Mama dropped me off at the Battery in Spartanburg.

"What's the CCF?" he asked.

"The Criminal Correction Facility!"

"No, I don't believe you ever told me that story, Jake."

FORT SILL IS AN ARMY BASIC TRAINING base. It's the home to the US Army Field Artillery School, the Marine Corps Field Artillery School, the US Army Air Defense Artillery School, the Thirty-first Air Defense Artillery Brigade, and the

Seventy-fifth Field Artillery Brigade. It was a hell of a place for a seventeen-year-old kid, still in high school, to take his first vacation out of state alone. It is one of the older forts on the US military history circuit, a remnant of the Indian Wars and a contributor of field artillery to all the major conflicts of the modern era. When the site was staked out in 1869, it was referred to by the Kiowa and Comanche Indians as the "Soldier House at Medicine Bluffs." Sometime later, it was named Fort Sill in honor of the Civil War brigadier general Joshua W. Sill. In the years since, it has grown into a sprawling, ten-thousand-acre complex lying just outside the shabby Oklahoma town of Lawton. In the summer of 2020, my wife, Beverly, and I took an overland trip, and as we passed through Lawton, Oklahoma, I was beset by a flood of memories. I thought it would be cool to stay overnight in Lawton and the next day take a look at the place, just for old time's sake.

By then I was a fifty-five-year-old retired lieutenant colonel with a long and varied service record behind me. Although my military career began easily enough, on that day in 1982, when I raised my right hand and signed up with the National Guard, that was just the beginning. At that time, I did not really picture myself as a career soldier, intending instead, like my dad, to just piggyback off a minimum of commitment to pick up a few easy bucks every month, and maybe some advanced education. I wanted to work the system a little bit. This was in keeping with his attitude of "throw a damned handful of sand in the fucker's face if you want to make the touchdown." Everyone who had an opinion to offer on the matter, from teachers to counselors to parents, told me I might be wasting my time even thinking about college, but as he told me, there is no fair fight, there is only winning. I made unashamed use of the National Guard and the ROTC to get where I wanted to go, working the system, and it was only as an afterthought that the Army became a full-time career.

This is the basic timeline of my military service: in 1988, while also a trained member of the National Guard, I was commissioned as a second lieutenant at the end of training with the ROTC at Clemson University. At Clemson, I also earned my bachelor's and first master's degree, both in agriculture education. My active-duty career began in 1992 as battalion chemical officer with the 10th Special Forces Group. I transferred in 1994 to the 154th Medical Detachment, serving with the Eighteenth Medical Command (MEDCOM) in Korea. From there, I climbed steadily through the ranks. I attended the Army Medical Department Advanced Course and Preventive Medicine Course, and served as an entomologist at the Center for Health Promotion and Preventive Medicine in Aberdeen Proving Ground, Maryland. In 1998, I was selected for Long Term Health Education and Training and earned my second master's degree in entomology from Colorado State University. From there, I returned to Korea in command of the Fifth Medical Detachment, 168th Area Support Medical Battalion, and Eighteenth MEDCOM in Yongsan. Between 2003 and 2007, I served as command entomologist at the Defense Logistics Agency at Fort Belvoir, Virginia. In 2007, I was back in Korea for the third time, this time serving as chief force health protection officer for the Eighth US Army. Between 2011 and 2012, I served in combat support during Operation *Enduring Freedom*, commanding the 452nd Medical Detachment in Shindand, Afghanistan. My last deployment was to Landstuhl, Germany, with the Public Health Command.

Returning to Fort Sill after all these years stirred up a bunch of memories, some good and some bad. A whole lot had changed, and although it is a softer, more humane process these days, it is still a tough experience for any kid to walk out of high school and in through the gates of a US military training facility. Finding my barracks and the central facilities was pretty easy, and it all looked somewhat the same, although most of the WWII-era accommodations that were still in commission when

I was under training had been torn down and replaced. It was tougher to locate the Criminal Correction Facility. However, after a few inquiries and some directions, I was back on that familiar route, and I found the complex looking weirdly unchanged. There were still guard towers, although they were empty, and it was still surrounded by a chain-link and razor-wire fence. Its function was no longer a correctional facility but an artillery Range Control Center (RCC). I stopped to chat with a guy smoking a cigarette outside, and pretending that I did not know, I asked him why an RCC facility was located in a stockade?

It used to be the CCF, he told me, and then he started bitching about having to work in an old correctional facility. It was a restricted area, and I could not gain access to the inside, and I don't really think I would have wanted to. That damned place was burned into my memory.

ONE MORNING IN JUNE 1983 I GOT OUT OF BED, stood in front of the mirror, and told myself that today was the day. After breakfast, my mom and dad drove me down to the National Guard Armory in Spartanburg, where a bus was waiting to transfer an intake of recruits to Spartanburg-Greenville airport. One of them I recognized was Dane Neves who lived across the road from Cora Pike, and he looked as anxious and uncertain of himself as I felt. From Spartanburg, we flew to Lawton, Oklahoma, and after a whole lot of hurry up and wait, we were herded onto another bus that took us across town to the entrance of Fort Sill. As we approached the gates, Dane Neves commented out loud, "Well boys, welcome to hell."

The bus swung round and came to a halt outside the reception center, and the doors opened like a landing craft ramp dropping on Omaha Beach. We filed out and walked into a shitstorm of confusion, yelling and screaming that began immediately, and did not stop. Following in quick succession came a spit-and-piss test for drugs, the contraband room, an introductory briefing, the Central Issuing Facility, duffle bags and uniforms. Go there, come back, sit down, stand up, all at maximum volume, and everything requiring a "Drill Sergeant, yes, Drill Sergeant." It was, as it was intended to be, as confusing and terrifying as the fog of war.

The strategy is to break a recruit down by coming at him from all directions, amplifying the stress and observing how each individual responds. Opinions are formed and performances quantified to quickly identify the weaker folk, the ones who probably would not still be around in thirteen weeks. Individuality was shattered, self-awareness crushed, and the idea of "I" and "me" obliterated. A recruit is deconstructed and reduced to nothing, from where he or she will be rebuilt as a soldier and a member of a team. The team becomes the single, basic element. There is no longer any such thing as an individual. Out of that individual, out of that young man or woman, for better or for worse, a soldier is created. Pressure is heaped on every recruit just to see how he or she functions under conditions of stress, and stress is about all I can remember.

Like much of the central facility, the barracks were of WWII vintage, with an upstairs and downstairs and the drill sergeant's office. The baffling progression of orders and sequences, the antiseptic backdrop, and a cohort of boys by now certain that they had made the biggest mistake of their lives. It could have come out of *Full Metal Jacket*, *Heartbreak Ridge*, or *Jarhead*, and every goddamned drill sergeant seemed to be a try-out for R. Lee Ermey's Gunnery Sergeant Hartman. It was Army basic training but it could have been Marine basic training, if you know what the difference would be. I am sure every recruit who ever felt the hot breath of a drill sergeant an inch from his face has the same type of thought.

I was assigned to a platoon of fifty-two basic trainees, some regular Army but most National Guard. We were placed under a senior drill sergeant by the name of William Ellenburg, who I recall as being pretty standard issue, about five-nine, muscular and compact, about five percent body fat, and a voice like a force-ten gale hurricane.

It was the South Carolina buddy platoon or possibly the SC redneck platoon according to Ellenburg At the time, the TV show "Dukes of Hazzard" was famous and it depicts a family living in the rural south on a farm always having run ins with the local police. One time a private said, "I am just a 'good ole boy' and Ellenburg lost his mind. We could all identify with the Dukes of Hazard because we probably lived it a bit. I doubt anyone of us were Rhodes scholar material. You see, I did not have a high school diploma yet, and many of us National Guard types did not. Ellenburg looked at us as 'less than', which was common at the time, as we were eventually going back home to "Fort Living Room" as they would call it.

Eighteen hours after stepping out of my bed in Fingerville, South Carolina, I put my head down on the white pillow of an army bunk in southern Oklahoma. I looked up at the bunk above, the silence eerie after hours of unrelenting mayhem, and I am thinking to myself, "Fuck!"

The next morning, all hell broke loose. Reveille was sounded at four in the morning, bringing privates to their feet. Physical training (PT) was scheduled for five o'clock sharp, with the hour or so in between reserved for cleaning the barracks and attending to private chores. Included in that discipline was trimming the grass on the walkway outside the barracks under the light of a flashlight because it was still dark outside. Breakfast was at seven o'clock, and training began exactly an hour later. We ran everywhere and never walked. Going to the restroom we ran, going to the chow hall we ran, and going anywhere in the outside area of the barracks we ran. If we weren't running, we were dropped for pushups. I was dropped for pushups many times, particularly exiting the chow hall, usually because I had just eaten, and I was relaxed and digesting my food. The only time we ever walked was inside the barracks.

My first significant problem was making up my bed. Basic training bed-making protocols are very specific and highly particular, like everything else in the Army. You have two sets of everything, one for practical use and another for inspection, and that there just screwed with my mind. Harry Moore, a kid from Spartanburg, helped me make my bed, and once it was done, it made sense to just not even make it anymore. The next night, and about every night after that, I slept on the floor underneath, maybe sometimes on top, and in the morning I'd just get up and tidy it up a bit.

This was just a minor thing that most of the other basic trainees seemed to find pretty easy, but a small issue can quickly become a really big problem in the Army. There were no kindly teachers or sports coaches to gloss over issues of low comprehension. The drill sergeants were conditioned to identify such weaknesses and pick at them like a scab until they become unsurvivable wounds. The Army is not like the Marine Corps that will reprocess a slow recruit until he or she is up to standard, very rarely cycling anyone out. In the Army, an informal quota of recruits is maintained to be failed as a process of selection, and as a means of motivating those with more promise. It is just part of the process, and it did not take long for Ellenburg and his sidekicks to spot me as a candidate for jerking around until I could take it no more. I had the same problem tying ties and shoelaces and numerous other petty procedures that required visual and spatial perception and quick hand-to-eye coordination. There was no time to experiment or practice and no opportunity was ever given for second tries. I understood that this was a crossroads for me because I knew very well that Ellenburg and his two subordinate drill sergeants, Joe Ragsdale and Michael Jackson, would spot any weakness in no time and would be all over my ass.

Harry Moore and I remained friends and met from time to time as the years passed, and he put it quite simple: "Being a slow learner is what it boiled down to." And he was right. Ellenburg fixated on me pretty much from day one. He was a drill sergeant in the original pattern, a career soldier in his early thirties, a combat engineer with Air Assault tabs and two years into his tour as a drill sergeant. He was in that crazy place that all drill sergeants get to after a while, which is the reason that a tour as a drill sergeant is limited to two years before rotation out. Drill sergeants play a particular role. Most of what they do is practiced and theatrical and designed to sow terror in the hearts of impressionable teenagers. While that malice and angry violence are mostly for show, the time comes when it starts to get real, and the Army measures that date as twenty-four months. Our platoon was Ellenburg's final intake, and he was not wasting time. They said that he was the toughest drill sergeant in the whole damned battery, and I believed it. Most of us were National Guard folks, and he didn't like that. National Guard meant Nasty Girls and he was probably pissed at that as well.

My infractions were minor, but they were consistent. It could be that I missed a square inch when I was shaving, had a twister in my webbing or my load-bearing equipment was misaligned or wrongly clipped and secured. It could be because, in the furious, rapid-fire, screaming, and unintelligible confusion, my mind froze, and my cognitive process was paralyzed. The more I fumbled and stuttered, the more it seemed to enrage him. Although sometimes Ragsdale and Ellenburg played good-cop, bad-cop, the good cop was always still pretty bad. Michael Jackson, who was a big, fit, and muscular black guy, a ghetto sergeant, standing over six feet tall, used to call every basic trainee a jackass.

"You jackasses are 'bout to piss me off!"

The truth is that if you want to survive Basic Training and move on in the Army, you have to do what you can not to disappoint your drill sergeant. Drill sergeants are predisposed to being disappointed and live to expose frailty and failure, and I was failing badly.

I guess the clearest way to illustrate how the whole process churned my guts is the weird fact that I would wake up and find myself alone on the parade ground in the dead of night, standing to attention in my skinnies, because of a dream or some damn thing, thinking it was time to fall in. When I became conscious, and when the fog cleared, I would realize that something was not right, and in a state of even greater confusion and self-loathing, I would creep back into my barracks and slide under my sheets on the top of the cool wooden floor. Guys told me I screamed and fought in my sleep. One day a private walked into the barracks pretending to be a drill sergeant. It was really nothing, just joking around and yelling about something the way that Ellenburg did, but it pissed me off, and inside of me something snapped. I jumped him and slammed him into the wall lockers, and then hurled him to the floor and began beating up on him. The guys pulled me off, and although he took it well, the news was out that I was so damned strung out that I couldn't hardly think straight. My mind and body were so completely over-geared in trying to digest everything, to drink out of that damned fire hose, that even while I was asleep, my mind was roiling in anxiety and stress.

Our platoon started with fifty-two guys, out of which thirteen either dropped out or were selected out. They started going to sick call to get out of PT, which is usually the beginning of the end. In those days, no serious basic trainee ever went on sick call, no matter what, and if he did, when drill sergeants took stock of it, that basic trainee was immediately on the shit list, no matter what. Sometime during those nine weeks, I picked up a serious bronchial infection and began hacking up mouthfuls of thick, green, foul-tasting phlegm that had specks of blood in it. To keep the fact quiet, I spat it out of the window of the second-floor barracks. Later I tried to clean it up with a hammer and a chisel, but it had become hard as cement. I never went on sick call. We were all suffering in different ways, and everybody's preoccupation was to grasp at any tactic and every strategy to survive. In a situation of such intensity, everyone is trying to find an edge, and if that edge is never going to sick call, then no matter how sick you get, you do not go on sick call.

Harry Moore was given notice of a trainee discharge program for poor marching and told to improve or his papers would be processed. He did improve, and survived to graduation, but for me the infractions just kept on coming. Although some of it might have been resistance and independence of mind, mostly it was just trying to drink out of that firehose again. Too much information, too many instructions, too much kit, too many acronyms, and too much incomprehensible jargon. I was not understanding everything—my equipment, my belt, my load-bearing equipment—things were misaligned or not properly secured during inspections. I may have a twister or something out of line, a button undone, a tuft of stubble on my chin, or my helmet sitting at an awkward angle. They were all minor infractions, but they were consistent. I was trying to understand everything I was supposed to do. I did the best I could, and I gnawed my fingernails to the quick in a state of continuous anxiety, but there were just too many infractions. Getting up multiple times in the middle of the night and going to stand outside on the parade ground just does not seem right. It was inevitable that some information on that would get back to Ellenburg, and his training was to pick up on and amplify odd or deviant behavior. I never back-talked to him, I was never disrespectful, and I tried my best, but there was no doubt that I was on his shit list.

Two basic trainees were identified to make an example of, to either get motivated or to get cycled out. One was Pvt. Sam Shaw, and the other was me. One day we were standing around at the rifle range waiting to be instructed when Ellenburg appeared and walked up the line, looking for trouble. He fixed his eye on Private Shaw and asked him in the usual tone,

"Did you shave today?"

"Yes, Drill Sergeant!"

"Shit! You know why your gear is all jacked up? I'll tell you why. Because you're sorry. You know what? I'm sending your ass to CCF."

With that, he walked off, and a couple of the basic trainees asked what was CCF. It's the damned Criminal Correction Facility! Jesus! Having wrapped up our rehearsal at the firing range, we returned to barracks and had lunch before attending a briefing. Briefings were becoming pretty routine by then, and right after that briefing, Ellenburg came into the room and roared, "Who all wants to go to CCF for observation?"

Private Neves put up his hand to attend CCF because he had not heard the bad news and thought it was an exercise or something that he would get to observe. It shocked the shit out of him in the end when he did not spectate but participated. Private Neves' attendance at CCF was his own damned misunderstanding. Ellenburg allowed his finger to hover over a sea of silent but expectant faces for a moment before he directed it at me. I know that it was not a random choice. He already had in mind who he wanted to weed out of the platoon. With that, the platoon filed out and moved on to something else while I was left standing in a state of confusion and shock. I'm thinking to myself what the hell had just happened?

Nothing was explained to me, and all that I understood was that somehow I had screwed up real bad. I was going to CCF. That is for bad people—criminals and serious screw-ups. It occurred to me that maybe if you do not do what the drill sergeants say in the Army that goes against the Uniform Code of Military Justice and is some type of a crime. I was out of the Army, and I was going into Criminal Correction. It was over, and it might take a long time to be processed out, so how long would I be in? I was thinking I would miss the next high school semester. I tried to process it all as me, Sammy Shaw, and a few other guys from other platoons rode the bus the mile or so to the CCF. A half-hour later, we arrived at that formidable place, surrounded by barbed wire and watched over by guard towers. In a state of almost paralyzed apprehension, I stepped out with the others and walked through the gate, and it was day one all over again, instantly, but this time much worse.

Get down, get up, get down, get up. Duck walk, log drill, low crawl over gravel until our sleeves were torn and arms scraped up and bloodied. Wielding a sledgehammer to make a big rock into small rocks. There were other soldiers around me trying to deal with the same shit, although I did not speak to or even take notice of them under a remorseless shitstorm of rapid-fire orders. I don't think I even went to the bathroom. It went on consistently until, quite abruptly, the drill sergeant said, "Go ahead, get up. You're going back to your platoon."

We arrived back at barracks at about six thirty that evening, and there Ellenburg gathered the rest of the platoon and told them to have a good look. Sammy and I stood there like a pair of sorry soldiers, and slowly, out of the fog, the whole thing began to make a bit more sense. The two of us were a hell of an example, a hell of a motivating factor for the others. We were standing there bloody, torn up, beaten up. In the years since, I have searched for some similar situations, such an extreme motivational method, and I have been unable to find anything. It could not have been a spontaneous thing on Ellenburg's part because an appointment would be required to book in a bunch of soldiers for some sort of session. The drill sergeants at the CCF were expecting us, and the program lasted exactly three hours, and it seems on reflection to have been preplanned and preconfigured, and maybe Ellenburg and others ran a lot of trainees through the same process.

Whatever the man was thinking, it worked. I call it my "Come to Jesus Moment." Although I process information slowly, I process it thoroughly, and everyone that I have kept up

54

with since those days tells me that the change in me was like night and day. Ellenburg took note of the fact that the experience had not broken me, as I am sure he expected, but had motivated and energized me. It seemed then that he switched from trying to weed me out of the platoon to thinking about how he could help me. One afternoon he called me into his office and asked me with apparently sincere concern, "Private Pike, are you fucking crazy or what?"

"No, Sergeant. My mama thinks I'm crazy, but I ain't crazy."

"You know," he said, this time in a kindlier, more fatherly tone, "we got programs here. We can help. You can get medical help if you need help."

"No, Drill Sergeant," I replied. "I don't need any help."

"Let me know if you need some help. We'll help you out. You want to go to a doctor?"

"No!" I replied, with a level of resolve and determination that surprised even me. "I don't want to go to the doctor, because I would miss out on training, and I need additional training. I need all the training that I can get."

He looked at me for a long time, flint hard and unsmiling, before, without further comment, and shaking his head, he dismissed me.

He seemed to like that, though. A soldier asking for more training is a soldier with commitment. I think that answer not only saved my ass, but it also set in motion a thought process within myself, and the development of a principle, one that I have used and reused time and again throughout my life. More training. Nothing is impossible if you can get enough training. Three days before graduation we had our end of cycle test and I was one of few who scored all gos. A go is a graded pass. Ellenburg handed out the results and then addressed the platoon.

"You see this Private Pike right here?" he said. "I was going to kick his ass out in the third week, but today, at the end

55

of cycle test, he got all gos. I want everybody here to applaud him."

In recognition of that achievement, he gave me an off-base pass, which the privates rarely if ever got. An off-base pass means you get to leave the base and head into town. I stayed on base because I had a suspicion that trouble favored me somehow, and Lawton, like all army towns, had plenty of potential for trouble. Besides that, like everyone, I was beat and just happy to have survived. In my packet of papers handed to me on my departure from Fort Sill was a certification titled "The Most Improved Private Award."

YEARS LATER I TRACED WILLIAM Ellenburg Jr to a family in Salisbury, North Carolina, from whom I was able to get his telephone number in Hawaii. He would have been in his mid to late forties by then and still an active-duty sergeant major on the island of Oahu. When I called, he did not remember me. "Too many damned privates!" he said, but I think he was touched that whoever I was, I made the effort. He may not have remembered me, but I remember him. As I stepped outside the gates of Fort Sill, a trained soldier of the US Army, I felt a new and satisfying surge of confidence. I had survived Basic Training, and I knew now that I could achieve so much more. I could achieve whatever the hell I set my mind to. In the Army, the dumber you are, the more likely you will be infantry, or artillery, or some other low-skill specialty, and that was not going to be me. Army Basic Training was the hardest experience of my life to that date, and probably ever since, and I don't think any kid who walks out of high school and through the gates of a training base can say any different. I survived, and now I had opportunities. For the first time in my life, I thought seriously about it, and figured that "college bound" might really be a possibility.

The Fort Sill Army Regional Correction Facility was deactivated in November 2010 after thirty-three years of function, transferring those inmates still serving sentences to Fort Leavenworth in Kansas. The same happened in Fort Carson, Colorado, and Fort Knox, Kentucky, along with numerous Marine and Navy correctional facilities and a number of disciplinary barracks scattered all over the country. The Fort Sill facility was integrated into the training program as a Range Control Center, its security features still in place and looking very much like a prison. As a retired soldier, I took it all in and remembered that brutal three hours as the most transformative of my life.

A interesting story is a fight with my dad. It was a playful fight. It was after I had come back from Basic Training. I had a skinned head, I was intense. I did not even know what happened to me. I was different, and he detected a little bit of bad-ass in me, and he wanted to test it. So, he started playing around, pushing me around until eventually he got me on the floor and tried to pin me. I turned him around and I picked him up about a foot or two and I body-slammed him on his back. That's when he yelled "no more! No more!". I though I'd hurt him. I though " Oh my God I can't believe I done this to my dad!" He had to be faking it! On the other hand I was thinking maybe I did beat his ass, maybe the only time anyone has beat his ass.

Dad listened with his eyes closed, and for a while I thought he was asleep. Diane Cole came in and out, and his vitals were checked. I was told that I really was messing with the rules, but he opened his eye, chuckled quietly, and said,

"No, you never told me that damn story. You always surprise the hell out of me, son."

WHERE THERE'S A WILL THERE'S AN 'A'

It's not what you achieve, it's what you overcome. That's what defines your career.

CARLTON FISK

A FEW YEARS AFTER MY RETIREMENT, I caught up with an old friend, Mark Stevens, at one time my gunnery sergeant in the National Guard, at Charlie Battery in Inman, South Carolina, who had also recently retired from the service. Over the years, I tried to keep in touch with him, and as I began the preliminary work on this memoir, I called him up, and we met over lunch at the Golden Corral in Spartanburg. I figured he would be a good place to start An angular man of expressive mannerism and lively wit, he has both the wry humor of a Southern man and the native love of telling stories. I figured he would be a good place to start as I tried to build a picture of how unpromising I must have looked to the guys in the unit when I made it home from Basic Training.

After Basic Training, the emphasis on artillery and gunnery remained, and so battery training became a fairly routine part of life in the National Guard. The National Guard does not deport itself as a regular, active-duty outfit, and so the rules of attendance and training are a little bit looser than active duty, and even the Army Reserve. Although a whole lot of drinking got done during battery training, we sent a shitload of bombs downrange without, at least as far as I recall, hitting anything that we shouldn't have. Often it seemed that the more beer we drank, the better we shot. Yes! We did drink beer and shoot rounds. One day I happened to mention to Sergeant Stevens that I was thinking of going to Clemson, and he laughed so hard, beer in his hand, that he almost fell off his ammunition box.

"Hell!" he hooted. "You'll never graduate from Clemson. You'll never graduate, boy. Never."

Now, thirty-five years later, as a retired lieutenant colonel with two advanced college degrees behind me and a significant amount of specialist training, I reminded him of that comment. He laughed.

"Well," he replied, "it sure amazed the hell out of me when I heard. How the fuck did a shithead like you manage that?"

I told him I owed him a favor. He was a pretty straightforward soldier, a left-right-left kind of guy, and in those days a lot of folks who enlisted stayed enlisted. It was kind of expected, and any ambition to break the mold and go beyond the norm is usually looked at with scorn. When he said that to me, laughing in my face, it kinda pissed me off and fired up my determination. He was just one of a bunch of different people who said the same thing, or thought the same thing, and when I hear that sort of shit, it just causes me to think, "Ah fuck that— I'm going to do it."

THE MOOD OF THE OUTBOUND JOURNEY from Fort Sill back to Spartanburg was noticeably less noisy and rambunctious than the inbound, as a small crop of local boys who had become men returned to their daily lives. My mom and dad collected me up at the Spartanburg-Greenville Airport and I guess, like every parent there, they sensed the change in me straight away. Apart from the usual hugs, handshakes, and inquiries, they asked no detailed questions, and I did not tell. The experience was still too fresh, too raw, and still unresolved in my mind.

Nothing was said about CCF for years. It was not until we got to talking there at the Mary Black Hospital that I even told my dad about it. I guess I wanted to try and explain to him, and maybe to myself, what it was that happened back then. The truth is I have no idea. All I know is that I owe it to Ellenburg for picking up the signs and God for the idea. In reply to Ellenburg's query about a referral to a psychiatrist, I told him I did not need a shrink, only more training. He's probably never heard a soldier say such a thing and I never thought about it before than moment, and yet, in the weeks that followed that CCF experience I woke up, and the penny dropped, and I discovered the simple strategy of more training. Work harder and longer really did seem to work.

Here are a few examples. Making my bed began as a severe challenge, and it remained so right until the end. My initial solution was to make my bed once and never sleep in it again, but as I gained confidence, I began to apply myself to repeating the procedure over and over until eventually, even though I never quite mastered it, I got a whole lot better. Even after that, I still preferred not to sleep in it, I didn't, because we were too damned tired, but I discovered that the idea was sound and it worked. Field-stripping an M16 is a basic drill fundamental to any soldier's training, and that also completely screwed me up. It is a simple procedure involving a couple of pins and a basic spring and bolt removal and replacement, designed to be soldier-proof, but it took me hours of endless repetition before I eventually nailed it down. Dealing with the small particulars of kit and presentation and all the other minor details that drill sergeants fixate on was improved by methodically going over the routines time and time again. I began to be given a little bit of latitude by my instructors, and as I passed through Individual Advanced Training, I managed to get by.

It took time, and it took time management, but in the end, it worked. This revelation was the first tiny light to shine in an infinite darkness, and once I fixed my attention on it, it seemed to grow brighter by the day. Although Ellenburg was the first to notice that change, my platoonmates also saw it, and so did my mom and dad. Back in my room on the evening of my return, I stood in front of the mirror in full uniform, and I saw a new and very different person looking back at me.

Back at school, things were different, too. I was now a trained soldier of the US Army, in high school, and in the South, a soldier is to be respected. I was also changed. Basic Training, even modern, softer versions of it, is a hardening, maturing process that instills self-confidence and self-reliance in a young person. This was probably more noticeable in me because I was still in high school and still surrounded by school kids. I became intense in my moods and responses, feeling separate, unique, and inspired in a way that I had never been before. Suddenly I had real confidence—true, life-altering confidence—which is something that I had never felt before. In the past, that sense of being different always came with expressions of sympathy and a pat on the head that said, "Never mind, you'll catch up someday." Now I felt that I had caught up a little bit. Stronger and smarter Basic Trainees than I was had quit when the going got tough, but I never did. I expected to be thrown out at any time, but I never thought about quitting. I came through in the end with a perfect score on my end-of-cycle test. Who would have guessed?

With my first National Guard paycheck, I bought a truck, a Toyota pickup, in the flatbed of which I lost my virginity to the first girl in my life. Her name was Dianne, and we met in church one day. I had had a few false starts in that department already. I recall taking a girl from a local family out to dinner one night, but when I picked up a bowl of soup and slurped it, and dripped some drips on my shirt, she threw down her napkin and told me I was a pig and asked me to take her home. I never saw her again after that.

Dianne was different. She was a simple, uncomplicated, unaffected girl from a working Southern Baptist working family who appreciated a strong and protective man. Although she was still a schoolgirl when we met, I was a soldier, and so her parents both liked and trusted me. We split up for a little while, and during that time, she began dating another boy I knew from the neighborhood. He owned a classic Ford Mustang, and one night I took my dad's twenty-gauge, grabbed a few shells, and staked out his place until the lights were turned out. I was feeling jealous. Then I walked up their driveway and put half a dozen loads of buckshot in the back of his car. She knew it was me, her mom knew it was me, so did her dad, and so did the new boy, but no one could prove a damn thing. Later, I ambushed him in the woods and beat the shit out of him. Word soon got around that it was a bad idea to mess with Pike's girlfriend.

Later, for a little while, we got back together, and when her mom asked – "Did you hear what happened to Robert's car?" I replied that I did not, and she smiled and said – "Someone shot it up!" Although she knew it was me she still allowed me to date the daughter. Both her mom and dad liked me even after that.

In the meantime, directly out of Basic Training, I was back at Boiling Springs High School to wrap up my senior year. My grades in that year did not improve much. Under the stress of the Criminal Correction Facility at Fort Sill, with drill sergeants screaming at me, I made the decision that I would work for a college degree, but that was easier said than done. I understood that to escape the fate of being a grunt, not only in the Army, but anywhere, I would need a college degree. My main motivation was only to never have to deal with any of that shit ever again. It was only later, when it was all over, and when the penny dropped and the lights came on, that I understood a college degree really was within my reach.

The Amy has a mantra they call the Five Ps, or 'Pre-planning Prevents Piss Poor Performance." Well, now that I was on the other side of Basic Training, I had a better idea of what that actually meant. I cannot recall exactly when I first heard it, but I think it was spending hours every night sitting on my bed stripping and reassembling an M16 that caught someone's attention, who pointed it out as "Pike drilling the Five Ps."

I thought about that a lot, and although it seemed to make a lot of sense and was easy when I was dealing with something as simple as tying a necktie or lacing up a pair of boots, in the more complex world of academia it was less obvious. Then, one day when I was at home watching TV, I caught an ad for an audiovisual learning seminar titled *Where There's a Will There's an A*. The ad featured the actor John Ritter in an infomercial format selling a learning system devised by a certain Professor Claude Olney of Arizona State University. The keywords that caught my attention were "study smart." That turned a switch in my head. Study smart and more training. Those two concepts seemed to go well together and made sense of the Five Ps. Work harder, work smarter, and plan for every eventuality. I sent off for the series, and a week or so later, a package arrived containing two VHF videocassette tapes. Although this new information did not come in time to help much with my high-school scores, it altered completely the direction of things when I enrolled in junior college.

THESE ARE THE PRINCIPLES MAPPED OUT in *Where There's a Will There's an A*, and in some ways they are self-evident and just a part of the general discipline of smart study. There are, however, also a few principles that are more esoteric, philosophic and sensory. For example, I always advise a student to use every one of their senses, especially when they are trying absorb some crazy or elusive concept.

Read aloud and record. Write because writing requires more than superficial reading. Use your finger to touch the paper. Listen to your voice. Study that paper while you are eating or drinking as a way to use your sense of taste and smell. Bring all of your senses into play as a kind of animal absorption of the idea or concept that you are trying to take in. The first and most important thing is enthusiasm. No system is going to work well unless you have a fundamental will to learn, Show up early at every class and sit in the front. Be interested, or act interested. Interest is what interest does. This is the early bird principle where the early bird gets the worm. It builds momentum, and the more you get into the habit of applying it the better it is. Be in class first, if you can try and sit in that front row. You can pick up all the choice nuggets that way. Your teacher will take note that you're always present and eager to learn, teachers like that, and when it come time to mark your paper your teacher will surely remember you.

Study your teacher too, because understanding the messenger helps in understanding the message. Mine an interrogate teachers, get intelligence from other students, and other people on how to strategize in advance before an upcoming semester or two. Do not load up on too many difficult classes in a semester. For every challenging class choose two that are less challenging. This can be true for both classes and teachers. Try to stack up more classes that you are stronger in than weaker. Go light on classes if necessary. Don't cram, don't over-study and take your time, and never be afraid to put up your hand. If you need clarification ask for clarification.

Be a regular at the library, and make use of the librarian. For me this was very important. Librarians love to answer question, and take a recording device into class and keep an audio record if you need. If you need a job then find one that gives you plenty of time to read and study. There are jobs out there. Security guard is a good example, I was a security guard and the junior college and I would study. Maybe a limo driver or night care. Study in short sessions and vary your locations. Shorter is always better than longer. Take frequent breaks. Take a nap if you need to. Take a walk around the block. Change your location from time to time. You will find information has a way of settling in when you do this. Use note cards because note cards speak to the brevity of study. A glance at a small three by five card does wonders. Take one more look at your notes no more than five minutes after you have left the class or the lecture. This could be difficult because you just got through listening. Just go ahead and do that shortly afterwards. Just a brief review. No need to write anything down. Just review the notes from the class within five minutes of leaving. Find a place where you can sit quietly and review those notes. Just five minutes.

IN 1984 I GRADUATED HIGH SCHOOL and enrolled at Spartanburg Methodist College (SMC). As I recall, I drove onto the campus in my Toyota pickup truck, walked into the Applications Office, and just filled out a couple of forms. I was not required to show any high school scores, no questions were asked, and I was accepted on the spot. SMC is a nonprofit junior college offering an associate degree in preparation for transfer to a university degree course. Although the cost was minimal, I paid for some of it, and the National Guard paid for some of it, through the Montgomery GI Bill.

I remember when I graduated college, my dad said to me, "Son, you are the only person I know who graduated college and took a cut in salary."

This was an inside joke. The reason was that I stacked up scholarships by religiously visiting the Spartanburg Methodist College Financial Aid Office until I was on first-name terms with all the counselors. One time I recall being criticized by another student whose comment was that the only way I got a 4.0 was because of my easy classes and lower load. That was exactly correct, and I was also being rewarded by the financial and scholarship systems. I probably had more money in the bank than he did. Anything that was on a scholarship offer, no matter how obscure, I applied for. I held down various jobs and gigs the entire time, so as a college student, I had plenty of resources. It seemed easy to me to conceptualize the college education scholarship system, the Veterans Administration disability system, and the US Army in general. Although I was unable to read or write well and I fumbled several applications, I could look at a complex system and understand in general, strategic terms how it worked and how to exploit it. If on my first shot I did not succeed, I just resubmitted my packet again, and then again, and many times more until I got exactly what I was looking for. The idea was just to wear them down with persistence.

Enrolling at junior college was a profound moment for me just because I *was* stepping so far out of my lane. I was scared. Everyone who ever took an interest in me told me I was not college bound and should not attempt it. I was just fearful a lot of the time at Spartanburg Methodist because I knew I had no real place there based on my grades and the opinions of my advisors and counselors, but I was determined to give it a try. My parents, although they never actively discouraged me, adopted a cautious line, damping down expectations and taking a "let's wait and see" approach. I guess they did not want to see me disappointed. I left school with very poor SAT scores, which was kind of predictable, and by that standard I certainly should not have been college bound, and there was no reason for anyone to think that I had any chance of succeeding.

So it was, with at best lukewarm encouragement, that I stepped blindly into a place where I did not belong. My pitch for a college degree had begun. My dad did it, and my brother did it, and now I was doing it. I can think of nothing more daring or ambitious than his coming down off that mountain at age thirteen with aspirations to study, to learn, to go to college, and to advance himself. No one ever told my dad he was college bound, but he did it anyway. Like him, I did not belong there. I was not college bound, but I was going anyway.

In the meantime, there was still the National Guard. One weekend a month and two weeks a year. Typically, a lot of beer got drunk, some cleaning up got done, and a whole lot of bullshitting. From the very start, I had a cat-and-mouse relationship with Sgt. Mark Stevens and others because my attitude was strictly academics first. My attitude to the Guard was just that it was the vehicle that would drive my education. I can recall to this day, as he tried to teach me the basic principles of an artillery aiming device, that Mark Stevens would scratch his head and look at me with the same bafflement as Drill Sergeant Ellenburg did a year earlier. It was a basic, old-school system with a leveling bubble for horizontal and another for vertical. "Listen, boy!" he said. "It ain't fuckin' rocket science. Any idiot can do it. I can't go any damned lower! You got to damn listen!"

It was worse at night. After fumbling in the dark for ten minutes, I asked him how was I supposed to do it?

"You got that flashlight in your pocket, ain't yer?" he asked.

Out came the flashlight with the white LED, and he almost lost his fucking mind.

"You got no fucking light or noise discipline at all. No white light on a live exercise, goddamn it!"

There is supposed to be a runner moving between groups to run dispatches, and I'd just holler.

"Shut the fuck up, boy!" he'd hiss at me. "Jesus fucking Christ!"

While under instruction to drive an M109 self-propelled howitzer, he gave up trying to connect with me through the helmet communications and took to hitting me on the head with a stick to get my attention. A smack on the right side of my helmet meant right, left meant left, and big smack on the top meant to go forward.

"You had the potential," he later admitted. "I could see it. But it seems as if you tried to push me, tryin' to push me to my limits. I could tell that you was smarter that what you acted like. You can read people. That's when you signed up, told me you was going to Clemson. I said, 'Hell, you'll never graduate from Clemson.' That's exactly what I told you. You'll never graduate. Never."

In my order of priorities, academics was always going to come first and Army training second. I was not looking for a successful career in uniform, just a college degree. He and other officers and NCOs interpreted my frequent absences as indiscipline, which they probably were, and that just added to his mounting frustration. It got so bad that one day he showed up at the Spartanburg Methodist College campus with a damn deputy intending to arrest and court-martial me. They couldn't find me.

"I think you had missed one or two tutorials," he remembered, "and you tried to blame it on school and this and that. To me, that was just a damned excuse. If you've got school, we usually work with you, but you just wouldn't show up. This went on for a month or two, and I told you, 'I'll put your ass in jail!' I seen potential in you; you was surely smarter than you was giving out. Sometimes you tried to get away with stuff. I put ol' Butch Collins in jail for three days, even though he was my buddy."

In fact, I was nowhere near campus at the time but studying in my truck in the parking lot of the Inman Armory. We might have three or four formations in a day, and although I would show up like I was supposed to, when it came time to study, I would just go to the car in the parking lot. I did what was necessary to get by in the Guard with my mind fully focused on college and studying. Academics was always going to come first. To me, the National Guard was just a means to an end. The ROTC was the same thing[1]. Besides that, the National Guard issued an easy paycheck, and I was not going to drop that.

I joined the Spartanburg Methodist College ROTC program because it offered easy college credits, but also because, in my mind, without telling a soul, I was starting to think about getting a commission. Not much had changed on the outside when I got home from Fort Sill, but a lot had changed on the inside. Surviving that experience taught me two things. The first was that if I could survive that, I could do any damn thing, and the second was that I did not plan to remain in the enlisted ranks forever. Since a commission required a college degree, and I was working towards that, it seemed to me to be an obvious way to go. For the time being, however, my strategy remained simply to put in the minimum requirement to stay in the Guard and the ROTC while at the same time making use of all the opportunities offered by both institutions to further my education. I got my Guard paycheck, I had the GI Bill, and I had a clear sense of the system and how to shake it. I continued to be a regular at the Financial Aid Office applying for any kind of scholarship. I learned more and more every day that *Where There's a Will There's an A.* Dad would always say, "Son, you need to understand the system!"

---

[1] ROTC, for those unfamiliar, means Reserve Officers' Training Corps. It described by Wikipedia as "a group of college and university-based officer training programs for training commissioned officers of the United States Armed Forces."

Well, I understood the system well enough, at the ten-thousand-foot level. The financial aid system is just another system. I learned that there are systems to everything. The scholarship process is a system. College is a system, and most of all, the Army is a system. I found I could understand the system far better than the minor details. I understood things at that ten-thousand-foot level way better than I did down there in the weeds. Non-Commissioned Officers are described often as enlisted soldiers with specific skills and duties, such as training, recruiting, tech, or military policing. The Army refers to these ranks as its "backbone." Commissioned officers, on the other hand, are management. They give NCOs and lower ranks their missions, their assignments, and their orders. That's why I figured that I could be an officer. They say NCOs are commissioned by the Grace of God, but regular officers are commissioned by Congress.

In Basic Training, and through my involvement with the Guard, I could see and understand how officers and men interacted. I could never be a sergeant because of my low capacity for detail, but I figured I could function well as an officer. Shit rolls down the hill. Send it down to the sergeant. If they have any issues, it comes back up to you, but it always goes back down. I can see things better from the top down. It is hard for me to turn the nut, and I could never wrap my head around righty-tighty, lefty-loosy, but I could understand how the mechanism functioned, how the *system* worked. While I might struggle to work a damn howitzer, I understood well enough how and when to deploy one, or a particular platoon or battalion, or even a regiment. I could instruct someone else to deal with the confusing details.

I knew how to take care of soldiers. I was humble and never came off with an attitude of arrogance or knowing everything, as I had seen so many other commissioned officers behave. Sometimes I approached soldiers with a request for help, simply because I did not know it all. I would never say a word about any academic difficulties. That was how I was taught by my father. No excuses. That's how I figured it. Relative competency levels are such that an officer requires an overall, three-dimensional view of the battlefield, while a senior NCO requires detailed knowledge of specifics and practical logistics. At the time, I did not realize that officers also have to write papers and reports. I just saw them coming out of their offices and giving orders to their first sergeants and platoon leaders. I thought I could more easily do that than bust my ass trying to deal with light and noise disciplines, trying to figure out forward, back, left, and right, and damned bomb-aiming devices. I saw it as being a general manager, and a general I could understand.

I ENROLLED IN THE SMC ROTC PROGRAM mostly for the sake of the college credits. After surviving Army Basic Training, and criminal correction, I figured out pretty quickly that ROTC was not much of anything. At the same time, the Wofford College ROTC Ranger Program was open to outside colleges, including Spartanburg Methodist College, so I joined that. The Ranger ROTC, which ran concurrently with National Guard, was extracurricular and a lot more hardcore, and so for a while I went hog wild with training. I was involved with the ROTC program, the Wofford Ranger program, and the National Guard all at the same. I figured I would eventually enter the officer corps, so I wanted to take on any extra training I could. The reason I joined the Ranger program was because ROTC grades leadership levels by basic infantry tactics, and since I was still artillery, I figured I needed extra training in the basics of leading an infantry squad. It was all about extra training and studying smart.

I did enjoy ROTC Ranger training because, as trainees, we got to do things way above and beyond the normal ROTC standard. Everything about the program was tougher, more rigorous, and more elitist in outlook. I had already been through Army Basic Training, and so my interest was in any additional training in leadership and infantry and assault tactics.

I recall during the ranger program a course at Camp Croft, Spartanburg, South Carolina, during which we were instructed on the correct handling and disposal of dead prisoners or enemy bodies in a combat zone. There is a particular method and procedure to approaching a dead body in relation to possible booby traps or contamination. The cadet playing the dead body objected to how I approached and sat up with a survival knife and stabbed me in the arm. At the time I did not know it because it was so fast. I guess he was trying to illustrate the risks of a faulty approach, and that a dead body could become a live body with a weapon at any time. It was winter and damned cold, and I was wearing layers, and so it was not until a few minutes had passed that I began to feel something warm under my uniform and I realized that I had actually been stabbed. I showed the wound to the captain, who immediately ordered me taken to Spartanburg General Hospital. Five stitches later, I was back, and when he saw me, the knifeman came over and apologized. No one was killed, no harm done, and no report made. He was a Ranger *cadre*, a senior student who had already been through the Ranger program and was now part of the support staff training the new Rangers. Shit happens. I was just happy to be in the program.

The Ranger program was certainly elite. With the equipment and opportunities we had, our training mimicked as closely as possible regular Army Ranger training. We did the ruck marches, ranges, survival, basic infantry tactics, how to react to ambushes, how to call for fire and just a wild amount of physical fitness training. I remember during a survival exercise they gave us a live chicken and said, "Hey, here's a chicken! Y'all figure this thing out.' We chased that chicken down, wrung its neck, cut it up and made a stew out of it. The idea was, I guess, to encourage ingenuity and resourcefulness and to promote team spirit. Ruck marches could be brutal. I recall trainees hallucinating from dehydration. We were at Camp Croft, and a kid walked off into the woods saying, "I've seen my daddy. I've seen my daddy out there!"

I grabbed him and hauled him back into line, saying, "No, you didn't. Just keep on walking. We are going to get this thing done. You can see your daddy later."

I remember seeing cadets trying to put quarters into a tree, thinking it was a Coke machine. Dehydration and exhaustion will do that. I once got dehydrated myself during an ROTC field exercise. I was out of water and asked another trainee if he would give me some of his. He refused, which was quite correct. Getting dehydrated is a big mistake on exercise, and usually a sergeant will drop a ton of shit on you if you start displaying signs of it. I asked again for the water, and when again he refused, so I attacked him and tried to forcefully take his water off him. Although a hell of a fight followed, he kept his water. I remember seeing him running off into the darkness after the fight with his water bottle, and I stayed thirsty.

One day, as I was set to rappel off the Viking football stadium at Spartanburg High School, a senior Ranger cadet checked my rigging and tied me off with a thumbs up. I was about to go over when the captain ran a second check and noticed an error in my gear and corrected it. The senior cadet got chewed out, and if I was sent over the edge without that second check I would have been seriously injured at the very least and likely killed. The ROTC Ranger Program was tough, but nothing like basic training.

The best part of it was that I picked up an Airborne patch. The course was conducted at Fort Benning, Georgia, and, according to the Ranger ROTC literature, "All it takes is three weeks at Fort Benning, a couple of gallons of sweat, a few thousand falls, and five little steps out of an aircraft twelve hundred feet up, and you will earn the coveted wings of the US

Army Paratrooper. Cadets have the opportunity to compete for a slot to the US Airborne School at Fort Benning, Georgia."

Again, I didn't think anything was difficult about the US Army Airborne School. I was much more scared of college than jumping out of a perfectly good airplane. They call the Airborne patch "Blood Wings," and it is pinned on with a bit of hazing and well-earned camaraderie. The blood wings tradition derives from a ritual of placing the badge on the graduate's chest with the pins facing inwards, and then slamming it into the chest to draw blood. I was still in the mindset that academics trumps Army training, but I was still sucking up good training, picking up a ton of credits, and building prestige as a soldier. Although I was still not thinking specifically of a long-term career in the military, each small achievement added more to the momentum, and in retrospect, it all seemed to be heading that way.

TWO YEARS AT SPARTANBURG Methodist College taught me truly that *Where There's a Will, There's an A*. I did not leave with an associate degree but with the maximum amount of course work necessary to transfer to a great university. In the first year at SMC, I pulled straight As and in the second, mostly As and Bs. I was scored at a 3.5 grade point average or higher, which at the time was well above the median. I refined and developed those principles of smart study and extra training, and for that, I won the math and biology awards in my final year. I came back a few years later and asked why I won the mathematics award, and the answer was because I was the only student who took all the courses from the bottom to the top. I started at general math, which I should have learned in high school, and went up as far as trigonometry. I won the biology award just for good grades, but I was always good in sciences. I did well at junior college, and that gave me a whole lot of solid confidence in moving on somewhere else. I was feeling unbelievably blessed, and I was hoping that my luck would hold. I call SMC my second-chance college. One day, my dad took a look around my room and found my four-point-zero perfect-score grades on the first semester. He said, "Jake, why did you not tell us about this?" I found it difficult to explain at the time. I felt that maybe it was luck and that maybe it might not ever happen again. Again, college was something I was not supposed to succeed at, at least according to the experts, and I was not yet on the other side, so bragging or informing my parents was something I was not comfortable with.

In the meantime, I badly wanted to go to Wofford College because my father went there, my brother went there, and eventually my sister did too, and of course I did the Wofford ROTC program too. all went there. I applied there for a three-year ROTC scholarship and went as far as to appear before the ROTC Board at Wofford College, but I was not accepted. Aggravated at being turned down by Wofford, I chose Clemson as an alternative because it was an agricultural college, and that was the clearest path that I could see to a four-year degree. I applied for an ROTC scholarship at Clemson, and I got it. It was a simple transfer from Spartanburg Methodist College, although it did aggravate me a little bit to be turned down by Wofford.

I also signed up to take the ROTC program at Clemson, which was a second and separate Ranger course from the one at Wofford College, but a lot more gung-ho, more focused on leadership, and with a much greater emphasis on active combat training. This was now my second Ranger program. Of course, it was hard core, but it was also a lot of fun, although it was also pretty clannish, and there was a tendency to look down on outsiders like me. Nonetheless, I stuck with the program as an extracurricular activity, did all the training, took the exam, and passed. I never showed up at graduation to pick up my certificate or the coveted black beret because I did not really want to identify with that group. I found their culture elitist, and since I had no feeling of personal superiority over anyone else, I had no interest in being part of that group.

In the order of things, once I picked up an ROTC scholarship at Clemson, I became a contract cadet, and that implied some advanced level of commitment to the Army. When the Army picks up the tab for your education, they always want something back for it, and now it was becoming less a vehicle to gain an education and more something I would be driving for its own sake. A contract cadet, serving the last two years of ROTC, and having entered into a contract in return for a stipend, is obligated to serve a specified time as an officer, either on Active Duty, in the Army Reserve or National Guard. I was now a bona fide college student on course to achieve a degree, and that implied that at the end of my period of training, I would be commissioned as a second lieutenant.

Still, in my mind, the ROTC, like the National Guard, was a means to an end, and academics would always come first. There was a rule of training that if academic coursework clashed with ROTC labs, the former prevailed. I purposely scheduled my academic coursework to clash with my ROTC labs, because I did not need the ROTC labs, so I was never around. I hardly attended any labs at all. I was confident that if I succeeded in earning a degree, a commission would follow. Academics was the greater challenge and the greater goal, and I kept that in mind. I was not in the four-year program but probably the five-and-a-half- or six-year program, so it took me a lot longer to graduate, even though it was an education degree. Although I picked up the checks and drew my money, I rarely showed up at the ROTC labs.

In the meantime, while I was on an ROTC scholarship, I remained a regular visitor to the Financial Aid Office at Clemson, applying for as many extra scholarships as I could make myself eligible for. Working the system. I held down various jobs, delivering pizza for Domino's and stuff like that, and in the spirit of "ask and you shall receive," I put an ad in the newspaper as a college student requesting free rent. Out of half a dozen replies, I chose an old farmhouse where I lived for about a year rent-free in exchange for mowing the lawn now and again and doing other odd jobs. The whole thing is a system.

I eventually finished ROTC second to last, because I was never around. I remember the poor cadet that finished last could barely speak English. I think he was from Puerto Rico. In December 1988, I was commissioned. The ceremony was held at the Littlejohn Coliseum at Clemson University, Clemson, South Carolina, where, dressed in my blues, my father pinned my second lieutenant's bars on me. After that I gave the sergeant major a dollar, which is a tradition, he saluted me, and I stepped out as an officer in the Armed Forces of the United States.

THE MOTION OF
THE OCEAN

Life is not linear; you have ups and downs. It's how you deal with the troughs that defines you.
MICHAEL LEE-CHIN

I N 1991, I VOLUNTEERED to serve in Operation *Desert Storm*, and although others in my National Guard Battalion went, my application was turned down. I remember having a conversation with my father about that, and he could not figure it out. In the past, a US military expeditionary force was a mass formation, with its mass comprising mostly infantry grunts, the artillery and the tanks, everything you see in the movies. In the era of the two world wars, Korea, and Vietnam, any man that raised his hand for selection was likely before long to find himself in a theater of operations. A modern US expeditionary force is different. It is like a circuit board. If your specific skillset plugs you into the correct port, you will be selected. If it does not, you will not. I was serving then as a communications officer with the National Guard, and my request was turned down.

"Hell son I can't figure it out." my dad grumbled, "Back in my day, if you wanted to go to war, they sure as hell would send your ass to war."

Although I was commissioned in 1988, it was not until 1992 that I was placed on active duty, which meant about three or four years hanging around the Armory as a National Guard platoon leader. During that time, I dated a National Guard private. She was an attractive woman, blond, with a great figure. It was consensual; we were both single and both part-time soldiers. We began to see each other at off-duty hours through annual training at Fort Gordon, Georgia, in the early 1990s. Although there was nothing inappropriate about it, according to me, and certainly nothing against formal regulations, I was given a written cease-and-desist order, which I tore up and ignored. In terms of regulations, fraternization was forbidden "within the chain of command," and we were outside one another's chain of command. She served in the battalion headquarters, and I was a platoon leader. Nonetheless, the battalion commander called me to his office and handed me a written letter to sign that I understood I was to cease and desist. I agreed, since I was ordered to understand the instruction, and I signed it, but I did not stop seeing the girl. Come time for my officer evaluation, however, I was pretty badly hosed because of it. You see, he is the commander and what he says goes. I did not know it at the time but there is a whole lot to do with perception as an officer. Perception is huge. When soldiers see something that just might be inappropriate, then it becomes a problem, even if its not.

So, on balance, I have to admit it was not an intelligent move, and it spoke to a certain maverick, cavalier tendency I had in me that ran contrary to military convention and discipline, and which dogged me often during my career. During that same training trip to Fort Gordon, Georgia, I tried to get a dental appointment as a National Guard officer on active service and kept running into a bureaucratic runaround, which is common in the Army. One day, I called impersonating a colonel from the

South Carolina National Guard, adopting an authoritarian tone and asking why my lieutenants were being denied proper dental care. The next day I called again, as a lieutenant, and had no problem getting an appointment. If I had been caught, though, no doubt I would have been court-martialed.

During that time, I took a very challenging course called COMSEC, or the Communications Security course, which I failed. It was a complex and detailed curriculum, dealing with the security of official communications involving a bewildering raft of details and procedures that flew totally over my head. I failed, and when I got back to the National Guard, my supervisor, whose name was Maj. Fred Thrailkill, brought me into his office and chewed me out.

"You are a damned waste of the taxpayers' money," he said. "And a waste of our time and money. We only got a limited training budget."

I acknowledged the fact that I failed and tried to explain that it was a difficult course and that I tried my best. On another occasion, Major Thrailkill got on to me because I did not want to donate to the Armory coffee-and-doughnut fund. I recall a particular command sergeant major going round and asking soldiers for donations and I told him, "No, I do not eat doughnuts or drink coffee."

"We'll see about that, young Lieutenant" he said, and soon afterwards I was back in Major Thrailkill's office getting my ass chewed out again.

"You are an officer," he said. "You need to learn to be an example to other soldiers and that we are all part of a team!" After that particular ass-chewing, I donated to any and all causes, and there were no problems on that issue again. In hindsight looking back I was feeling that he was doing his job…he was a little bit uptight maybe, but was doing his job according to how he saw fit. Mostly I tried to keep my distance from him.

My first serious job after graduating from Clemson University was a federal appointment in the local US

Department of Agriculture Soil Conservation Service, based in Barnwell, South Carolina, and it was a good job. My function was to advise farmers on the conservation of land and soil and offer various programs to assist with it. That job did not last long. I took a joyride alone in my official vehicle in a county not assigned to me, ran a stop sign, and totaled the truck. The supervisor was glad I was alive, and I was too. I was hit on the driver's side which slammed me all the way to the passenger side, and the entire driver's side was crushed. I walked away without a scratch, and I felt very lucky. Although I was not directly reprimanded, the fact was taken note of, and before long I was let go.

During this time I recorded multiple traffic violations. I would regularly speed, run stop signs and red lights. All minor issues, but it was all consistent and it stacked up. I eventually ran out of points on my driver's license, and then my license was taken away. I kept on driving and the next time I was pulled over I was cuffed and stuffed and sent to jail, charged with a DUS, or Driving Under Suspension. As I was getting into the squad car, in handcuffs, my brother was driving by and he saw me entering the back of a police car. He was on his way home on Highway 9 to Boiling Springs. When he got home he told my dad and my dad and my brother came down to help get me out of jail. I was not in jail long, and my Dad was pretty agitated about it all. He was concerned about my attitude, about going to jail more or less. He saw that I was not upset by it and commented – "Son, is there anything you give a shit about? You act like nothing happened!"

And he was correct.

"Is there anything you give a shit about? You act like nothing happened."

I kept up that fuck-it attitude and that dogged me a lot during that time.

Then I took a job in Spartanburg as an air sampler with a company called AAA Environmental Solutions, testing air for asbestos and working on its removal. I did not get along particularly well with my boss, and before long I was fired from there, too. From there, I put in an unemployment package in Spartanburg County.

It was a worthwhile lesson, because despite now holding a master's degree, I still found myself in exactly the types of situations that I had difficulty dealing with. The air sampling work was tedious, repetitive, detail-oriented and deep in the weeds. That is not the ten-thousand-foot view I was working towards. Besides that, I was still an arrogant youth with a fuck-you attitude, and in less than a year, I was drawing unemployment. Civilian life did not seem to be working out.

And it got worse. One weekend in Myrtle Beach, continuing with the principle of working systems, I had a set of cards printed up, and I trawled up and down the beachfront looking to pick up some women. It was a simple line: "I like you. I'm having a party, and you're invited." That was it really. Just wanted to meet some women. The cards had my name and phone number on them, along with a handwritten venue that was usually a hotel. Mostly it worked well, but one day, after a couple of hours of working it, I looked down the beach and I saw some woman talking to the cops and they were pointing me out. Apparently they were saying this that I wasn't doing. Two police officers approached me, asked me who I was and what I was doing, and told me they were going to lock me up for solicitation of prostitution. I was cuffed and stuffed and put in Myrtle Beach jail for a little while. I was questioned and released. My first and only thought was how long is this likely to sit on my record. I asked, and the answer was five years. Now I acknowledged guilt just to get out, but really I was just looking for some women and after that I was more careful. I am my father's son, and some systems are ill-advised.

By then I was in my mid-twenties and filled with attitude and self-confidence. A quiet self-confidence, the cocky type. I had graduated Basic Training and survived Criminal

Correction Facility, jump out of airplanes, been to ROTC Ranger School, got my Bachelors and Masters degree and I was a commissioned officer in the ranks of Uncle Sam's uniformed services. I felt untouchable.

Then, a week or two later, sitting at dinner with Mom and Dad, the phone rang, and I answered it. At the other end was Human Resources Command in Washington, DC, an officer, and the message was that I was finally going on active duty, and would I like to join the 10th Special Forces Group as a chemical officer? My answer was "Hell Yeah!", and putting the phone down, I retook my seat with a wide smile on my face.

"Guess what?" I said.

Within a few days, I was off unemployment and on active duty. Spartanburg is a patriotic town, and the unemployment office got word I was getting off unemployment and heading towards a full-time gig in the Army, and when I went into the office to sign off on unemployment I was greeted in the office with wide smiles and many congratulations, and I felt like a little star.

THE ASSIGNMENT TO THE 10th Special Forces Group came right out of the blue. I get questions about this. According to the Army website, "The 10th Special Forces Group is an active-duty United States Army Special Forces Group. The 10th Group is designed to deploy and execute nine doctrinal missions: unconventional warfare, foreign internal defense, direct action, counter-insurgency, special reconnaissance, counterterrorism, information operations, counterproliferation of weapons of mass destruction, and security force assistance."

Human Resources Command, used to be called Personnel Command, or PERSCOM, is a mysterious agency in the hands of which lie the fates of career soldiers across the entire spectrum of the US uniformed services. Human

Resources Command puts you where you need to go. Now, why was I selected for a Special Forces assignment is a question I am often asked. It is a bit of a mystery, and all that I can think of is that, as a young, commissioned officer, I was probably a bit more mature than most. They knew I had enlisted time and with a higher standard of training thanks to the Ranger ROTC. I had an Airborne patch on me, and I was a little older. Either way, it was a perfect fit for me because straight off the bat I knew that I was in a world where the orthodoxies of regular military service meant little, if anything. Thinking outside the box was a cultivated skill, the lines of division between the ranks were less defined, and the left-right-left school of military doctrine was abandoned at the gates of the barracks. I liked that. I got along with that. Now, as a chemical officer, I was not assigned to a combat role but a to specialized branch within the group dealing specifically with threats related to chemical, nuclear, radiological, and biological defense.

The Basic Training course to qualify as a chemical officer was conducted at Fort McClellan outside Anniston, Alabama, a huge installation that they say sometimes trains up to a quarter of a million personnel. It is home to the Chemical Corps, the Military Police and what was at one time the Women's Army Corps. I drove down to Alabama in September 1992 and there I joined with about forty other trainees from various other places around the United States. Although it was mapped out that we would all end up as staff officers in whatever unit we were assigned to, I was the only lieutenant that had been earmarked to serve with a Special Forces group. For this reason, I kinda stood out, and in fact, I was offered money by a few other lieutenants to trade assignments. They wanted to go where I was going. The course was scheduled for five months, and I stepped into shit almost at the moment I walked through the gates.

I looked around and pretty quickly got the measure of my surroundings and slipped into what was, by then, becoming

84

an established strategy. The Five Ps. Work hard and work smart. I posted an advertisement in the classified section of the Fort McClellan Post newspaper asking for any old exam and study papers. This was really stupid in hindsight. Within hours, I was standing to attention in the office of Capt. Ted Ropes with Sergeant Goins standing behind me, and I knew without having to be told that somehow I was back on the shitlist. Although he was short, stiff as a board, and by-the-book, Captain Ropes was also good-looking, charismatic, and an excellent leader. Not only was he running the course, but he was also earmarked for assignment with the 10th Special Forces Group where I was going at. The classified advertisement had been brought to his attention, and he did not like it, which was a fact that he made plainly understood.

Under the lash of an Army ass-chewing, I tried to explain that I suffer specific learning difficulties, and that I need any additional help that I can find. This was the first and only time in my thirty-one year military career that I admitted that I had a learning disability, but it was a huge ass chewing. I was trying to prevent failure at another Army school like I did in the South Carolina National Guard. I never did tell Captain Ropes about that. Despite it being, to my mind at least, a pretty logical course of action and against no formal regulations, Captain Ropes was unmoved. He had never seen or heard of anything like that before, and that was all that he needed to know.

Again, it is just a matter of perception. It was a strategy that had worked for me in the past and would work again many times in the future, but under this command, it was perceived somehow as cheating, and it was shut down. I got no reply from the advertisement in any case. I was told that command would be keeping its eye on me for the duration of the course, and they would, and that eye was Sergeant Goins, a Cajun with a grim, humorless aspect and a no-bullshit attitude. I remarked to Captain Ropes as I walked out the door that I was looking forward to serving with him in the 10th Special Forces Group, and his reply was, "Just get the fuck out of my office!"

I do remember coming back in for my end-of-course counseling to discover that Captain Ropes was unexpectedly pleased with my end result. "You have done well," he said. "No fucking off like the other lieutenants, good on physical fitness, and good on academics, we tried to look for something to complain about but you are all good to go."

And that was that. No mention was made of the business of the advertisement and past papers, of cheating or plagiarism, and not one word of it passed beyond Captain Ropes' office. He was a good guy. He could easily have made life pretty difficult for me, but he did not, and as I would discover as my career progressed, that can be pretty rare. In the end, he and I came to terms because I did not fail, as he had assumed I would. I did everything I was supposed to do, working and refining my Five Ps, and I gave him no further grounds for a reprimand. Later he made major at Fort Devens, and in the full range of my military career, he is perhaps one of the men that I admired most.

BY THE EARLY 1990S, THE CHEMICAL CORPS had mostly dropped its original offensive role and had become principally an agency of chemical defense and mitigation. A Google search of "Fort McClellan" will likely throw up a whole bunch of injury and disability attorneys drift-netting for class actions, which in itself tells a story. Exposure to nerve agents and toxins was at one time a daily risk of serving on the site, and there are countless horror stories of GIs left permanently disabled. Fort McClellan was part of the original storage network of the US chemical and biological arsenal, and it specialized, according to the legal press, in turning out "Chemical Warfare Service officers."

Although in reality, it was more mundane than that, it was still an edgy training program. NCOs were trained as chemical instructors for various conventional units, alongside a handful of other military trainees from friendly foreign countries who were similarly instructed. Every frontline unit of the Army is invested to a greater or lesser extent with the tactical capability of dealing with chemical or biological hazards, and that doctrine can trace its origins to Fort McClellan. We learned about nuclear radiation fallout and chemical and biological weapons and about anthrax, botulinum, and smallpox. We worked in MOPP suits in the gas chamber exposed to live nerve agents.[1] We brought in a goat and knocked it out with nerve agent and then revived it with atropine just to show that that stuff works.[2] The most unsettling part of it was being in a gas chamber filled with that live nerve agent and relying on nothing for survival but protective gear. That sort of shit will screw your head up if you think too much about it. The instructors were constantly checking our eyes for any sign of panic. A panic attack or an uncontrolled freak-out under those conditions is life-threatening to everyone involved.

One time the senior NCO on staff said – "What the hell! We got a dumb-assed Lieutenant Pike here, and apparently he has a masters degree. How the hell did he ever end up with a masters degree is beyond me. His name was Master Sergeant Michael Conman and I liked him a lot. I never told him I had a masters degree but he found out somewhere. I did not answer, but just smiled at him. He was the senior NCO and I needed him on my side. One day I came clean with him and said – "I don't know a damn thing about what you guys are talking about. You are all talking in this damned special forces jargon with

---

[1] MOPP: Mission-oriented protective posture.

[2] According to Wikipedia, "Atropine is a tropane alkaloid and anticholinergic medication used to treat certain types of nerve agent and pesticide poisonings as well as some types of slow heart rate, and to decrease saliva production during surgery."

acronyms and stuff. Its all new to me so I am a dumb-ass. I don't even know what going on around here."

He seemed to respect that comment a lot. I never told him that I had any problem learning, but he understood me. He would be like one of those real Rambo folks, if there ever is one. He once told us – "I got to go away." And he did, and he returned back. He was on some super-secret mission. I did not know what he did, and no one ever asked him about it.

In the end, I came through and was sent to Fort Devens in Massachusetts, which is the home of the 10th Special Forces Group. A chemical officer attached to a Special Forces unit is typically assigned to the operations section to take care of the ash and the trash of the battalion staff. Despite the prestige of serving in Special Forces, it is essentially a junior staff position, and most of my days were spent crunching numbers, compiling charts for presentations and publications, putting slides on a computer, and generally acting as an assistant to the operations officer. Most people assigned to the Chemical Corps ultimately end up trying to get a branch transfer, because it is not a desirable corps to be in. A branch transfer is an almost impossible feat in the Army. I had the opportunity at the end of the Basic Chemical course to go to Army Ranger School, and one of the few regrets that I have is that I did not seize that opportunity. I had definitely trained to Ranger standard in the ROTC, no doubt. In retrospect, though, I probably would not have had the physical or mental capacity to pass selection, so maybe it was for the best.

In total, I served for one year with the 10th Special Forces Group, and as I reflect on my career, that was probably the most enjoyable assignment in my entire thirty-one years in the Army. Although once or twice I thought very seriously about staying in and getting my Special Forces tab and becoming a Green Beret, I was again put off by the heavy demands of selection, training, and operation. The personal lives of most Special Forces soldiers that I knew were in shambles thanks to multiple failed marriages and the demands of deployment that meant long periods away from home. The number of parachute jumps, the weight that they carry. Special Forces operations folks are often broken by the time they are in their mid-thirties, and even just the experience that I had of it as a staff officer was enough to convince me it was probably not for me. I enjoyed the culture very, very much . I was also now convinced that I wanted to remain on active duty and make a career out of the military, and it was my objective to get into another unique niche of the Army.

One particular memory I have of that time is of the Airborne prop blast initiation. Although the tradition has been officially discontinued, the prop blast initiation was at one time a rite of passage for all US Army Airborne officers who had graduated from Jump School with the required five training jumps—making a candidate a "five-jump-chump." Until you make your sixth jump, which traditionally is with your unit, you are known as a "cherry-jumper." These days it is more of an informal club which to join requires a period of training and selection. As I recall, it was a three- or four-day event featuring the usual surplus of physical fitness, road marching, general harassment, and some jumping out of airplanes, and a whole lot of aggravation and mocking on the ground. In the end, assuming that an initiate can stand up to the stress, he is then required to appear before a committee in a hanger, where he must recite the Prop Blast Mantra under some sort of hazing. In my case, I had to stand naked in the doorway of an aircraft, it was a mock aircraft, holding on to the sides that had been rigged with an electrical current. Stress, of course, shrinks your male organs, and through gales of raucous laughter came the comment, "Hey Pike, why the fuck is your dick so small?"

"Sir!" I replied. "It ain't the size of the ship but the motion of the ocean."

That prompted another gale of laughter.

"All right, Pike. You're in!"

A concoction of alcohol was mixed in what they call a "sink grog" and poured down my throat, and we all got drunk after that. My feeling about it all is that it was all way outa line but I was just happy to be in the group, and I was proud of another small achievement.

Other experiences now were less friendly. During jump training at Fort Devens, we were required to do at least one water jump, which is usually a low-level approach over a body of water, and typically, because you are landing on water, you can tolerate a higher wind speeds. The training doctrine on this is iron clad, and it requires that turn yourself always *into* the wind to damp down your speed and help achieve a better and more controlled landing. I am not sure why, it could have been personal, or it could just have been some hazing, but a particular major whose name I will withhold took me to one side and said, "Hey, Pike. I'm going to be turning away from the wind, and I want you to do the same thing."

"Are you sure about that?" I asked.

"Yeah, yeah, sure. Just follow me."

At the time I only had only a handful of jumps under my belt, and in the Army you do what you are told. He was the jumpmaster, the "master-blaster" as we called him, and he had to be taken seriously. He had upwards of thirty jumps under his belt, he was a major, and the tone of the instruction did not invite argument.

As we approached the drop, he reminded me, "Make sure you do what I told you." We jumped, and while everyone tacked into the wind when their chutes opened, he and I broke ranks and turned away from the wind. We started hauling ass. This created instant consternation on the ground. I looked down and saw the inflatable zodiacs arcing away and speeding up the lake to intercept us. When I saw that, I knew I was in trouble. We were coming down at high speed, moving away from the rest of the group and bearing down on the opposite bank. There were jetties and lake houses and a line of trees fringing the shore.

If I hit land or a building at this speed, I would either be badly injured or dead. No doubt. At the last minute, I had some sense, I turned into the wind and came down barley on the shore in about three or four feet of water. I was pretty shaken up.

When we were picked up, a sergeant yelled in fury, "What the fuck y'all doing?"

I told them, pointing at the major, "This guy told repeatedly me to turn away from the wind!" The way the sergeant greeted that news told me he knew it was true. I guess he had seen it go down before. He was a sergeant, and the major was a major, so he kept his mouth shut. After this event, I kept my distance from that major, because someone who knowingly put a young soldier's life in danger for no good reason cannot be regarded as a trustworthy leader. That major was a weird guy, not widely respected, and I learned a damn good lesson that day. On other assignments during training, I saw guys making bad landings and being carried away on stretchers. It was a strange episode. Nothing was said about it after that day, and no explanation was ever given.

MY ORIGINAL IDEA WAS TO SERVE out the three years of active duty service required of me as a contract cadet, and as required by my ROTC scholarship, and then return to the South Carolina National Guard as a weekend warrior with its routine obligation of two days a month and two week a year. As I progressed through my first year of service in a Special Forces environment, however, I began to change my mind.

The credo of Special Forces is very different from the regular branches of the service. Individual soldiers are encouraged to develop their creativity and independence of mind under a much looser general code of conduct. Noncommissioned officers are allowed to openly express their views and opinions with the expectation that their advice will be respected and often implemented. Sometimes the conventional branches of the Army look at special forces as rogue and rebellious. That is not something you will find very often in conventional units. It also functions around that ten-thousand-foot view, which I was beginning to like and understand. Perhaps for the first time in my life, I found that I fit in somewhere. My shambling style of walking—they used to call it "Pike's monkey walk"—and my stooping posture did not stand out quite so sharply, and my general attitude of familiarity—belching, farting, and scratching my balls, scorning discipline, and embracing independence—blended in well in the world of the Special Forces soldier. It was kinda looked up to an rewarded.

Most importantly, though, I did not find myself bringing up the rear as I had all my life, struggling to keep up with the stragglers and drinking from the damned fire hose. The idea, therefore, of eventually being rotated back into a conventional assignment and then back into the National Guard, back into the left-right-left military mindset, had diminishing appeal. I decided, in the end, to specialize, stay on active duty, and embark on a career in uniform. I had also begun to figure out the long-term benefits of staying in uniform for the full term, until retirement, which really did offer many advantages. Not only does a retired officer qualify for a pension after twenty years, but the health benefits and all kinds of other veterans' benefits stack up after retirement. I had arrived at a point where the ordinariness of the National Guard and the mundane prospect of civilian life no longer held any real interest for me. I was also in a much better position now to appreciate the almost unlimited potential available in the military structure to men and women of resourcefulness and above-average intelligence.

At that point, I came up against one of the great myths of the armed forces. It is a widely understood fact that it is *not* possible, once you have been assigned to a particular branch, in my case the Chemical Corps, to switch to another. One more myth is the requirements needed to enter a medical branch. I recall during ROTC training being instructed in all the various branches of the Army, and when I asked a question about the different medical branches, and if I could get in, the reply was, "Oh, you can't go into the Army medical department unless you're a PhD, a doctor, a veterinarian, or a dentist."

This is not the case. After digging into it a little, I discovered that there are numerous medical specialties as diverse as biochemists, dieticians, environmental engineers, environmental scientists, audiologists, occupational therapists, podiatrists, nutritionists, preventive medicine officers, and many others. In none of these specialties does one need a PhD, or even a medical degree. At Clemson, I studied animal sciences, biology and agriculture, so I already had a grounding in the basics, and since I was generally interested in the sciences, I figured I could reasonably think about a Medical Department specialty. I think I can maybe trace my interest in the Medical Department to Basic Training when, deep in the mud and the blood, I saw that the ambulance drivers got to ride around in an air-conditioned vehicle and pull light duties. I guess it occurred to me that a better option than working on an assembly line was to study towards a specific specialty, to get better paid, to break the tedium, and to pitch for more meaningful work.

The Army is a strange animal. Often if you ask the same question on a different day, or ask the same person on a different day, or a different person on the same day, you will get a different answer every time. The military establishment is a huge, complex organization driven by a code of practice that is mostly convention and tradition and not necessarily always regulation. The system has a well-earned reputation for unyielding orthodoxy, but there are ways around that. There is actually no hard and fast regulation against a branch transfer, it's just a matter of chancing upon the right person at the right time.

A lot of people get frustrated dealing with it all and just give up, but I became pretty good at planning ahead. I made a point of following up on an action one or two weeks after I had initiated it. In any large government department, things have a way of getting lost. I kept everything and would resubmit again and again when no action seemed to be taken or any response forthcoming. Often, if one set of paperwork was required, I would make five copies of the same correspondence on the assumption that at least four of them would fall into the great black hole. It was never anything that I took personally, but just learned to accept as a fact of Army life. On the rare occasion that something was achieved first time round, I was really surprised. One time I tried submitting something into my record, and after failing eight or nine times, I paper-clipped a dollar bill on the first page and it worked. It pissed off someone who called me up on the phone and told me, "Please do not send cash through Army distribution as it is against regulations!" Nonetheless, it got someone's attention, and I felt rewarded.

So I began bombarding the medical departments with applications. I first tried environmental sciences and got nowhere. For some reason, that door was shut tight no matter how much I hammered on it. Then someone suggested entomology as kind of a sister specialty to environmental science. Before then I did not know that there was such a thing as an Army entomologist, but since I had done entomology at Clemson, I figured I had the basics down, I knew about the sciences, so I was going to give it a try . I called them up, and they said sure, you can give it a try, put your packet in. That's it just how it goes sometimes, and that is how I transferred from the Chemical Corps to the Medical Service Corps, when they said it could not be done.

FARTING, BELCHING, AND SCRATCHING

Culture is the widening of the mind and of the spirit.
JAWAHARLAL NEHRU

ARLY IN THE NEW YEAR OF 1994, the 10th Special Forces Group was deployed on a training exercise to Canada. The unit was co-located with Canadian units also undergoing what they called "Cold Weather Survival Training." It was January and February in Quebec Province, and it sure was damn cold. The daytime high probably hit around five or six degrees on a good day and it regularly dropped at night to twenty or thirty below. Operating with Special Forces, you always get the best kit and equipment, the kind of stuff that would be on the top shelf in an outdoors or ski shop, which is usually the stuff no one can afford. The training was in basic cold weather operations and survival—building ice shelters, cross-country skiing, cold weather vehicle maintenance and operation, and anything else necessary to function and maneuver in arctic conditions.

Interestingly, it was also a mission within a mission. While supposedly we were there on a training operation in cooperation with Canadian forces, we were also on an intelligence-gathering mission on behalf of the Central Intelligence Agency. Although none of us knew what the specific objective was, we were told to take as many casual photographs of our surroundings as possible and pass them on to a CIA agent embedded in the unit. I remember asking him once, "Hey, what are y'all gonna do with the pictures?" And the reply came, as I recall, it was only on a need-to-know basis.

This is what they call "pooping and snooping" on suspicious activity, probably gun running or drug smuggling, or maybe just keeping an eye on what the Canadians were up to north of the forty-eighth parallel. Then, sometime early in February, my orders came down from above, and I was released and assigned to Korea. Jumping on a transport convoy, I headed back down to Fort Devens. There I picked up my gear and my old truck and, with a heavy heart, said goodbye to the 10th Special Forces Group. From Massachusetts I drove down to South Carolina, parked my truck in the back of Cora Pike's house, because my mom did not want to see the truck in her yard. Then I had a few beers with my dad, and that was it.

"What the hell, son!" he said with a laugh. "You a damned bug person now?"

"Well, you know," I replied. "I'm going to be in the sciences."

"Okay. Well, whatever."

I ARRIVED IN KOREA from South Carolina in march 1994. From Incheon International Airport, on the outskirts of Seoul, I took a train south to Daegu, a journey of two or three hours. I sat on that train as it snaked through a clean, highly developed, and heavily urbanized landscape, surrounded on all sides by rolling hill country and mist-covered mountains. I fell asleep on that train and I remember, I had a dream. When the train came to a stop, it squealed, and I woke up in fright thinking my mama was screaming at me.

This was my first long-term deployment overseas and my first serious trip outside the United States, and I was amazed.[1] I had kind of expected South Korea to be some third-world shithole, but it was not at all that way. The train passed through a major areas such as Daejeon, and I was blown away by how well ordered and clean it all was. By the time the train pulled into Dongdaegu Station, that's in Daegu, later that afternoon, I was already beginning to feel the first pull of that attraction to Asia that would never leave me.

I was met at the train station by Capt. Tom Delk, environmental science officer and commander of the 154th Medical Detachment. Under his supervision, I would serve for twelve months as executive officer and medical entomologist. We left the station and drove through downtown Daegu, a sizable city of about 2.5 million people, the fourth largest in Korea. It was early spring, and the boulevard trees were flush with new leaf, and lots of cherry blossoms were beginning to appear. It was so clean and well ordered, it was so different, and it was really pretty. Then, as we turned into the gates of Camp Walker, we were suddenly back in America.

Camp Walker is a sprawling, one-hundred-acre US military complex set in the southern precincts of the city. To the south of the perimeter lies Apsan Park, an urban wilderness area surrounding a two-thousand-foot peak, and home to one of a handful of notable Buddhist temples that are scattered throughout the city. Camp Walker is home to, among other units

---

[1] I did briefly visit Italy for a training exercise with the National Guard, and of course, I was deployed for a few weeks on a training exercise in Canada.

and detachments, the Army-Air Force Exchange Service, it's got the Military Police Company, Signals Company and of course the 168th Medical Battalion under the Eight Army, which controls all of the units in South Korea. I was with the 154th Medical Detachment, and, of course, that is within the 168th Medical Battalion. It is the largest of three US military bases in Daegu, the others being Camp Henry and Camp George. There is also a Camp Carroll, located about twenty miles north in the village of Waegwan.

Like most major US Army overseas facilities, Camp Walker is a self-contained environment with an eighteen-hole golf course, state-of-the-art facilities, first-world accommodations, a school, a commissary with all the main US brands and franchises, a bowling alley, and a branch of the US Postal Service. It houses a population mostly comprising soft-body US military administrative personnel, augmented by a civilian staff and a good number of uniformed and non-uniformed Korean personnel. The facility is part of US Army Garrison Daegu IV, Area Four, which also includes Camp Henry, Camp George and Camp Carol. According to the US Army website, U.S. Army Garrison Daegu Area IV provides "essential community service, facilities, and infrastructure for soldiers, civilians, contractors, and their families, while enabling the 'Fight Tonight' capability. Supports noncombatant evacuation operations and provides Army fixed-base command and control."

I went through in-processing, picked up my equipment and security clearance, passes and so forth, and was introduced to the folk in my department. As part of that general umbrella of support services were the various departments concerned with preventive medicine, and as a public health officer myself, my assignment was general and administrative, concerned mainly with maintaining standards of health and sanitation on base and anywhere else troops were stationed. I was executive officer to Capt. Tom Delk, and I was assigned to a team of preventive medical people, including women, augmented by a small support staff of Koreans. My daily routine was to inspect dining, kitchen, and restaurant facilities and to submit reports and make recommendations. I was also assigned to manage the motor-pool, which required yet more inspections and reports. As far as entomology was concerned, besides mosquito surveillance, roach and rat control, we did not do very much. South Korea in the 1990s was not a tropical hellhole and was certainly not an environment of endemic disease or systemic sanitation failures. Detachments like mine tended to be comparatively small, comprising no more than twelve US Army soldiers, and perhaps seven South Koreans. These we called KATUSAs, or "Korean Augmentees to the United States Army." KATUSAs are interpreters and they are also training in preventive medicine with us.

The US military garrison in Daegu is pretty well integrated into the surrounding community. A lot of Koreans worked or were associated with the garrison and made regular use of the gym, the aquatic center, the golf course and other entertainments. Although there were family and singles quarters on base, many chose to live off base, and it was common for servicemen to marry into the local communities and end up staying after the end of their time. Some stayed on as civilian contractors to the military and integrated more or less completely into Korean life. In order to function in the military environment there was no need to learn Korean because many of the Koreans associated with the garrison spoke English as a basic requirement. I remember if you talked to the Koreans slowly they could understand, and they definitely knew how to read English.

It seemed to me that the Koreans were a little bit standoffish I would say, mostly tolerating the US presence without any particular interest in getting to know us better. We were just transits, there for one, maybe two years and then we're gone. Although there were prostitutes and bar owners who welcomed greenback business, getting to know Korean women was a bit tough to do. Korea is a wealthy, developed, and educated country and so the incentive for a woman to hook up with a GI to get a green card or military benefits was not quite so acute maybe as it once was—and still is—in some other places.

It was spring when I arrived, and the famous Korean cherry blossom festivals were beginning all over the peninsula. My first trip out of town was down south to the coastal city of Jinhae where one of the most famous of them is held. Jinhae, or Chinhae, is also the site of the main US naval base in South Korea, so the place was swarming with drifters. On the bus down, a woman who spoke a little bit of English struck up a conversation with me and offered to guide me through the festival. Because Korean women are in general very reserved that immediately got my gut sense to tingling. At some point, she suggested that we hire a boat and take it out onto a lake or lagoon, and I felt real suspicious about that. She kept pushing that idea, and I thought after a while that I needed to get the hell out of there. I figured she was just trying to get me someplace where I could be jumped and robbed. I made some excuses and I told her I was okay on my own, but she would just not leave me. A few times I excused myself to use the bathroom until I found one that had a window that was big enough to climb through. I climbed out of the bathroom window, scaled a wall and took off running. I did not see her again after that.

When I got back to Camp Walker, I got to talking to a very pretty woman, she was about thirty-three-years-old, local Korean, and her name was Mi-jeong who worked as an administrative assistant in the office. She was married to a US Army warrant officer by the name of Wilhoit and they lived off-base. I told her about what had happened, and she suggested that in future it would be a lot safer if she showed me around. She told me, in a half-joking way, that her ass was worth a million dollars. That was the beginning of an affair that went on for the duration of my tour. She sure did show me around, and with her I took a deep dive into Korean food and culture, which helped reinforce an already strong and growing fascination for the place. For a while we were able to keep our relationship low-key and clandestine. Since I did not have a whole lot of social interaction with my colleagues and fellow officers, it was pretty easy, at least in the beginning, to keep it that way.

A little side story I would like to tell now. Since I was considered a new guy, a new Army entomologist, my commander Tom Delk told me to go up to the 5th Medical Detachment to meet the senior entomologist who was Major George Korch. He was the commander of the 5th Medical Detachment. A detachment that I would command later in my career. Major George Korch, his was of training was go to the barracks for the entire week and read Army Regulation 40-5. This was a preventive medicine regulation. I never did tell him that I couldn't read well anyway but I definitely could not read legal jargon inside a regulation, and even if I could understand it, my brain don't think regulation style. The bad news is that whole week was a waste of time, because I could understand not a damned thing in that regulation, but the good news is I never got in trouble.

Trouble was not far behind though. I never completely managed to break the ice with my colleagues in the office. Tom Delk was probably the only exception. He and I have bumped into one another many times over the years, and we have remained friends. He was an orthodox staff officer, not much older than me, serious in outlook and somewhat of the left-right-left school. I, on the other hand, walked into the office environment of a medical detachment with exactly the same attitude and behavior that I had become accustomed to in Special Forces.

In a Special Forces unit, even as a staff officer, every established convention or code of conduct is routinely disregarded. I recall it was common for officers and NCOs to drink until three o'clock in the morning and then get out and go do a jump at daybreak. We grew our hair longer, we slouched around with our hands in our pockets, and we were on easy and familiar terms with both senior officers and the enlisted ranks. In a conventional unit, officers are generally not encouraged to fraternize with the enlisted ranks, mainly because it is possible that one day it might be necessary to send them out to die. I was prior enlisted myself, I came from that background, and I generally got on better with the enlisted ranks than the typical cadet school officer. I wanted to get to know the men that, in theory at least, I might one day have to send out to die, and in any case, few if any of my fellow officers would socialize with me. I was a good ol' boy, academically challenged, rough mannered and just too far beyond the pale for a cadet school medical officer to handle.

One day, Tom called me into his office. "I can't believe that I actually have to even do this," he said. "Having a counseling session with my XO over your hygiene! But you've got to understand, Lieutenant Pike, that you are in a medical unit now. You are not with a bunch of Special Forces guys. You can't just walk into the office and rip a fart or scratch your balls or dig in your ass in front of female soldiers. I have been getting complaints."

He showed me the official complaint, which was listed as "gender insensitivity." Although I was definitely embarrassed by it, I don't think there is anything in the regulations regarding gender insensitivity, I read the tea leaves and took a typical "fuck-it" attitude and just moved on. There were two senior female soldiers in the unit called Garland and Castro. Garland was black and Castro was Hispanic, and they hated me, and I am pretty sure they were the ones who lodged the complaint. They hated me, I guess, because they had figured out what was going on with of Mi-jeong, realizing that I was carrying on a pretty much open relationship with a married woman who worked in the office. They were specialists in preventive medicine, and they took that shit real serious.

There was a bar district in Daegu they called the *Ville*. It was only a few miles from base, and there were clubs and bars that, according to the Status of Forces Agreement of the time, only US personnel and Korean women could go to. Kind of difficult to imagine that now, but that's how it was then. One evening I got a little bit too drunk on base and decided to head down there. I was short on some cash and did not want to take a taxi, so I borrowed a bicycle that was parked outside our office building. I had no clue whose bike it was, and the damned thing got run over and destroyed, I can't remember exactly how. I was not hurt, so it must have been while I was in the bar. While I was drinking. When I was done drinking, I staggered back to base carrying the bike, and I left it where I had found it. Next day Specialist Castro came into the office saying:

"The darndest thing happened last night. I parked my bike where I always park it, and this morning I came down, and it is completely destroyed! Like it got hit by a truck. Who would *do* such a thing?"

I heard this, and it came back to me, and I walked out of my office and said, "Ah—that would be me."

"Sir!" she exclaimed, and then completely lost her cool and began yelling at me. "What is *wrong* with you! Goddamn it! Why would you *do* that!"

"I wanted to go downtown," I said.

She glared at me for a moment before she spun on her heels and stormed off, speechless with fury.

Captain Delk asked me the same thing. "Lieutenant Pike!" he said. "Why would you do that? And why the fuck would you admit it?"

Another time I was holding the phones down at the office while everyone else was on lunch. I was just pulling a phone duty then and I got hungry, so I went to the refrigerator and looked around for something to east. Later, Specialist

Castro came out of the kitchen, seething in another fury. "All right!" she yelled. "I'm sick of this crap! Who took a bite out of my goddamned sandwich?"

"Ah," I said. "That would be me."

"*Sir!* You are an officer! Why would you steal an enlisted person's lunch?"

"Because I was hungry," I replied, and then followed up with, "It wasn't that good anyway, so I put it back."

I don't even remember what she said, but after she was done raging, she could hardly even address me in a professional context, let along in private. I was pretty sure it was Specialist Castro who was behind a lot of the shit that was stirred up around me. I recall when she discovered I was hanging out pretty regularly with a private first class by the name of Troy Cardieu, who was in her chain of command, entertaining him at the officers' club, she put him on a warning not to fraternize with the commissioned ranks, and with me in particular. That was a shame because he and I got along well, or at least I thought so. I guess when I invited him back to my quarters, and as my guest at the officers' club, he saw it as part of an invitation and part of an order. One time at the officers' club, I got into a pissing match with a Sergeant Major Schnakenberg, the highest enlisted rank in our specialty in the entire Army. He was a hulking, red-headed guy, and the issue was Mi-jeong. He was also trying to get something started with her. I ended up winning that fight because I guess she saw sense in sticking with an officer. Either way, because of that fight, my affair with Mi-jeong came out in the open and my name really was dirt in the office. I figured it was time to take my adventures abroad.

There were different ways in those days that you could take time out. You could apply for leave, which meant that you were free to leave the country and travel back home or anywhere else, or you could apply for a four-day pass. Although a four-day pass did not count against your accumulated leave, you were required to remain in-country. I took numerous four-day passes and just flew to the Philippines. Mi-jeong knew where I was headed, and she knew why.

The problem with Korean women is just that Korea is not an impoverished third-world country and so there is no particular advantage anymore for local women to make themselves available to a GI. Korean women are a bit standoffish as well, its part of their culture. Unless a woman has already crossed that line, they generally will not. I made friends with a guy in the Navy who was stationed for a few months at Jinhae, and he knew the Southeast Asian circuit pretty well. He told me that if I like Asian women I should go on down to the Philippines. I took a four-day pass and technically went AWOL, or Absent Without Leave, jumping on a scheduled flight to Manila. I asked around onboard the flight for intel and was told by other soldiers to take a bus up north to Angeles City in Olongapo. That was where the old Clark Air Base was located, and there were still facilities and places for US military personnel to bunk down.

It was in the Philippines that my cultural emersion in Asia really got into high gear. It was such a different experience from Korea. I found Filipino women charming, and not uninterested at all, but friendly, sensual and engaging. It was easy to get around, and English is widely spoken and understood everywhere. The cost-of-living index is a whole lot lower than Korea, and because people are much poorer, the greenback gets attention. US service members are pretty common on the streets, a lot of retirees and expats, and a lot of Filipino women get their tickets out that way. Hanging out with them in a permissive sexual environment completely altered my worldview. The urban culture was diverse and cosmopolitan, the nightlife wild and the party ongoing.

And it was not only the women that grabbed my attention. The Philippines is an archipelago of islands in the South China Sea, with a tropical flavor and a diversity of population and culture. There's mangos, there's coconuts, there's fishes. It is a Catholic country, Spanish-speaking, with beautiful churches in the Spanish style everywhere, even in the smallest villages. I enjoyed traveling in the chicken trucks and pig trucks, eating street food, drinking in local bars and talking with the expats. After a couple of days I flew back to Korea and walked back into the office without a word to anyone. I took a few of those trips, and in combination with my experiences in Korea, I began to really fall in love in Asia. They say once you are in, it is tough to go back. Although the Koreans can be unfriendly to outsiders, they are also cerebral, cultured, and educated, and I liked that. I was excited at the thought of exploring the region more. In my mind, I was beginning to build a picture of maybe someday retiring from the Army, marrying an Asian woman and moving out there. Mi-jeong was the only one that I talked to about that.

ONE OF MY DAD'S FAVORITE STORIES was one that he called "Jake falling into a honey bucket."

"Hey, Jake," he would say, "tell me the one about you falling in the honey bucket!" When he had company, he would never fail to dig that one up. "Y'know," he would say. Pointing at me, "Jake one time fell in a damn honey bucket," he would say and laugh until tears rolled down his cheeks.

It happened in the summer of 1994, a few months after I arrived in-country. I signed up to take the Expert Field Medical Badge. The EFMB is one of the most sought-after badges in all the medical department. It is a two-to three-week course and it was conducted at Warrior Base, which is a US Army training facility located north of the Imjin River, and just a few miles south of the DMZ, the demilitarized zone. Warrior Base was close enough to the DMZ that the loudspeakers on the North Korean side that push out propaganda to the South were clearly audible. It was never silent. Although the badge is primarily to certify competence in battlefield triage, and stabilizing patients in a war, and taking them off the battlefield, it also included many other military disciplines that are regular to a soldier's life. The intention of these disciplines is to mimic battlefield conditions and to limit sleep so that a soldier is operating under constant stress and fatigue that would mimic a wartime environment. It is hot, it is dirty, there are millions of mosquitos because of the paddy fields, and the course is tough enough to keep the pass rate between ten and fifteen percent. Very few trainees get through on the first try. One of many lanes included in the course was one on daytime and nighttime field navigation.

When you start on the day version of land navigation, they equip you with a grid coordinate and an azimuth on a compass bearing that you are required to follow. You set off at a certain coordinate for however many kilometers in order to locate that particular point. From there, you proceed off on another grid coordinate in order to find another point, and there are a series of points. There are usually a bunch of decoy points, so it is easy to get it wrong, and if you screwed up the first one, you can try to reassess and get pack in sequence. The nighttime version is much more challenging. It is pitch dark with no ambient light, at least when I went, and the otherworldly blare of communist propaganda coming in from the other side is very disorienting. We were briefed before we set off that this was farm country. "There is no light." The instructor warned us. "so *do not* follow your azimuth as the crow flies. Do not turn on your lights at all. Do not just walk from point A to point B in a straight line because there are farmers, fields out there, and ponds and rice paddies. You could fall and hurt yourself, you could drown, or you could get bitten by a snake."

Most of soldiers taking that course were coming in from medical units and did not function well under those conditions. I, on the other hand, was right at home. I was raised in the country and I recall that I did well land naving in all of my ROTC training, Ranger ROTC, during Basic Training and when I was in special forces, so I have had a lot of land navigating. There was no real pressure on me at that time to earn this badge. I was pretty confident. There was no actual requirement at that time to earn this patch, but it is sought after and very highly regarded.

Besides the standard infantry disciplines, the key segment of testing is battlefield triage, which is typically conducted under very authentic combat conditions, and usually it involves an entire cadre of people drawn from various other places to function as actors, supervisors, and adjudicators. Under simulated battle conditions, with actors playing the parts of wounded soldiers, a medical officer like me must determine under extreme stress the severity and priority of injuries and administer the appropriate field medical response. You can train and study, and I surely did, maxing out the Five Ps, but this is a challenging course, and you can never really master the requirements of judgement by study and training alone. All the scenarios are complicated by different factors, almost like trick questions, with numerous possible decisions and solutions to any given one. If, for example, a soldier has a serious head wound and is bleeding heavily, with his brains all out o him, then probably he is going to die, that's called expectant, so no time need be wasted on him. But he might also have a compound fracture, and be positioned on a slope, so moving him technically becomes necessary to deal with the compound fracture, but moving him is also potentially fatal for a brain injury. Most soldiers in the end fail at the triage section. Because there are no defined rules, a field medic is obliged, under authentic battlefield conditions, with realistically simulated injuries and with flash-bangs and rounds going off all over, to rely on solid training and his or her own judgment in a specific allotment of time.

In the order of things, the trainees who applied to take the course are required to pass all of these field disciplines first. The terrain over which this particular selection was conducted was made up of the signature rural, small-scale farming country that straddles the DMZ. The landscape in that part of Korea is defined by hills and low mountains with expanses of flat, low-lying floodplain where rice is planted out in seasonally flooded paddies. In the summer, it is hot and humid, even at night, and it is the season when most agricultural activity is taking place. The fields are flooded and there is a heavy and pervasive smell of fresh feces.

They say when you arrive on the DMZ the first thing you smell is shit and garlic, and there is plenty of truth in that. Garlic is everywhere. It is cooked with every meal and often eaten raw. I eat it raw now. The smell of shit comes from the ditches on the edges of the rice paddies where animal and human feces, or "night soil," is gathered in deep ponds as fertilizer. The preliminary brief before going out into the field on a night navigation is pretty clear about what will happen if a soldier falls into a cesspool. This will result in an immediate medical evacuation for reasons of likely infection, and should anything be detected, an early trip home.

I joined a group of twenty or so soldiers and was dropped off by truck at about nine o'clock in the evening. Each soldier carried a basic complement of load-bearing and battle equipment, a map, a compass, a gas-mask and a rifle. We were each given several widely separated waypoints to locate and mark without the use of light.

Although I was easily able to identify the first land navigation point by crossing an open paddy field, on the second leg I walked right into a ditch full of stinking sludge. I was going good, I knew it was there on my left side, so I tried to stay away from it, but my right foot hit some kind of a mud slick, and before I could correct myself, I lost my footing and landed on my ass, slid down a shallow bank and plunged into it. With the weight of my equipment pulling me down, I was struck by the godawful thought that I was going to drown in this shit. It was an ugly situation. It then occurred to me that even should I somehow make it out, I probably would want to be dead anyway, because I was guaranteed to be the laughing stock of the entire fucking garrison. UI would be called "Poopin' Pike" or something like that, and if I died the headline would be that "Lieutenant Pike Dies in Shit". I really did think I was going to die there because it was pulling me down. My thoughts at the time was that I never would have a family, I don't have a wife and I don't have any children. I'm still a young man, I can't die like this.

I tried to keep calm and control my gag impulse. By slow and careful maneuver I was able to position my body horizontal, keeping my head above the surface, and then, in a moving swamp of liquefied feces, I inched my way carefully towards the road, caterpillaring until I could feel the edge of the ditch. By degrees I eased my ass out onto solid ground, wow that felt good, and there I lay looking up at the stars, thinking, "What the hell! Why does this shit happen to me?"

Pvt. First Class Troy Cardieu, a specialist in my detachment back at Camp Walker, was also on that course, and I think I will let him take up the story. This is how he remembered it:

DON'T JUST WALK IN A STRAIGHT LINE from point A to point B, they told us, because there are farmers' fields out here and rice paddies, and you could fall and hurt yourself, or you could drown in a pool of shit. Well, nobody tells Lieutenant Pike what to do. I already had my points, so I was taking my remaining time to nap under a tree before turning in my answers. I was just sitting underneath that tree with my Kevlar helmet down over my eyes, catching forty winks. All of a sudden, this stench of feces and urine just washes over me, enough that it woke me up. I look up and I see one of those chem lights that we had to use so they could find us if they needed to, and I turn on my tac light, and I shine it up at the person standing in front of me. I see Lieutenant Pike in a red glow, and all he is wearing is his Kevlar helmet and his LBE with a gas mask on it, but he is completely naked and barefoot, and he has just got shit *all* over him.

I look up and I go, "Sir!"

"Ah," he says. "I fell in some shit."

"I can smell that, Sir."

And he's like, "I was walking on the rice paddies."

I said, "Sir they told us not to walk on the rice paddies."

"I know."

"Sir, where is your uniform?"

He told me that after he fell in the pig shit, he walked over to the farmer's house and knocked on the door—the balls of this man! He knocks on their door. He's standing there covered in pig and human shit, and he tells the woman who came to the door,

"I fell in your pig shit."

The poor woman can see that, and she can smell it. She doesn't speak any English, but motions to him to come inside, strip out of all his clothes, and somehow, even though he didn't speak any Korean, he complies. He strips down to his underwear in front of this unfamiliar woman and she promises to bring his uniform back after she cleans it, and he is okay with that. So he was on his way back to camp when he ran into me.

He gets back to camp and pulls his stretcher out of the tent and sleeps that night under a tree. Next morning, he has a shower and appears on parade in his PT kit, and everyone was like, "Do you plan on participating today?" And he was like, "Yeah, I am just waiting on someone."

And they all looked at each other, asking who the hell Lieutenant Pike could be waiting for in the middle of the woods on the DMZ? Next thing you know, here comes this little *ajumma* woman; she comes running up, and she bows, and she's got his clothes folded and pressed, and he ends up wearing the crispest uniform.[1] He just takes it, bows back to her, and walks back to his tent as if nothing happened.

YEARS LATER, I TOLD TOM DELK THAT STORY, and he laughed like hell. He told me he had no idea at the time, but I figured word must have got out. His answer was that if any soldier was likely to fall into a pool of shit, it would be a Pike. My old man had a different take. If any soldier could fall into a pool of shit and come out of it smelling like roses, then it could only have been a Pike. Of course, I failed the land navigation lane, although that was not what caused me to fail the course. It was screwing up the emergency triage that did that, as it did for Troy and many others. I was okay with that, though. I had gotten away with falling in a cesspool. If Castro and Garland thought that was what I deserved, they never said so, but I figured that is probably what they thought.

I SHIPPED OUT OF SOUTH KOREA IN FEBRUARY 1995, under a cloud. I walked off base alone with a duffle bag over my shoulder and hailed a taxi. No one offered to drive me, and probably no one would have if I asked. Mi-jeong had begun putting pressure on me as I was preparing to ship out, and I told her plainly that I did not intend to marry her. That pissed her off real good. By then, it was generally known that I had been going AWOL and taking regular flights to the Philippines. When she was brought in and questioned about it, she told them everything she knew. By then I guess it was too late for them to do much about it, and I slipped away without reprimand. It was

---

[1] *Ajumma* is a term of defining a mother, a matron, or a middle-aged woman.

112

a close-run thing. My promotion came through a few weeks before, so I left base with the rank of captain. I skated on pretty thin ice a few times on that tour, but I got away with it, so I was feeling good. I had my orders to report to Fort Sam Houston in San Antonio, Texas, for what would likely be a long stretch of training. I felt good about that, too. I felt pretty untouchable.

Back in the States, I took a couple of weeks' leave and drove back home to Fingerville. My dad and I spent time sitting around in the yard, with the dogs all around, chatting about this and that. One evening as he sipped his pre-dinner scotch and soda, I shared my impressions of Korea and the Philippines and tried to explain to him the appeal it had for me—the food, the women, and the society. He and Mom did not care much for Asian food, and they would often remark on it. He would say, "You been eating that damn *kimchi* again. I can smell the garlic coming out of you. Damn, son, can you lay off that shit every once in a while?"

It was more than just food and women. It was just the behavior of men, men being men. It was the spitting on sidewalks, slurping soup, farting, and how businessmen would quite openly piss in the shrubbery. I liked all of that. I could relate to it. I told him how great I was adapting to that life. I also told him about my interest in Asian women. That was a brief conversation. He cut me off with the comment, "Son, you can screw them chinks all you want, but do me a favor and don't, for God's sake, marry one."

*Myself at Basic Training. Forgot to wear
an undershirt for an official picture.
More Trouble!*

Myself at Airborne School

Beverly, my wife, and I at a military ball. She helped me out of a lot of trouble

115

Afghanistan

My dad, the most influential man in my life

Drill SGT. Ellenburg, the most feared man in my life

Unit Photo Germany

116

My dad doing what he loved best, building and tending a fire

Training at Fort Polk Louisiana

Chantel, my daughter, and I, after Afghanistan

Commander's Ball Korea

118

Mrs Drake, my high school counsellor who advised me not to go to college, and then me as a senior officer with two Masters Degrees

The 5th Medical Detachment, Korea

In Afghanistan: taking cover during direct fire at a remote base with the police behind me

Afghanistan. Outside the office tent, Shindand

Afghanistan. A soldier and I waiting for aircraft. Shindand Airbase

*Figure 1South Korea. I went 'native' much in Korea and eventually was a
US Army community relations officer award winner*

Myself and daughter far left. Yongsan Army Garrison. I was a soccer coach in Korea

A family visit to the White House for an Easter Egg event

Dennis Earl Pike

RED SHIT

When life knocks you down, try to land on your back. Because if you can look up, you can get up.
LES BROWN

EARLY IN FEBRUARY 1995, I packed up my old Toyota truck, wished the old folks goodbye, and got on the road, on to the I-85, for the long drive to San Antonio, through Georgia, Alabama, and the Gulf States. I felt emboldened, maybe even just a little bit cocky, exalting in the sensation of going where I was never meant to be and achieving what no one ever expected. My first tour is South Korea was complete. I was a bit changed, not only by Asian food but Asian women. In fact I never dated another white woman again. I was stacking up experience and training, moving ahead not only in the eyes of my family, but among other soldiers too. I must have communicated some of that brimming confidence in my conversations with my father, who said to me as I was leaving South Carolina something along the lines of, "Careful, son. Pride comes before the fall."

FORT SAM HOUSTON IN SAN ANTONIO, TEXAS, is known as the home of Army medicine. It is the headquarters of the US Army Medical Command, the US Medical Corps, and all of its various branches, elements and departments that make it the largest medical training facility of the uniformed services. It was a good feeling to arrive in San Antonio and report according to my orders. Ahead of me lay a year of intense training and entry at last into the club of trained US Army Medical Department personnel. The facility was full of young officers from first-class schools and universities, serious-minded people entering a serious branch of military service, and with the kind of academic experience and background that I could not ever match.

As I shambled in with my monkey walk and my Southern manners, a little bit of redneck. prior-enlisted and an academic insurgent, I will not deny that I felt more than a little bit intimidated. The informal reprimand delivered to me by fellow soldiers in Korea seemed to underscore the fact that I was an outlier, which tended to stir up in me a rebellious spirit. Most men of my age and background who enlisted remained enlisted, so a good 'ol country boy with rough manners and a hardscrabble attitude was a rarity at that level. I had been raised by a man who grew up wiping his ass with mountain laurel leaves and eating from dumpsters, who got a kick out of firing bottle rockets at cars, and who taught me the art of watermelon theft. I arrived at Fort Sam with the residue of that mindset and the heart of a mountain man. My Special Forces experience set me apart, and my independence of spirit was still fundamentally at odds with the establishment. I might even have been a little reactionary and aggressive, and that curious, rebellious impulse to self-destruct was still glowing warm in the belly.

I anticipated an easy ride at Fort Sam, and that was for sound reason. At this point in any officer's career, so much money has been poured into training and capacity building that there is no real incentive to mark up a failure. At the same time, because no officer arrives at this point without an authentic interest and a will to succeed, there was a mood about the place of serious study and advancement. I was fortunate to have been given the opportunity to stack up a whole lot of training at one time, and I was proud of being part of a corps of men and women poised to enter the specialized field of military medical services. I saw it as the first major step in my career, which promised more of the same if I could just keep a firm grip. Using those Five Ps I tried to see if old Tom Delk could get me some papers and background on how to pass through these gates, but he was a regulation guy and he shut the door on that one.

I took four principal courses that year, of which two were required and the others elective. These were, in order of importance: the Principles of Preventive Medicine; the Army Medical Department Advanced Course; the Department of Defense Pesticide Application Course; and the Air Force Operational Entomology Course. In the interest of sustaining high pass rates, most of the examinations and assessments were either oral or practical, or they took the form of multiple-choice questions. In general, the instructors seemed inclined to offer help or a heads-up on anything that needed particular attention. The only one that really concerned me was the Army Medical Department Advanced Course, an intense, five-month course with elements of analysis and deduction and a whole lot of reading and writing.

At any one time, there are hundreds of courses ongoing at Fort Sam, often interlinked, so if you successfully complete one, it tends to sometimes lead into another. For the sake of those interested in entering this branch of the uniformed services, here are a few facts and details of the courses and the general expectation placed on Army Medical Department personnel.

The role of a medical entomologist is almost exclusively limited to preventive medicine. It is not the world of the PhD, the army doctor or the field surgeon, but the medic and the preventive medicine officer. In the United States, as in most military establishments, the preventive medicine branches of the general Army medical service corps came long after the establishment of an ambulance corps and the development of battlefield surgery as a specialization. In fact, the emergence of preventive medicine in the military ran parallel to its development in the civilian sphere. The annals of military history are full of wars and campaigns where the death toll from disease far outstripped the number of soldiers killed on the battlefield. The best example of this is the Civil War, during which more than six hundred thousand young men lost their lives. While the odds of an active-duty soldier surviving were only about one in four, more than twice as many died of disease and other causes than fell on the battlefield. Out of some 200,000 troops killed on both sides, 224,480 Union soldiers and 164,000 Confederates died of diseases such as measles, typhoid fever, and pneumonia, contracted mainly in camps, prisoner of war holding facilities and field hospitals. The concept of a specialist, preventive medicine branch was pioneered at the beginning of the sixteenth century by the Royal Navy. The job of an onboard medical attendant, known as a "scab-lifter," was often a punishment duty, certainly not a professional assignment, and one that often killed as many caregivers as it did patients.

The preventive branch of the US military medical establishment can trace its formal origins to July 27, 1775, when the Congress established the "Army Hospital," overseen at the time by the director-general and chief physician. It was not until 1818, during the First Seminole War, that the Army Medical Department was established as a full-time branch of the US military, leading to the development over the next century of the Army Nurse Corps, Dental Corps, Veterinary Corps, Medical Service Corps and, finally, in 1947, the Army Medical Specialist Corps. Under the terms of the Army Organization Act of 1950, the Army Medical Department was renamed Army Medical

Service, and in 1968, it finally became the Army Medical Department.

According to the archives of the Army, "The Army Medical Department, or the AMEDD, is the US Army's healthcare organization and is present in the Active Army, the US Army Reserve, and the Army National Guard components. It is headquartered at Fort Sam Houston, San Antonio, Texas, which hosts the AMEDD Center and School. Large numbers of AMEDD senior leaders can also be found in the Washington, DC, area, divided between the Pentagon and the Walter Reed National Military Medical Center."

The Principles of Preventive Medicine is an entry-level course that establishes a trainee with the essential knowledge base and skills necessary to function in one or other of the preventive medicine specialties. In addition, each trainee is required to undergo detailed instruction unique to his or her particular specialty. One of the most important skills, whatever specialty a trainee might choose, is management and administration. Every overseas deployment is accompanied by a detachment of preventive medicine personnel, usually in small units of between ten and fifteen soldiers, who are responsible for a bunch of programs, each of which requires detailed organization, management and problem-solving.

General subjects covered by the course include managing preventive medicine operations at home and abroad, knowledge of population health for force health protection; employment of operational risk management techniques for preventive medicine and health surveillance; identification of current issues affecting preventive medicine, and managing preventive medicine support for homeland security operations. More detailed instruction deals with community health practices, communicable and infectious diseases, operational preventive medicine, epidemiology, statistics, medical entomology, industrial hygiene, health physics, sanitary engineering, and environmental science. The objective of this part of the course is to provide a broad overview of each of the specialty areas, preparing each trainee to function as part of a multidisciplinary team. Each specialty group also receives additional instruction in appropriate specialty topics, preparing them to function independently at an entry level within their specialties. Usually, the whole thing wraps up with a three-day field training exercise, after which the Army Medical Department Advanced Course begins.

FOR THAT THREE-DAY FIELD EXERCISE, a unit of six or seven trainee entomologists traveled down to Sinton in South Texas to gather, survey, and catalog medically important insects. Sinton is on the Gulf Coast a few miles north of Corpus Christi, a relic of the oil and cattle boom, and a fine old Texas town. It is home to the 851st Transportation Company and the US Army Reserve. Our unit comprised junior officers under the instructional leadership of a major, a herpetologist by the name of Richard Whittle.

Major Whittle was an academic with military rank but without what I would describe as a natural feeling for soldiering and no real grasp on leadership. He was a good entomologist and snake expert, no doubt. I was a captain, one rank lower, but I was older and prior-enlisted with a whole lot more real military experience than any of them. The others were all lieutenants, and so they sorta look up to me a little, and take their lead from me rather than the officer in charge. I remember one time one of them said to me, "Damn, I wish I could have done Special Forces." This put Whittle a little bit out of the loop. We were a small, collegial community on a technical assignment, so there was no real rank formality, and since he was uncertain of himself, Major Whittle sometimes responded peevishly, alienating others from himself even more. Again, the environment was collegial and it was for learning.

We were working off base as the temporary guests of a local rancher and his family. It was a private environment, and Major Whittle was anxious to present a good picture and not to weigh too heavily on the hospitality of our host. This was an obligation that he felt very keenly, and since it was his responsibility to liaise with the landowner, he was anxious that nothing happen to embarrass him or discredit the unit. The house was an old-style Texas ranch property with limited amenities, and the facility assigned to us was pretty much a shack with no indoor plumbing. We arrived on the property in the evening, and before anything could be set up, I was caught short and relieved the urge in a nearby cattle enclosure. I thought no more about it until the next morning when I heard Major Whittle outside in the yard erupt in a rage, demanding to know who shit in the cattle enclosure. That sort of behavior within a small group of medical service officers was very unusual, unheard of in fact.

"I say again!" He demanded. "Who shit in the animal corral?"

I stepped up, stood to attention, and replied, "That would be me, Sir."

"What the fuck. *What the fuck!* You are a goddamned public health officer, for Christ's sake! Why did you not cover it up?"

"Because," I replied, completely blindsided, "it is an animal corral. I thought it would be covered cow shit by the morning."

"No! It is a fucking *vacant* animal corral! We are guests of the farmer and he stepped in your damn turd this morning! And why the *fuck* is your shit *red*?"

I explained, as my fellow officers struggled to keep a straight face, that I had just come off a tour in Korea. I happen to like Korean food, and Korean food uses red pepper paste that turns a person's stools red, some people more than others. This seemed to turn him speechless with rage, and he spun on his

131

heels and stormed out of the room. At the moment he left, the others fell around and bust a gut laughing.

Even though the whole thing was embarrassing, unnecessary, and very out of character in a fraternal group of medical officers, he certainly did have a point. If I had been older and holding the position of executive officer of a unit myself, I probably would have been more sympathetic to him, but I was not, and nor were my fellow officers. The incident was funny, but it also pissed the squad off, establishing a mood of rebellion against Major Whittle that I thought was also kind of unnecessary and unfair. As medical officers, none of us were really used to the left-right-left army doctrine, and we definitely did not function under heavy discipline the way a regular infantry combat unit might. For sure he was at fault in reprimanding me like that in front of everyone else, but I did not take it as bad as the others. It was an odd situation, and almost from that point on he lost control. In a way, I became the de-facto squad leader, defending him and trying to keep the program on course. All the others were at Fort Sam only for this course and would be shipping out when it was over, while I would likely be sticking around for a while and seeing Major Whittle again. After the whole red shit thing, he began to lean on me a little as a fortification against the crap he was taking from the others. It was a situation I had never seen or heard of before. I began to get the feeling that a mutiny was brewing.

Pretty soon, the squad was working to rule, following orders only to the degree that it was absolutely necessary, and dragging their feet over everything else. In a conventional combat unit, there would have been a heavy, disciplinary intervention, but not in a unit like ours. Major Whittle really had no choice but to power through it. I had never experienced a mutiny like this before and never since. Infantrymen, officer or enlisted, get chewed out like that all the time and lose no sleep over it. To me it seemed unfair, and even though I had been the cause of it all, I did not support making Major Whittle's life difficult.

Then, a few days before we were scheduled to leave, the others approached me and asked me to ask Major Whittle if we could ship out early. Everything that needed to be done had been done, and they wanted to get back to Fort Sam Houston. I asked them why me? I was at the top of Major Whittle's shit list. They told me that as a captain I was the senior officer, besides which, despite being the cause of it all, I was on better terms with him than anyone else. I did like the man. I put it to him, and he said absolutely. He was done with the whole shitshow himself. None of the others would ride back in the same bus as him, so he and I rode back together.

He was pissed, but he held it together. As we were driving up out of Sinton towards San Antonio, he saw a snake on the side of the road. He said, "Hey, Pike, let's get that snake." He was a herpetologist, so he knew snakes. I was scared of snakes, and I said, "Na, let's just keep going." In the end, we got out, and he had me take the back end of the snake, which I did, and it shit all over my arm. He laughed. That was his way of getting back at me a little bit, I guess.

Back at Fort Sam, as we were unloading the van, he said to the squad, "Y'all wanted to go home. Well, here we are. You sure did miss out on free beer and steaks. The farmer invited us over tonight." It was poor shot, a little bit passive-aggressive, but it was the best he had. Later, when we handed in a really piss-poor collection of insects, his comment was, "Jesus! My damn enlisted soldiers could have done better than you." And he was right. We were all well-educated and all holding master's and some PhDs. We could have, and should have done better.

The performance of the group shut down due to me taking a shit and being reprimanded for it. I guess the moral of the story is that the group is more powerful than the individual. I stayed on good terms with Major Whittle for the remainder of my time at Fort Sam. Talking about it later raised a laugh. In the end, I got on pretty well with him. Talking about it all later, it raised a laugh. Training officers are often just university professors in uniform, and they often do not have any interest or incentive to push discipline. The world of the medical service officer is small, and I figured I might need him one day.

BACK AT FORT SAM, I BEGAN IMMEDIATELY to prepare myself for the Army Medical Department Advanced Course. The word 'advanced' got me a little nervous because I was not advanced in anything. This is typically a five-month course with an emphasis on both classroom and hands-on training. It is for the most part a big-picture program with some of the more important themes being the military decision-making process, Army health systems support and force health protection doctrines, unit training management, leadership skills, and staff officer functions. Having mastered the military decision-making process, trainees are then required to deliver an individual concept-of-support brief in the presence of course instructors. This comprises a seven-step process in developing the concept of general medical support to large-scale ground combat operations. Embedded in this are the many established doctrinal principles of the Army health systems and force health protection. As a whole, the course lays heavy emphasis on presentation and communication skills, and expertise in the course material. It is usually a required course, and although in the normal run of things, it is not intended to be that difficult; it presented a tremendous hurdle for me simply because of the amount of reading and writing involved, and the emphasis on presentation and public speaking. For me just public speaking alone, among these academic giants, rattled me a bit. I would feel more comfortable jumping out of an airplane.

By then, the Five Ps had become a well-developed and practiced routine for me, and knowing in advance what was likely to be required, I applied a little creative thinking and ingenuity. To deal with public speaking, I began attending meetings of the local Toastmasters chapter, a public speakers club, which I recommend to anyone, no matter what their level of competence. Then I took a deep dive into the faculty dumpsters and unearthed a wealth of past papers, discarded reports and briefings from earlier courses and outgoing trainees. I even found evaluation reports. This time I said nothing to anyone. I built up a comprehensive file of material and studied it hard. The result was that I passed, and although not with spectacular results, all things considered, it was a successful transition. That is the principle of the Five Ps. Thanks to my Five Ps, I earned my stripes and got to call myself a Medical Service Corps officer.

As a Medical Service Corps officer, my specialty was to be entomology. According to the standard US Army doctrine, "Medical entomologists are commissioned officers in the Army Medical Service Corps. Their overall mission is to prevent arthropod-borne disease among the soldiers and civilians who support military operations."

Besides these standard principles, the courses also included the usual elements of leadership and administration and staff functions in the field of preventive medicine. We were also taught the principles of training and instruction, consultation, and product development and research. Fortunately, I had a good background in the sciences thanks to my degrees in agriculture, and so I found the practical aspects of this fairly straightforward. Of my elective courses, one was Air Force Entomology. This comprised general military entomology with the addition of a few details specific to Air Force deployments and insect control as it affected the safety and smooth function of aircraft. Again, according to the standard doctrine, "During that two-week course, students receive instruction and training on proper surveillance and control techniques for arthropods and arthropod-borne diseases.

Through the use of informal lectures, laboratories, and field and scenario exercises, emphasis is placed on major arthropods and arthropod-borne diseases, as well as environmental and cultural conditions which deploying personnel are likely to encounter during deployments."

The emphasis, once again, was on a team approach in dealing with and solving problems related to pest management and vector-borne diseases during military exercises, in war zones, and in the case of natural disasters. In the 1990s, the emphasis was on "operations other than war," but this changed later to "other operations," or OO, because other operations can sometimes become war. Again, scenarios and field exercises are the backbone of instruction, allowing trainees to practice hands-on and display their abilities to implement in the field what they learn in class.

The responsibilities and duties of an Army or Air Force entomologist may be defined mostly by survey, identification, and mitigation strategies. Identification is the most important part, and the most difficult part for me. I picked up on all of this pretty well because, for most critters, their priorities are simple survival, and competition for food, water, and reproduction. Within the context of the standard training doctrine, these procedures are regulated, regimented, and run according to clearly defined methods and protocols. As a staff officer, a senior medical officer is also typically expected to develop and consult on the entomological portion of operational and educational programs in the area of preventive medicine. What is more, he or she must be capable of formulating policies, plans, and procedures for military pest management programs, to advise and consult on environmental matters, to coordinate pest management and biological activities with military and civilian agencies and to instruct and conduct research in medical biology.

A major part of practical disease prevention in a field setting is the application of pesticides, which today are bound up in environmental issues and other essential protocols of safety and environmental responsibility. The Department of Defense Pesticide Application Course runs through a gamut of issues related to the use of pesticides in the field, dealing with a variety of different types, how to handle them, how to dispose of them, and the equipment necessary for their application and safety. Then there are more general subjects related to state and federal laws and statutes and the environmental laws and protocols of any host nation.

What I learned from all of this was twofold. First, that preventive medicine is a military discipline that leans heavily on administration and organization; and second, that education and training run as an ongoing thread in the career of a Medical Service Corps officer. Medical officers receive regular refreshers and are constantly enlarging and building on their skills with ongoing training. They are also expected to provide training and lectures in the field in support of disease prevention among troops on active deployment.

As I approached the end of that year, I had stacked up a significant amount of training, and although very much in the average range, I passed. I was very proud of myself. Then, two things happened that would completely alter my life. The first was meeting my future wife, and the second was picking up a DUI.

IT IS CONVENTIONAL WISDOM IN MILITARY circles that a DUI on a soldier's official record is a career death sentence. After drinking fairly heavily one night at the Midnight Rodeo in the El Dorado neighborhood of San Antonio, I got into my truck and drove a few blocks to the Taco Cabana. I was standing in line inside the restaurant when I noticed a cop sitting in his squad car in the parking lot with its blue lights, on motioning me to come outside. Initially, I thought he needed help, and as a fellow uniformed public servant, I did not think twice. When I came up alongside him, he pointed to my truck and asked me if it was mine. I replied in the affirmative. He introduced himself as Officer Molina and then asked if I had been drinking, and like a dumbass, I admitted that I had. Based on a claim that I had been speeding, he required a field sobriety test, and when I failed that, I was cuffed and stuffed. I was taken to downtown San Antonio, and there I blew a 0.112. My truck was impounded, and I stayed in the jail all night until I was retrieved by the Military Police and driven back to my apartment.

"Fuck!" I thought to myself. "This is the end."

I felt it was the end, and I accepted that it was the end, because I definitely did ignore all of our briefings and instructions about drinking and driving.

A few days later, I was summoned before a battalion commander of the US Army Medical Department Center and School, Fort Sam Houston, Maj. Gen. John J. Cuddy. Standing to attention I was read a General Officer Memorandum of Reprimand, the much-feared GOMOR. Although the language of a GOMOR is standardized and not necessarily specific to any individual, it nonetheless hit me in the gut when it was read to me. After the details were recited, that on 12 December 1995 I operated my vehicle while intoxicated and was subsequently cited by an officer of the San Antonio Police Department, the document went on to record that "because your conduct falls far short of the sort of the self-discipline and mature judgment expected of commissioned officers, this incident calls to question your character for continued service in the US Army."

I basically replied 'Yes! I fucked up and I am going to face the consequences.

The preamble emphasized that this was to be regarded strictly as an administrative reprimand and not a nonjudicial punishment under the Uniform Code of Military Justice. Barring a successful rebuttal, an opportunity for which was available to me through the chain of command within fourteen days, the GOMOR was to be placed in my Official Military Personnel File. As a routine response, and through the army legal system and the official chain of command, I submitted a rebuttal the following day.

It is important to emphasize here that no charges of driving under the influence were ultimately made against me. The reasons the charges were dropped have never been entirely clear to me, although there was a clear discrepancy between the wording of the police report and what actually happened. According to the arresting officer, I was observed to be speeding and was pulled over in the parking lot of the Taco Cabana, and there found to be under the influence, with speech slurred, emitting a strong odor of alcohol, and of disorderly appearance. A sobriety test was conducted there and then, including a nystagmus test, which I failed.[1] This is not what happened. I turned into the parking lot of the Taco Cabana and entered the restaurant. It was only as I was standing in the line that I noticed the police officer outside, who then motioned to me. On the assumption that he needed help, I complied. Under cross-examination, this might be construed as irregular, possibly even entrapment, and perhaps the officer and his superiors understood this. The police report comprised a single, brief paragraph, uncharacteristically simplistic and noncommittal, and within a few days it was swept under the carpet.

I was, therefore, in a position to state in my rebuttal that no formal charges had been pursued against me and that I had no DUI on my civilian record. My rebuttal began with an apology to my unit, my fellow officers, and my command for my error of judgment, followed by a plea that such an error of judgment not be allowed to destroy an otherwise unblemished

---

[1] According to the DUI Foundation, a nystagmus test is as follows: "In the horizontal gaze nystagmus test used by law enforcement officials, the officer positions an object, usually a pen or a finger, about one foot from the driver's face and then moves the object from one side to another while observing the driver's eye movements."

military career. This appeal was submitted to the office of Maj. Gen. James Peake, the officer commanding the US Army Medical Department Center and School, Fort Sam Houston. His response was this: "I have carefully reviewed your rebuttal and all matters in your case. I consider the allegations against you to be very serious and have directed the official reprimand to be filed in your Official Military Personnel Folder."

And so it was. I had cause then to remember my dad's words of warning—pride comes before a fall. The long-term effect of an official reprimand on a charge as serious as a DUI is usually to end any advancement through the ranks, any future training, and any hope of a military career. I was thirty years old, holding the rank of captain and on the cusp of entering a field of service that both interested me and answered to many of my callings. With a GOMOR in my file, my horizons were diminished, and it seemed inevitable that my service to the armed forces of the United States would revert to the rank of a captain in the National Guard—a weekend warrior, two days a month and two weeks a year. It was a brutal personal reprimand. Needless to say, word got around, and as I stood to attention in the auditorium at Fort Sam Houston, dressed in my blues, to have my name read out and collect my certification, I was aware that everyone there who knew me knew that it was over for me. Beverly, my future wife, was in the audience to comfort me and she was there for the good, the bad and the ugly.

Then, as we were wrapping up and preparing to shut down, I fell into conversation with a senior NCO who had once had a similar experience. Somewhere in the manual, he told me, there is a regulation stating that if, within one year, the general officer who issued the GOMOR can be persuaded that a soldier has performed well and remained a potential asset to the Army, he had the authority to entirely expunge the GOMOR. It seemed doubtful, a real long shot, seldom if ever used and rarely successful, but it gave me hope. Two things I can say in conclusion: the first is that I had met the woman I knew I would marry, and the second is that my independence of mind, scorn for military discipline, and that urge to self-destruct ended with the filing of that GOMOR. I promised myself that if I survived this, things would be very different.

SMELLING LIKE ROSES

Failure is not falling down but refusing to get up.
REV. ROBERT SCHULLER

B ACK IN SOUTH CAROLINA, and over a couple of cold beers, Dad's advice to me was the same as it had always been. "Get on your feet son, keep moving forward, and never give up."

From my years in the army I felt I would probably not recover from this major screw-up. The issue weighed heavily on my spirit. My name was mud, and there was good reason to believe that the GOMOR would end me, as a captain, with no hope for advancement. Although I had been thrown a lifeline in the form of one year at a minimum to prove my worth, it still seemed like a long shot. My father was proud of me for achieving so much, much more than he had ever imagined, and he cast no judgments on my behavior. He had once been given a DUI coming back home from Fred's house in the 1970s, but at that time, the stigma of it was different. We were in the era of MADD, or Mothers Against Drunk Driving. I was more allied with DAMM, or Drunks Against Mad Mothers. Even if I did find myself back at the National Guard, he reminded me, one weekend a month and two weeks a year, I would still be an officer, I would probably be promoted, and I could still anticipate a good civilian career.

He said, "Hell Son, you are still an officer with two college degrees!"

But I, on he other hand, knew the mountain I needed to climb. It would be very difficult, even if I was able to gather all the evidence needed to expunge the record. It was a gut-check. The language of the GOMOR brought into question my character, judgment, and fitness to serve, the essential material of a soldier. Yes, it was standardized language, read to me according to regulations and without prejudice, but it struck me down, nonetheless. One day, long ago, I faced what I also thought was the end of my career, during those few transformational hours in a Criminal Correctional Facility, confused about how and why I got there, but clear in my mind that I had done nothing wrong. This, however, was a dishonorable business. No one confronted me about it directly, or told me to my face that I was an asshole, but it was widely known. Word gets out. Pike had a DUI. As much as it was terminal to my career, it was also a harsh personal rebuke.

When I asked my dad's advice, he thought for a long while before he answered. As an enlisted man only for a few years, and now a civilian, he had no real sense of how the military establishment functioned, and so he applied the more intuitive logic of business. Thinking out loud, he said, "Well, not so many bug men in the army that they can afford to throw one away, especially after so much of my damn tax money has been put into your training. The way I see it is all you do is training."

And he was right. It was a thought that gave me hope. It would make no sense for the Army to discard someone like me, a member of a relatively obscure specialty, into whose training and education so much investment had been made. I figured, as I reflected on it, that all I needed to do was to give them a sound reason to reconsider, and they probably would. It had to be worth a try.

My new position, in the meantime, was project officer with the entomological department of the Center for Health Promotion and Preventive Medicine located in Aberdeen Proving Ground in Maryland. The CHPPM, or "Chipmunk" as it was known, is a combined civilian and military agency, and my appointment was in a general staff capacity. I performed basic administrative functions, dealt with liaisons, and by way of a pesticide hotline, worked with research bodies and other similar facilities across the military sphere. Although on the whole, it was a routine and unremarkable assignment—certainly not a whole lot of water coming out of that firehose—it was what I had to work with, and I approached it determined to make the best use of it. I was answerable to a civilian director by the name of Ed Evans, who responded to this enthusiasm in kind, signing off with a minimum of reflection on every application for additional training that I put on his desk. I had one year of grace to prove to the Army that I was both reformed and indispensable, and to do that I needed to stack up training, lots of training, to display above-average commitment and have something solid at the end of that period to show.

The fact remained, meanwhile, that to date I had been charged with no crime related to my DUI arrest. Despite that, the arrest itself remained on the record. It occurred to me that if I could get that arrest record expunged from the archives of whichever agencies held it, including military command, that it would add weight to any later appeal to an Army Suitability Evaluation Board. My first course of action, therefore, was to hire a lawyer in San Antonio to file an appeal in civil court.

In those days, it was a question of sitting down with a copy of the yellow pages and making phone calls, and to narrow down the search, I came up with a strategy. To each of the dozen or so lawyers I contacted, I asked for one name out of a handful that I would propose, not including themselves, who they would consider best suited to take on a case like this. The name put forward by everyone, other than himself, was John Brown. John Brown was the best kind of lawyer: he was expensive, and a self-opinionated, argumentative and unpleasant asshole with an ego about the size of the Grand Canyon, and as soon as I sized him up, I hired him. The first thing he asked me when he looked over the police report was, "What the fuck did you do to that cop? Did you give him a goddamned blowjob or something?"

Over the course of fifteen years with the San Antonio Police Department, Officer Molina and John Brown had crossed paths many times. Molina had a reputation as a bloodhound, ambitious and committed, and at the time of writing, he held the rank of captain in the Bexar County Sheriff's Office. John Brown had never seen a report authored by Officer Molina that was so brief and unspecific, and rarely if ever did he drop a charge once it had been filed. Possibly he sensed the potential of entrapment in the manner in which he effected the arrest, or maybe, when he discovered I was an Army officer, a fellow member of the uniformed services, whose career would likely be killed by a DUI, he thought better of it. Either way, all I can recall of that episode is that I rode in a squad car from the 8400 block on Perrin Beitel Road to the precinct feeling quite relaxed. I guess I took the attitude that what would happen now would happen. Our conversation was collegial and humorous, and I think he was probably amused by the good-old-boy shit and the rough military humor. I was processed, my alcohol count recorded, and I was locked up. My truck was impounded, and I sat in jail until eventually, after about eighteen hours, I was released without charge.

According to John Brown, this was more than adequate grounds to file an appeal for the complete removal of my arrest record, and this he did. Although technically it was a simple argument and a fairly straightforward petition, procedurally it was lengthy and convoluted. I was required to return to San Antonio frequently for hearings and deferrals and suchlike,

145

which, besides the inconvenience, all added to a mounting expense. The petition was submitted in October 1997, and a ruling in my favor was handed down two months later in December. Among the agencies ordered to delete their record of my arrest, and there were quite a number of them, was the Department of the Army.

I was working on the assumption that a decree of this nature delivered by a civilian court and ordered to include the Department of the Army would, as a matter of procedure, obligate them to do as ordered. Not so. I was apprised, through various exchanges, of some details that had not at the time been clear to me. In the first instance, the military does not hold itself subject to the jurisdiction of a civilian court, and in the second, the GOMOR was not a prescribed punishment but an administrative action with no record of arrest. It was also made clear to me that the complete removal of a GOMOR was only possible if the charge was manifestly and provably untrue. I had already acknowledged that I was guilty of driving under the influence and, notwithstanding that the charge had been dropped, I had blown a 0.112 and was unarguably driving above the legal limit. This, in the eyes of the military, was sufficient grounds to confirm the reprimand and to order its retention in my Official Military Personnel File. As advised by the US Army Trial Defense Service, I filed an immediate appeal. In response, Maj. Gen. James Peake replied that the matter of driving under the influence was not disputed and had been correctly processed, and so the reprimand had been appropriately filed. And that, at least for the time being, was the end of the matter.

It was a bitter disappointment, particularly after all the time, effort, and expense that I had gone through to mount an action in civilian court. It was a failure of the Five Ps. A glimmer of hope, however, remained in another procedural angle. This was to appeal for the reprimand to be moved from my Official Military Personnel File, where it was accessible to any department or branch, to the restricted portion of my file. To achieve this, it was now even more important to prove my commitment to my career and the fact that I was indispensable to the Army.

"Not so many damn bug men in the Army that they can afford to throw one away." Is what my dad always said.

In the meantime I had two small encounters with the police not having to do anything with drinking and driving. Word came down from the army that it was important to burn your sensitive files such as your travel vouchers and your receipts and all the wicked amount of paperwork collected over the years in the Army. The Army runs on paper and I had a huge trash bag full of it, and I was going to go ahead and burn them. I walked a ways out into the woods, at night, and alone outside my apartment. Some one passing on the road stopped and looked at me from about one hundred yards away. I knew this was not a good thing so I started pee on the fire and toss dirt on the remains and get the hell out of there.

Then, out of the blue a helicopter with a spotlight arrived overhead. It was one of those helicopters that you see on the television chasing people on the ground. I started running through the woods taking care to stay uncover of the thick bushes, and I went the long way to get back to my apartment. I was scared because I had no damned Idea what it was about. I went into the office next day and said, "Hey Y'all, I got chased by a helicopter yesterday and I don't know why. You have any idea?"

They laughed at that story and told me that there was no open burning in city limits. I asked, "what is that?"

"You can't make a fire because there's and ordnance or something."

"Wow. I ain't never heard nothing like that before."

I never did any open burning after that.

I had another small experience with the military police on base. They chased me into the gym sauna. Now I was driving on a Saturday on base. A lot of times in the evenings or in the mornings they have a bugle call. Usually in the evening they would play the Retreat, and what you are supposed to do is stop your car. A lot of people stop the car and get out and stand to attention. Well, I just kept on driving. The Military Police spotted me ignoring the sounding of Retreat and they started to take on after me. I sped up my car to try and get away from him. My plan was to get to the gym and then hide. I made it to the gym and ran inside and hid in the sauna. When he found me the Military Policeman began to chew out my ass on the correct procedure of stopping a car during the sounding of Retreat. I could only think what all the other soldier at the gym were thinking. I acknowledge the instructions and was polite towards the police officer and I was let off without charge.

MY DAD TOLD US THE STORIES—barefoot and hungry stories, teaching his sons how to survive, how to steal watermelons, to overcome, to never quit no matter what. I could survive, too, and fuck them all! "You are who you are," I told myself. "You are not white trash. You can be whatever you want to be. Never give up, and keep moving forward, no matter what. That, after all, is fundamental to military training."

I began networking among colleagues and superiors to gather what was a nonspecific number of letters and endorsements required to support any claim of rehabilitation and proof of future value to the Army. I made no secret about why. I had screwed up real bad, and I needed help. Another cornerstone principle of the Five Ps: Never be afraid of asking for help. At the same time, I put in applications for every scrap of training I could, and in the belief that nothing could better illustrate my commitment to the Army than availability for deployment, I made myself available to the Sixty-first Medical Detachment, a medical unit attached to the XVIII Airborne Corps. During the course of that year, I twice retook the Expert

Medical Field Badge, first in Fort Drum in New York State, where I failed again, and for the third time at Fort Indian Town Gap in Pennsylvania, where I passed by the narrowest margin.

There is a moral in the story of that pass that is probably worth telling you here. During my second attempt at Fort Drum, I was placed in charge of the van that transported the various support personnel who acted out the roles of casualties and who carried out the multiple functions necessary to stage the course. As the course was wrapping up, a small group of privates asked me to drive them into town for drink and food. I tossed them the keys to the van and told them to take it. They were pretty impressed by that. The next time around, as I went through my third effort, two of them were again assigned to support the course. I failed the triage lanes over a particular detail of how casualties were to be loaded into vehicles. This put me right on the knife-edge, and I was summoned to appear before the committee to discuss it. I probably would have failed but for those two privates who spoke to sergeant major on my behalf, and that tipped the balance. That same sergeant major later told me that he pretty much took care of me over that. The moral of the story is to be nice to everyone, even people at the bottom. I would probably have failed for the third time, but for those two privates giving a heads-up to the sergeant major, saying, "Hey this guy is a good guy. We need to give him his badge."

Also that year, I attended the Combined Arms Services and Staff School at Fort Leavenworth, Kansas. This was a big one, and it was particularly challenging to me for the number of presentations and PowerPoint displays that were required. As the only captain out of a dozen or more to come up short on one important presentation, I was called before the committee and told that I would be thrown a lifeline and allowed to repeat the presentation in a private setting. It was the day before Veterans Day, and that gave me time to prepare two presentations in the hope that one at least would pass. That display of unusual determination and commitment seemed to impress the board members, and I think I probably passed for that one reason alone.

Later, in his official assessment, Ed Evans added in the comments section, "Captain Pike is one of the finest company-grade officers I have known and supervised. His dedicated and enthusiastic approach to assigned duties, without exception, exceeded performance objectives. Particularly outstanding were his lectures to field sanitation team members on arthropods and disease field preventive medicine measures, the control of arthropods with pesticides, and rodent management."

The most challenging and enjoyable two weeks of that year were those spent at Fort Drum earning my Air Assault Badge. According to official documentation, "The Air Assault Badge is awarded by the US Army for successful completion of the Air Assault School. The course includes three phases of instruction involving US Army rotary-wing aircraft: combat air assault operations; rigging and sling-loading operations; and rappelling from a helicopter."

My justification for applying to take the badge was that sometime in the future, I might be required to sling-load a pesticide dispersal unit via a helicopter. I owe Ed Evans for that one.

This time I made sure to stick to the Five Ps. I practiced ruck marching and the obstacle course, making a point of getting to grips with the rope. I had never climbed a rope before, and so I put in a lot of time at local gym, making sure that I had that down, and it paid off. A lot of trainees failed on the rope, but I passed.

The preliminaries to the course require a trainee to illustrate basic soldiering skills and fitness through route marches and an obstacle course to weed out the lazy or crazy early on. This aspect of the course is run along standard infantry training lines with a drill sergeant—in this case, an Air Assault Sergeant—working through the usual repertoire of screaming, yelling, cursing, and hurling personal insults at you. They seem to pick on officers with particular relish, because a situation like this is probably the only opportunity they ever get to do that. As I was working my way through the obstacle course, the sergeant noticed the *caduceus* badge on my left shoulder that indicated my unit. It was an unusual badge, and he called me over.

"Hey, what do you do?" he asked me.

I told him, "I'm a Medical Service Corps Officer, an entomologist."

"What the fuck is that?"

"It is insect management and control of disease."

"Oh, I see. You sit in a fuckin' air-conditioned office, and you look at shit in a microscope?"

"Yes, Sergeant Air Assault," I said. "I do that."

He thought about that for a while and then pointed back down the obstacle course. "Why don't you go over to that mud puddle over there and stick your head in it and look for bugs underwater?"

"Yes, Sergeant Air Assault," I replied, and I jogged over to the mud puddle and plunged my head into it for a little while, moving it around as if I was looking for something. In a few minutes, I was back, and said,

"Air Assault Sergeant, I can't find any bugs under water."

He turned away. "Just get the fuck outa here."

IN APRIL 1998, I SUBMITTED AN APPEAL to the Army Suitability Evaluation Board under Army Regulation 600-37, Chapter 7. This regulation, if it was found to be justified, allowed for the complete removal of any unfavorable information contained in an Official Military Personnel or, alternately, its relocation to a restricted file. By then I understood that complete removal of the GOMOR from my record was near enough impossible, for the reason that the charges were basically accurate. Although there was nothing to be gained by arguing against that, as a matter of formality, I submitted a request to have all documentation relating to the GOMOR removed from the record. I had by then been informed by the Department of the Army Suitability and Evaluation Board that the ruling of a civilian court had no bearing on military administrative issues. In due course, I was advised that any request for the removal of the GOMOR would attract no serious consideration. It was suggested by the assistant president that the only way forward now was to request that the GOMOR be transferred from the performance portion of my Official Military Personnel File to the restricted section.

In support of the appeal, I was required to include as many letters of support I could get from anyone who could be persuaded to help. I took the position from the beginning that I screwed up and screwed up badly and that I needed help. The Chipmunk was a largely civilian-administered body, and most of my colleagues rallied to my support, including Ed Evans, and even Maj. Richard Whittle, by then chief of the medical zoology branch, and the protagonist in the red shit story. When he heard, he said, "Hell yeah! I'll sign on for that shit." I guess he remembered me standing in his corner when his unit mutinied over that ol' red shit story.

Putting the Five Ps in overdrive, I wrote hundreds of dispatches, bombarding the various medical departments, composing letters of support on my behalf for others to amend and sign. Besides emphasizing the progress I had made and the accreditations and certificates I had earned, I highlighted the idea that entomologists are such a rarity in the service, and so difficult and expensive to train and recruit, that I was indispensable.

A good example of what came out of it was a letter from Col. Phillip Lawyer, entomology consultant with the Office of the Surgeon General, who noted, "The GOMOR has served its purpose. Captain Pike has paid for it professionally. In July 1997, he submitted an application packet for Long Term Health Education & Training (LTHET) to pursue a master's degree in medical entomology. In October 1997, I received notice from PERSCOM, MSC Branch, that he was not selected for LTHET due to the GOMOR in his permanent record."

Probably the most influential letter came from the office of Glenn Reese, member of the South Carolina Senate. The process of nailing him down began with the telephone book and passed through numerous members of his staff and interns in response to a persistent barrage of letters and telephone calls. The result of it all was a letter signed by Senator Reese that was just a slightly modified version of a sample letter requested from me. It read in part, "Captain Pike has been extensively trained by the US Army. To leave this GOMOR on his record will undoubtedly end his career in the Army. I understand that it takes much money to train officers in the Army. If Captain Pike were to be involuntarily separated in the future because of his GOMOR, it would be a waste for the taxpayers."

During that critical period, as a PROFIS, or part of the Professional Filler System, for the Sixty-first Medical Detachment, I was deployed twice to El Salvador.[1] The first deployment was for five weeks as part of a combined US humanitarian mission to several Central American countries in the wake of Hurricane Mitch, and the second as a contribution to Operation *New Horizons*, an ongoing aid and development operation in Central and South America. These deployments were regarded as "other operations," adding significant ballast to my general resume of achievement and chances of

---

[1] The PROFIS or Professional Filler System is used by the US military to fill voids in personnel when a unit deploys on a combat or humanitarian mission. Due to the high financial cost of employing physicians, civil engineers, lawyers, or other "high-dollar-specialists" in a military unit, usually at the battalion and sometimes at the brigade level, a full-time "specialist" is not permanently assigned to these units. When a unit deploys to an austere location, the demand for a specialist increases. The military's solution is to have a PROFIS or assigned specialist to these units who only serves with the unit when it deploys.

redemption. In totality, the appeal package was carefully put together. It was strongly backed by influential individuals of various backgrounds, and it displayed a record of exceptional service, varied training, and a commitment to a continued career in the Army. It was powerful medicine, and when eventually it found its way onto the desk of Gen. James Peake, although he, too, confirmed that the reprimand had been correctly filed, he added his own letter of support. The appeal was granted in the fall of 1998, three years after the event, and the reprimand moved to the restricted file. In September of that year, the Long Term Health Education & Training Board met, and my application to take a master's degree in entomology was approved. This was huge, and I knew it. It was a huge deal, and I know folks in the grapevine said, "What the fuck just happened?"

ONE OF MY DEPLOYMENTS TO EL SALVADOR was as part of the international response to Hurricane Mitch, which hit Central America in 1998, causing mass fatalities and immense infrastructural damage. We used to say "Mitch is a Bitch!" I was detailed as a PROFIS for the Sixty-first Medical Detachment, a unit out of Fort Campbell, Kentucky, and sent down there to help clean up and support the local public health services. The other deployment, in the same capacity, was as part of Operation *New Horizons*, an ongoing, multigenerational effort augmenting US capacity-building operations in Central and South America.[1]

---

[1] Operation New Horizons is a series of recurring US–led operations in Central and South America and the Caribbean Islands. It has had several names over the years, including New Horizons and Beyond the Horizons (as of 2008). US Southern Command sponsors these operations and uses active-duty, Reserve and National Guard forces from throughout the United States to conduct the missions. The units involved focus on engineering-type endeavors to enhance the infrastructure of a region by building schools,

The role of the detachment was basically to support crisis relief work underway on the part of numerous branches of the US Army and various NGOs, picking up the pieces after Hurricane Mitch. This detachment was preventive medicine. The number of fatalities caused by the hurricane was eleven thousand, mostly in Honduras and Nicaragua, and across the region, an already shaky system of public health was teetering on the brink of collapse. Just as the Corps of Engineers worked on roads and schools, we medical folk supported hospitals and clinics, importing huge quantities of pesticides and pest control equipment. This was both to keep our bases healthy, pest-free and clean, and to deal with mosquito abatement and rodent control in the wider countryside.

One day, a particular female soldier, in a tent full of other soldiers, complained of snakes. I investigated, but I did not see any snakes, nor any evidence of snakes. She was adamant, however, that she had seen a snake. Understanding that even false reports of things like snakes can stir panic in soldiers, I instructed everyone to leave the tent for three hours while I got out my "snake repellent spray." I pulled in two other soldiers and we filled our sprayer tanks up with water and put a light dusting of it on the grass in and around the tent. I never heard another word about snakes after that.

Another problem was that personnel were sternly warned off of eating anything other than the standard issue MREs, or "Meals Rejected by Ethiopians," as the soldiers called them. There was so much good, fresh food about that it seemed crazy to me to honor those regulations and resist all the fantastic-looking local street food that was all around. One day I thought screw it and sat down at the stall of a local El

---

medical clinics, and roads and similar projects. The units also conduct medical assistance by providing such support to an area. Joint Task Force Bravo coordinates a number of these activities. In addition, these operations often include nonmilitary assistance, such as from the US Agency for International Development and the US Department of Agriculture.

Salvadorian vendor and settled into some homemade street food. I found it very good. A couple of soldiers came by and said to me, "Hey, we're not allowed to eat local food unless it is approved."

I replied, "I am the damn authority that gets to decide if food is good or not, and I declare this food good to eat."

They looked around, and before long, they were all eating at my table.

The Sixty-first Medical Detachment was a small unit of about fifteen preventive medicine technicians responsible for inspecting water supplies and sanitation, setting out mosquito traps, spraying pesticides and rodenticides, and basically doing the work of civilian public health officials. It was during this deployment that I met a young, hard-charging, red-headed corporal by the name of Malisha Palmer, a native of Alabama, who impressed me with her no-bullshit approach to what was, under those conditions, a pretty challenging job. She was a roll-up-your-sleeves kind of gal, and although I did not have a whole lot to do with her on a professional level—she was under the direct supervision of a sergeant—I was impressed. That would not be the last time that I would run into Malisha Palmer.

On the whole, it was a pretty routine deployment, although it did come on the back of a handful of calamitous foreign interventions, so the chain of command was anxious as hell. One of these was the US contribution to UNISOM II in Somalia, that ended in 1993 with the disastrous Battle of Mogadishu, the basis for the film *Black Hawk Down*.[1] That episode generally depressed US enthusiasm for armed intervention overseas. For this reason, the rules of engagement for both deployments were very specific. It was strongly emphasized that any use of force, except in absolute extreme

---

[1] According to Wikipedia, "United Nations Operation in Somalia II (UNOSOM II) was the second phase of the United Nations intervention in Somalia, from March 1993 until March 1995, after the country had become involved in civil war in 1991."

circumstances, was forbidden. We did get our hazardous duty pay. Charged clips were to remain in our ammo pouches and never carried in the gun. I recall, before leaving Fort Campbell, that a senior officer advised me, "Make sure that you don't shoot unless you absolutely need to. If you don't understand the rules of engagement, just do not shoot. If you come out of this thing without shooting, that's fine."

We all came away from that briefing with the clear understanding that shooting an El Salvadorian would be a hanging offense, regardless of the circumstances. On both deployments, we were escorted everywhere by Salvadorian guards who were armed and who were not bound by those rules of engagement, but who were probably just as sketchy as the bandits who were the biggest threat.

One evening, I recall, we were moving in a small convoy between a village and the hotel complex where we were billeted when our Humvees were stopped by a group of bandits. It was an extremely tense situation. On that occasion, we had no guards but only a group of Salvadorian interpreters who carried on a rapid-fire and highly animated conversation with the bandits. They seemed to be debating on whether or not to rob and kill us and dump us on the side of the road, probably to report back to their bosses that they had scrubbed out a bunch of US soldiers.

The US military advisory teams in El Salvador tend to be involved in one way or another with the war on drugs. They demanded our passports and military IDs, which were handed over, and it was pointed out as we did that our Geneva Convention code indicated that we were medical and not combatant personnel. This provoked another round of furious conversation as we stood around, not understanding any of it, but knowing that we were in some kind of deep shit. I think understanding that we were not narcs but medical people on a humanitarian mission cooled the temperature down a little bit. A few cautious smiles were exchanged after that. We were doing good in the community, and they were community members, so they let us go, and we geared up and quickly drove away.

One time the team was working in a small village preparing equipment and pesticides for a big spray operation when a drugged-up local began menacing me with his machete raised. I told the guard to waste no time and just take him out. Weapons were cocked and shots almost fired before the man turned his back and drifted back into the crowd. I had no idea what it was about.

Mostly we were advised to keep to ourselves, not to visit local bars and restaurants and not to interact with the local people. This was a zero-defect environment. To me that was a real shame, because most of my pleasure in overseas deployments has been meeting and engaging with local people. I like visiting bars and markets and sampling local food, and to be in Central America and forced to live off the damned MREs was disappointing. I never cared for those rules, and so I broke them regularly. I spent time hanging out with the children, kicking a ball around, and learning basic Spanish, from the kids . Most of them had never seen a blond-haired, white-skinned *gringo* like me before.

On our last day, we decided to distribute a load of uneaten MREs to the local villagers. In an exercise in poor planning, we loaded up a Humvee and dumped them in the village square, which immediately provoked a riot. MREs are full of tasty stuff for the Salvadorians like chocolate and dried fruit and meat, packing huge amounts of calories into a small bag, and with cups and cutlery and all the rest. As a rule they are usually highly sought after by local people. We watched amazed as big kids beat up on the small kids, and the small kids ran around with armfuls of food as well as the miscellaneous contents of hundreds of care packages that had come from home. It was a fucking riot that turned mean when the stuff ran out. Suddenly they were hurling rocks and mudballs at us, demanding more. *Más comida, más comida!* We took refuge in the hotel, which was attacked and defaced, and that really pissed off the management. It occurred to me afterward that we maybe should have donated the whole lot to a church or to the village elders for them to distribute. We put together a collection and gave it to the hotel manager to try and help with the cleanup. It was a sobering experience.

Back home in Maryland, I applied my Five Ps and volunteered with the Baltimore American Red Cross, serving on their disaster assistance team. After my experience in El Salvador, and during the Hurricane Mitch deployment, I was awarded the honor of being named the Red Cross "Hometown Hero." I guess they were short of heroes that year. What I found interesting is that my service during Hurricane Mitch was with the Army, not the Red Cross, and typically those two agencies— Army and Red Cross—do not overlap in that way. The Red Cross gave me that award and requested that my general officer at the time award it to me. In a ceremonial banquet, dressed up to the nines, he did. Soon afterward, the commanding general of Chipmunk found out, and not to be outdone, she awarded me the Army Volunteer just for volunteering with the Red Cross. It was kind of a strange thing, getting recognition in that way for just going about my daily life, doing shit that I enjoyed.

IN A SIMPLE CIVIL CEREMONY in San Antonio on December 20, 1997, Beverly and I were married. I think we got a military discount. We met one night at the Midnight Rodeo in San Antonio, and our relationship developed during my frequent visits to the city to make my obligations to the court. In keeping with the Five Ps, I ran a background check on her before I proposed. She came out clean. She stood alongside me during that whole, long legal journey, and was there as it resolved itself. She owned her own home, had a good job at the USAA Federal Savings Bank, and she came from an affluent, self-made immigrant family from Vietnam. I knew I had made the right decision when her mother made up a five-gallon container of fish sauce. I picked it up in my truck and was pretty damn worried that if it broke I'd need a hazmat team to deal with it. Beverly's mother was a first-generation immigrant, and her family were self-made people. Maybe thanks to my own background, I understood and appreciated their sense of the value of a dollar. I felt a connection that was more than just physical and emotional.

This marked a significant turning point in my life for more than the obvious reasons. The appeal against the GOMOR had been a difficult and exhausting process that deployed all my ingenuity, acquired strategy, and determination to succeed. I came out of it a better soldier and a better man. I was proud and have since been complimented by many people for the determination and thoroughness of the effort. At the same time, I was chastened and humbled. The pride of the past and my reckless and sometimes self-destructive behavior were purged from my nature. Beverly, my wife, was a buffer between me and the outside world. She joined me in Maryland briefly before the commencement of my next phase of study. As an active-duty officer, I was now able to select the university of my choice, and I chose Colorado State. I packed up my old Toyota and drove the two thousand miles across the country to Fort Collins, Colorado. A few months later, she joined me there, and we put down a deposit and closed on our first home.

THE BEST OF TIMES

Good times become good memories and bad times become good lessons in life.

ANURAG PRAKASH RAY

I N THE SPRING OF 1997, in preparation for college selection, I took the GRE, or Graduate Record Examinations. According to the *Educational Testing Service*, the GRE is a standardized test that measures "verbal reasoning, quantitative reasoning, critical thinking, and analytical writing skills that have been developed over a long period and are required for success in today's demanding programs."

This was always going to be a difficult hill for me to climb. I never did well in standardized tests. Guaranteed.

My first stab at the GRE was in October 1995, while I was stationed at Fort Sam Huston, a few months before my DUI, and the results were not encouraging. My score was fifteen, twenty-eight, and five percent respectively for verbal, quantitative, and reasoning, each significantly below average. The test was taken under what is termed "no special conditions," in other words, strictly within the allotted time. Later, an educational psychologist in Maryland recommended on my behalf that I be allowed to take the test in twice the allotted time. This was an huge moment for me, on many levels, but not least because upon it depended my entry into college for my second master's program. I studied hard, going to the extent of hiring a private tutor, covering all the bases according to the Five Ps. Many people asked me why did you get two masters degrees? The thing is the first masters degree was in agriculture education, something that I had been through and understood. This was going to be a solid masters degree in entomology, which is my study area. I did not want to go get a PhD because I know my limitations. I did the Five Ps.

The fact remained, as it always had, and still does, that although my processing abilities are slow, they are thorough, and given time and opportunity to approach a course or an examination in a measured and repetitive way, I can almost always get where I am going. The result of it all was a significantly improved GRE score, with forty-six, seventy-two, and forty-two respectively. Although, in terms of the median, those were average scores at best, and I only narrowly passed, for me it was an almighty success. The funny thing is, when I submitted my application to the Army for my second master's degree, I took some liquid white out and erased the note that said "Special Conditions Allowed" in regards to my improved GRE score. I did not want anyone to be forewarned or apprised of my academic disabilities. I felt ashamed.

The test was sponsored for four colleges: Colorado State University, University of Florida, Texas A&M, and Louisiana State. I was now in a position to choose any one of these to attend as a full-time, paid student in pursuit of a master's degree in medical entomology. I chose Colorado State in Fort Collins for several reasons. Partly because my mom had studied there and it was close to the mountains, but mainly it was because I could earn my degree on the successful completion of a given amount of coursework without having to write a thesis. It was the non-thesis option. Another reason was that the Geer family owned a cabin that I could use part time, or any time I wanted to, to go hiking or fishing and snow skiing. The Pikes always enjoyed their visits to that cabin.

Although I was still under the administrative control of the Army, in every other respect I was a private citizen, temporarily released from the chain of command. I could pack away my uniform, grow my hair, and wear a beard if I felt like it. I recall one time I stopped by the Colorado State University ROTC department to use the copy and fax machine, and while there I hung out and chewed the fat with some of the cadets. I was wearing shorts and sandals and sporting a ragged beard and long hair, and as I was sitting around, the commandant came by and asked me, "Where is your command at?"

"I don't know," I replied. "I guess somewhere down at Fort Sam Houston. I am a student, and I never visited the command."

He looked confused. "We are in the business of training future Army officers," he said. "I need for them to look up to someone as an example, and you are not the example. Never come in here looking like that again!"

I left and never went back.

In the meantime, with the worst year of my life behind me, I packed up my truck and set off overland, leaving Beverly to wrap up her affairs in Maryland before she would join me a few weeks later. By then I was pretty certain I would make the rank of major, which in the military establishment is the equivalent of university tenure. Transitioning from company-grade ranks to a field-grade rank traditionally sets an officer up for his twenty years of career service and retirement at a senior rank. Wicked indeed would have to be my misbehavior from now on for me not to achieve that. It was a good place to be. It was a time to reflect on the past and anticipate the future, to reign in the devils, and take time out for a few wounds to heal.

The greatest threat to my career in uniform had always been myself, and at times in the last few years, I had come pretty close to bringing it all crashing down around me. Now things were different. I was married, and I was a mature soldier, a student, and a man of respectable accomplishment. Ultimately, it is not what you achieve in life, but what you overcome to achieve it. Therein lies the measure of a career and the character of a man. I had dragged myself up from the lowest academic expectations, broken barriers, and pushed forward a few boundaries, and all of it was testimony to the slow, methodical process by which I had found that most things in life can be achieved. It was a triumph of the Five Ps, and a vision forward.

Although no part of my success to date could be measured on the standard scale as anything more than average, averting failure was always to me a success in itself. As I counted the white lines on the great American open road, my mind settled by degrees. The anxiety and stress of the last two years were replaced by anticipation, and the pleasant thought of that boy, who was never meant to be college bound, immersing himself in study in the rarified corridors of a fine university. It was an opportunity to settle into married life, and perhaps contemplate a family. What lay beyond that was unimportant, because I was at last safely established in my career, and secure in the love of a good woman.

SOMEWHERE IN IOWA OR NEBRASKA, on a rural highway off the I-80, and tired of eating fast food, I saw a congregation of folks at an outdoor gathering in the garden of a country home. I pulled in on an impulse, parked up, casually walked in, stood in line, and helped myself to great food. It was a family reunion, and when asked, I gave a false name and said I had been out of town for a while and had been out of touch. I was made welcome. I ate, drank, and enjoyed good company before I slipped away and got back on the road.

Later, passing through Cheyenne, Wyoming, I swung into the Francis E. Warren Air Force Base and parked up on the edge of a pond where I laid out my bedroll in the bed of my truck. At three o'clock in the morning, I was awakened by a squad of MPs demanding to see my orders and my military ID. I was thinking oh my God, I'm in trouble again. Once they established who I was and where I was heading, they told me to go back to sleep.

"How can I go back to sleep?" I grumbled. "Y'all done woke me up."

From one end of the country to the other, I had been sleeping in the back of my truck, in parks, malls, and parking lots without a single disturbance, and lo and behold, I stop at a military base, and they want to see my ID and my orders. I did not realize it at the time, but there were sensitive missile silos in the area, which pretty much explains it.

ABOUT THOSE TWO YEARS IN COLORADO, there is not much to say, other than they were the best of times. Beverly arrived a few weeks after me, and we settled in our new house together. She found a job at the local district attorney's office, and in the new semester I began school. The regimen was easy, and I had all the time in the world to study, apply my methodology, and work towards my degree. As an additional accreditation, I completed a summer internship with a local laboratory of the Centers for Disease Control, engaged in research and surveillance into mosquitoes and other disease-carrying vectors. For some reason, after years of applying and being turned down, I was invited to take the Army Master of Fitness Course. The lead instructor had seen all my applications over the years and was eventually moved by my sheer persistence to give me a break. "You are pretty damned determined to be on this course," he remarked when we finally met. I had not been approved by the Army to take the course, mainly for reasons of funding, and I was only accepted this time around because I took my own personal leave and took the course at my own expense.

I attended the course at Fort Jackson, South Carolina and passed, gaining an additional skill identifier as a master fitness trainer. In Colorado, I also gained certification as a Registered Environmental Health Sanitarian, which is one of the respected certifications in the field of Army preventive medicine. It is a tough one. Applying the Five Ps once again, I attended a conference and a series of classes on how to study for and pass a test. I locked myself in the library for a full three weeks to study for this test, using multiple examples and past test papers that I picked up at the conference. I passed on the first try, although only by a hair.

During down times, I liked to hike and ride my bike in the mountains around Fort Collins, spending quite a lot of time in the Geer family cabin near Golden, Colorado. I enjoyed the time I spent there, and when I discovered that the family intended to put the property on the market, I offered to buy it. I put down a detailed proposal on paper, expressing my interest and outlining in bulleted points all that I could and wanted to do with the place. No reply ever came. I heard that one of the sisters really wanted to sell the place, but there seemed to be some resistance to selling it to me. My dad was pretty interested in the place too, and he tried to liaise between my mother and her sisters over the issue, but choosing his battles, he figured it was better just to keep the peace at home. I never figured out why they would not sell to me. They just would not.

Despite living only a few miles up the I-25, relations between us were, as they had always been, remote, distant, and aloof. When we did meet, conversations were again never more than superficial and general. Nothing was ever volunteered, and no sincere inquiries ever made. As a mature man, raised in the rough and tumble of rural South Carolina, schooled in the military and the fraternal order of Southern storytellers, I found it all very bizarre. Then one day I discovered why.

166

I spent a lot of time in the campus library, which doubled as my office, my spiritual retreat, and my second home. Sometimes I sat and studied and at other times I explored the internet or just browsed through the magazines and periodicals. One day I happened to be paging through back copies of the old student-run newspaper when I stumbled on a short note on the 1959 marriage of Nancy Carol Geer to a man whose name I had never heard before. The last name was Wafer. It was an astonishing piece of intelligence. Not a word had ever been spoken in my family about my mother having been married before she met my father.

A little more research took me to the central cemetery in Denver, where I discovered the grave of "Baby Boy," who died of unknown causes at just three months, and whose brief life told a story that both families had kept a firm secret. In the Victorian world of upper-middle-class Denver of the 1950s, a well-bred girl of good birth did not fall pregnant out of wedlock, and when she did, the matter was made right by a shotgun wedding. Beyond those superficial details, nothing more was to be found. The matter was not spoken about or made known to the family until 2014, when, after my mother's funeral, her sister, Aunt Betty, passed on the information only in its essential details, bringing it at last out into the open.

In January 2001, my own family came into being when my daughter Chantel was born. When I heard that Beverly was into labor, I rode my bike like a madman from campus directly to the Poudre Valley Hospital, arriving just in time to witness the birth. When the umbilical cord was cut, the child was briefly handed to me, and within those precious few seconds, my emotions conflicted between fear that I would break her or drop her or fuck it up in some way and a soaring elation and tearful joy that I could not in my wildest dreams have anticipated. My bond with my daughter was absolute and instantaneous. People have told me since that fatherhood is my best skill, and I believe this is true. Beverly's mother, Yen, arrived to help, but she hurried back to San Antonio as soon as the cold weather set in. These were truly the best of times, and in the afterglow of that momentous moment came my orders. I was going back to Korea.

I remember making a road trip to see the Geer family. I went to Pueblo, Durango, Boulder, saw all the Geers with my new baby, all the people that I could coordinate with. I told one of the cousins how scared I was being a parent, and his comment was, "Well you have already formed an opinion of yourself, so it doesn't really matter does it?"

I found it all really bizarre. I was thinking after that road trip fuck 'em all!

AS I DISCUSSED A LITTLE EARLIER, the relationship between my mom and I was a bit challenging just to say the least. I could write a whole memoir on my mother's ass chewings. She was a good mom, she did her best, but she was dealing with a very wicked past that she kept a secret. In her earlier years I know she had been married and divorced, and we know that she had an infant child that died a few months after birth. In retrospect I know that must have bothered her a lot. Another parallel story that probably bothered her even more had to do with me. In 1991 I met a girl named Angie who lived near Fingerville in South Carolina. She was petit, pretty, but pregnant when we met. She was clearly not carrying my child. We had a relationship, and when the baby was born it was named Jason Geer Pike.

The bad news is that it died of Sudden Infant Death Syndrome in 1991. The even more bad news is that the obituary showed up in the Spartanburg Herald News. My mom got a hold of the story and she unleashed a wrath of ass-chewings, questioning me about the birth, the father an the baby…all kinds of rapid fire questions and all hell was breaking loose. Dad heard the shitstorm below and he came down and also listened to my story, and the gale questions and third degree from my mom, screaming and yelling at the top of her lungs, like I had never heard before.

I pleaded with he that it was not my child. She demanded to see a photo of the baby so she could decide if it was my baby or not.

"Mom! It's not my child! Yes, we had a relationship."

"Why would you date a pregnant woman?"

She questioned why the baby was named after me, and I told her that I did not know. It's her baby and she has the right to name it whatever she wants!

My dad then saved my ass. He agreed, it was her baby she could call it what she wants. Mom stormed off, and then returned about five minutes later with another ass-chewing. "You better talk to that damned whore to tweak the name with the name of that birth father!"

I promised I would, and I did. I pleaded with Angie to tweak the name to something named after the father, and she did. In the second obituary, and on the headstone, the baby was named Jason Geer Loiret Pike.

KOREA AGAIN: THE POLITICS OF EXECUTIVE COMMAND

How good and pleasant it is when God's people live together in unity!
PSALM 133:1

O N 13 JUNE 2003, *The Morning Calm*, the US Armed Forces newspaper for the Korean Peninsula, published a lead article titled *"Good Neighbor Program Sets Standard for Alliance's Next Fifty Years."*

"This year," the article said, "marks the 50th year of the Republic of Korea and US alliance. Forged by the blood of war and strengthened through military and economic ties, the alliance has remained viable and strong through half a century. To ensure the alliance remains strong in this century, Gen. Leon LaPorte, commander, United Nations Command, Combined Forces Command, and US Forces Korea, designed a new policy to thank Koreans for their continued friendship: the Good Neighbor Program ... all the leaders of the peninsula have taken the ideals expressed by LaPorte in his new policy and applied

170

them by creating numerous Good Neighbor events. One leader who has really taken those ideals to heart is Major Jason Pike, commander, Fifth Medical Detachment."

I ARRIVED IN KOREA IN THE FALL OF 2001 to take command of the Fifth Medical Detachment headquartered at the Yongsan Garrison in metropolitan Seoul. Known informally as the "White House," Yongsan was at that time headquarters to the entire US military operation in South Korea. As such, it was home to a disproportionate contingent of senior officers and commanders, including three and four-star generals, who ran the various departments and sectors that deal with every aspect of the US military presence in South Korea.[1] It was a high-pressure environment and a very busy and active place where the fire hose was cranked up to the maximum all the time. You could think of this deployment as a bunch of rats in a cage. Korea is different. It is the only place that I know in the US Army where you have a three and a four star commander within the size of something relatively small. Korea is about the size of Indiana. Most three and four star commands go globally or definitely multi-state in the United States. Every time you have a three or four star command you have multiple staffs and many people. Oh, and by the way, Korea does not have a whole lot of training area to go and stretch out in anyway. It was just busy, a busy, busy time. Lots of politics.

The US military establishment in Korea is arguably one of the most important peacetime overseas deployments across the entire defense spectrum, with only Germany and Japan hosting more US troops and support personnel. South Korea is home not only to the Eighth Army and all its ancillary structures

---

[1] The headquarters of the US deployment to South Korea relocated in 2018 to Camp Humphreys in Pyeongtaek, south of Seoul.

but also to the Seventh Air Force, Naval Forces Korea, Marine Forces Korea, and Special Operations Command Korea. It is a noncombat command insofar as it is not attendant on a hot war, so it tends to be top heavy with administrative departments and personnel, many of them civilians, dealing with the practicalities of a rotating deployment of more than twenty-eight thousand uniformed members. As an integrated, self-contained city within a city, it presents a huge public health challenge. After an easy assignment with the Chipmunk in Maryland and a stress-free two years on campus at Fort Collins, checking in at Yongsan was a wake-up call. It was my first command and my first real experience of the complex political environments at a command level.

Every few years, a Tri-Service Entomology Conference is held at the Naval Air Base at Fort Jackson in Florida. Here, members of what is a very small fraternity of military entomologists gather from the three main branches to mingle, meet and greet, and compare notes. Entomology is a small professional community within the armed forces, so everyone tends to know everyone anyway, and in most cases, the gathering is just an opportunity to put names to faces, sit through a few presentations, enhance our skills and socialize. I had heard of Ted Small many times in the past, and in 1997, standing in a line at a Tri-Service Human Resources meeting, we met for the first time. He was a fortysomething lieutenant colonel, bookish in appearance and highly personable. I was standing there with Beverly, a petit and attractive Asian woman, and it was evident to me that the thing he liked most about me was my woman. I thought to myself that it takes a lot of balls to openly flirt with a man's girlfriend when he is standing right there. That was Ted Small.

A Google search of Doctor Ted Small in relation to entomology in the Korean Peninsula yields an impressive weight of academic and research publications that back up his reputation as one of the foremost international authorities in that field. He has, for example, a species of mosquito endemic to the Korean Peninsula named after him. He was maybe the best known and most widely respected member of the fraternity and, depending on who you talk to, well-liked and widely admired.

It was interesting to finally meet a person whose work I had studied and who was so highly regarded in his field. I remarked to that effect to Ed Evans when I was back in Maryland, and while he agreed that Ted Small was an impressive character, and certainly at the cutting edge of research in Korea, he was inclined to add that I should keep an eye on my six o'clock.

I knew that Colonel Small would be in Korea when I got there—he was chief of preventive medicine with Eighteenth MEDCOM, whereas I was earmarked to command a separate medical detachment, so we were safely outside of one another's chain of command. I cannot recall precisely when we bumped into each other, but when we did, it was a collegial reintroduction accompanied by the usual bullshit and small talk of a small network. While he was functioning at a brigade level, I was at a battalion level, and I figured out quickly that he was pretty damned interested in what was taking place in my department. I had under my supervision two Korean scientists attached to the US Army whose job it was to run most of the legwork on species identification and research papers. We were a preventive medicine group, and our job was mostly practical within the context of a large military establishment. Our main responsibility was to maintain a healthful environment within the garrison and beyond, and the mechanics of that were fairly straightforward. It was a matter of maintaining health and sanitation protocols, undertaking inspections, and writing reports.

Ted Small, on the other hand, was a researcher. He had been doing this his entire career. He was highly academic in outlook, supporting multiple outreaches, and sustaining a steady outflow of published material. That was not my work. He had been there for years, was married to a Korean woman, and had integrated himself deeply into the local establishment. He seemed to have a proprietorial view of it all and was unashamedly scathing of the workhorses of the field whose job was not to document the reproductive cycles of some unnamed species of mosquitos but to measure the appropriate distance between a rank of portable toilets and the chow hall. In my world, that was an administrative function, and having Doctor Small showing up at all times needing personnel to undertake some damn obscure research job, or mosquito or rat survey, irritated the shit out of me. He would complain sometimes, saying that it was our job. I dug in my heels. I had other stuff to do. You got to make priorities in the in the day. It was not all about entomology. That's how I came across, and we failed to communicate. He was always passive, speaking in a soft, light tone, smiling, and ingratiating, but insistent, eyes always searching, interested, possessive, and dogged. This guy was a workaholic. He worked all the time.

In the end, I began to play him, promising but never delivering. One time he sent down an order through the chain of command requesting mosquito traps to be set up behind the Child Development building in the middle of November, when it was too damn cold for mosquitos. I ignored the command, which I am pretty certain pissed him off good. As a PhD, and a highly accomplished academic, I am sure it annoyed him a lot to have some barely literate Southern boy with a second-class degree calling himself an entomologist and not paying homage to him.

He remarked to me once, "Your writing is worthless." He said it in a calm and passive voice, almost in passing, as he walking out of my office. I never trusted him enough to tell him exactly why he was right about that. He did name me in one or two professional publications, in recognition of my contribution, which was good of him. It was not done for any

174

love of me, of course, or desire to advance my career, but just to correctly dot his Is and cross his Ts.

At the time, it was all more of an irritation than a real problem to me, but my gut instinct warned me to watch my back. Our roles and responsibilities did not technically overlap, and if I went out of my way on occasion to piss him off, it was a fairly safe bet that there would eventually be trouble. I knew that under the surface, there was a seed of real animus beginning to germinate between us, but at the time I could not have give a damn. I had a life, and I had a wife and a child. I was active in the community, and if he wanted to burn the midnight oil, then that's on him. My claim to the title of entomologist was accidental. I was a commander running an outfit with the object of doing a specific job. When that job was over, I shut down my computer, went home and played with my daughter. I knew it chapped his ass, but there was nothing he could really do about it. In retrospect, maybe I should have been more tolerant because, in the long game, it turned out that there was a lot he could do.

Now I was commander of the 5th Medical Detachment. It was my first command, and it was a high pressure executive-level situation, and I am working with a lot of the higher ranking officers and things were a bit stressful, and really the worst thing about it was the politics. The political gamesmanship among brother and sister officers that really tore me down. That's just the way it is sometimes. You get a bunch of people, you put them together, and there is a lot of competition, especially in a high pressure environment, and not a lot of good things are going to come out of it.

IN THE MEANTIME, as I had the first time around, I derived much pleasure from my social interactions with the local Koreans. I was a married family man now, so whoring trips to the Philippines were a thing of the past, but hanging out and spending time with my Korean officers was a very cool alternative. This time it did not win me a reputation for insubordination and a cavalier attitude to the rules, but caused me to be recognized at a command level.

The US military structure overseas is organic and has evolved and been modified since WWII according to the ebb and flow of foreign wars and strategic alliances. At the time, South Korea fell under Unified Forces Korea. There were other commands, such as SOUTHCOM, concerned with deployments and strategic alliances in South America, then you got CENTCOM with the Middle East, and hen, of course, you got AFRICOM which is African affairs.

Most Americans, even those with no particular interest or background in the military, will appreciate and understand the origins and importance of the strategic alliance between the United States and the Republic of Korea. While combat operations ended in July 1953, the war technically never ended. North and South Korea remain theoretically at war and separated by a demilitarized zone negotiated as part of the terms of armistice. Across this divide, the two sides remain frozen in an effective ceasefire position. North Korea exists as a rogue state and the last of the old-style totalitarian communist regimes of the Cold War period. Its unpredictability and status as a nuclear power, its often stated objective of controlling the entire peninsula, and its ideological loathing for the United States all tend to place the defense of South Korea very high on the list of US foreign policy priorities. The importance and sheer scope of the US military presence in South Korea require that many US servicemen and staff personnel interact closely with their Korean counterparts. For this, a detailed and highly engaged liaison operation exists that is backed up by a diligent public relations effort. Under the broad support of this, Gen. Leon LaPorte conceived what he called the "good neighbor" exercise.

According to the US Army website, "Although we may have been strangers seventy years ago, with the passed-on torch of Freedom, the inextricable bond the ROK and US now share is unfathomable. An example of this is illustrated in the combined combat division led by US and ROK Flag officers located in the Republic of Korea, the Eighth US Army's Second Infantry Division. Service members of this unique alliance work together shoulder to shoulder every day to maintain peace and stability during this time of armistice. There are also several thousand Korean Augmentees to the US Army (KATUSA) soldiers living and working with US soldiers at bases throughout the Republic of Korea."

My contribution to the good neighbor program came about completely by accident. At the time, most of the KATUSAs were draftees or national servicemen with the Republic of Korea Armed Forces who were selected for their education and proficiency in English. Besides their work in research and preventive medicine, they also served in a liaison role and occasionally as interpreters. Attachment to the US military in any capacity was regarded as a prestigious assignment, and as a consequence, most KATUSAs tended to be young men of exceptional education and often from wealth families. In command of my KATUSAs, and serving as a liaison officer to keep the whole thing running smoothly, was a regular ROK Major by the name of Seong-ha Park.

At the time Beverly, Chantel and I were lodged in embassy housing in the diplomatic compound within the Yongsan Garrison, which was very comfortable. It was a social environment where Korean personnel were not particularly well represented, and it was Beverly who suggested that I make an effort to become friends with Major Park. He was fluent in English and well educated, and with many shared interests, he and I pretty quickly became friends. This was not at all a common thing. I recall an anecdote of that period that helps to illustrate this fact. During one of our regular Command and

Staff meetings, otherwise known as "Command and Shaft," unit commanders and first sergeants would assemble to give and to get updates from higher HQ. We would gather in a small briefing room for long hours, and I recall once sitting beside a peer commander by the name of Capt. Steve Patterson, who took out an air freshener and shook it in front of me saying, "This is a solution for you Major Pike. You smell worse than my damned KATUSAS." It was a joke, it was true, and it raised a laugh, but it was also a little dig at me for my over-familiarity with the Koreans, especially the food, onions and garlic, that stuff comes out of your skin.

Major Park and I got into the habit of hanging out and drinking, exploring local wilderness areas, and occasionally going on drinking and fishing expeditions in the countryside. This went on for a while until one day we decided to invite someone from the Eighth Army Public Affairs Office to join us, to take a few pictures and write up a story. That someone was S.Sgt. Russell C. Bassett, whose office was just down the corridor from mine. In June 2003, Major Park and I planned a trip to a farm village outside Wonju-si on the eastern edge of the Chiak National Park. The press release and subsequent article, written by S.Sgt. Russell Barratt, tells the story very well.

THE GOOD NEIGHBOR PROGRAM. What does it really mean to you? At the macro level, this new and innovative policy involves commands implementing programs such as Korean National Police Appreciation, Adopt A School, Educator Outreach, and Good Neighbor Award programs. But this program will be truly effective when taken to heart at the individual level. Two soldiers who exemplify the potential the Good Neighbor Program has for strengthening the ROK–US alliance are Maj. Jason Pike, Fifth Medical Detachment commander, and Maj. Park, Seong-ha, Eighteenth MEDCOM's Republic of Korea liaison officer.

These two officers have taken the ideals outlined in the Good Neighbor Program and applied them, not only to their units but also to their personal value systems.

Recently, I had the privilege of joining Pike and Park on their overnight visit to Kang Lim farm village in Wonju Province. We were joined by Capt. Oh, Chul-min, of the Third ROK Army's Troop Medical Center and several members of the village for a day of fishing, a night of drinking, and a morning of hiking in Chiak National Park.

"In Korea, part of the things that are encouraged by the command is to go out and bond with the Koreans," said Pike. "The whole key to serving in Korea is to learn from your ROK counterparts, have some fun with the Korean people, and bond with them. In the end, you are going to be a better person, and you will be doing your part to keep the alliance strong."

Pike's favorite part of the overnight stay was getting to eat the fish that we caught. Lee, Hyun-deuk, who, according to Park, is the village's resident fishing expert, showed us the finer points of using a net to catch fish in a river. After several hours, we had enough for a meal and went to the Kang Lim noodle restaurant to sample our catch. At the restaurant, we were joined by Kang, Ung-man, a Wonju Province politician and two of his friends for a night of bonding—Korean style. After eating the fish, we joined in some singing, dancing, arm-wrestling, and eating lots and lots of food. It seemed like the food and drink just kept coming. The fish were small and fried up whole without any cleaning, so we ate the tail, head, and guts of the fish.

"I always like to go out and eat and drink with the Koreans, because that is how you really connect with them," explained Pike.

There were some cultural differences, but we all had the right attitude, and a good time seemed to be had by all. Much later that night, we retired to the home of Song, Kum-sun, and Lee, Tong-Rae, to get some rest. Song and Lee are old friends of Park, and their hospitality was very congenial. Lee is the owner of The Original Ahn Heung Chin Bong store, which, according to Park, is famous throughout Korea for its sweet bread. Early the next morning, Song took us hiking up Chiak Mountain, where we followed a beautifully clear stream up the scenic mountain. For Park, getting out of the city and getting up in the mountains was the best part of the overnight stay.

"Sunday morning, when we climbed the mountain, was very enjoyable to me," he said. "I loved the fresh air, the flowing water, and the birds singing—it was so great."

One of Park's jobs as the Eighteenth MEDCOM's ROK liaison officer is to organize events like this, but his friendship with Pike transcends the workplace. The two medical officers have had each other in their homes for dinner numerous times, and they can often be found eating lunch together, or going on events such as the farm village visit. After spending a weekend with them, I realized that I have never seen the ROK–US alliance stronger and the Good Neighbor Program more exemplified than I did with them. Pike, who has coordinated several of these types of events, as well as training events with his unit and their ROK counterparts, said that getting involved is not difficult.

"Going out and bonding with the Korean people is easy and fun," he said. "You have got ROK liaison officers, and it is not difficult to do these types of events."

Park and Pike told me they really enjoyed themselves and were invited by the villagers to come back in August and bring more Americans with them. Pike said he would definitely come back and would try to get more people from his unit to come with him.

Everyone seemed to really have a good time—I know I sure did. The real beauty of the trip, though, is that we are working to strengthen the ROK/US alliance while having command-directed fun. So what does the Good Neighbor Program mean to you?

IN HINDSIGHT THIS WAS VERY EASY. Some places in the world you are not aloud to go out and eat and drink with the local because of certain rules and regulations. In South Korea, this was an objective of the general. Yes, go out and bond with them. The rule I guess was, do it, and have fun doing it. I just thought it was easy and fun and it spoke to my natural ability to get out and integrate with the locals.

To finish this story, I'll need to leap forward a little bit in chronology. In 2007, four years after these events, I was promoted to lieutenant colonel, and among the letters and notes of congratulations that I received was one from Maj. Gen. Phillip Volpe, sent not to my office but to my home address.

Three years earlier, at the rank of colonel, Phillip Volpe was also in Korea, serving as the commander of the Eighteenth Medical Command, MEDCOM, and second in my particular chain of command. It appears that as the first of Russell Barratt's stories began to appear in print, Colonel Volpe took a very keen interest. Any outstanding activity or success of this sort on the part of a subordinate officer tends to reflect well on a senior officer's command, and he was eager to claim credit. Unbeknownst to me, he began accumulating a packet for submission to a Pentagon panel judging the community relations efforts of the various regional commands. The Army Community Relations Award of Excellence is presented annually to outstanding members of the various commands for their efforts in establishing good working relationships with their host nations and generally to strengthen strategic alliances. I would guess that PACOM's third-place ranking out of all the superstars worldwide went some way towards Colonel Phillip Volpe's eventual promotion to a one-star general, and hence his letter of warm congratulation when I achieved the rank of lieutenant colonel. It was sent to my home, and we were not at that time in one another's chain of command.

When I think back on this thing, I think that I could probably have made a wonderful foreign officer or someone whose mission it is to build international relationships because I was awarded for something that I find very easy.

In the meantime, between my second and third deployments to Korea, I was assigned in part to the Defense Logistics Agency in Fort Belvoir, Virginia, and it was there in March 2004 that I received a puzzling telephone call from the Pentagon. The voice at the other end informed me that I was expected in DC within a week for a special award ceremony. I had no clue what this could mean. DC is just a thirty-minute drive up I-95 from Fort Belvoir, but I had promised Chantel that I would take her skiing that weekend with my brother Denny. When asked if I could postpone the trip, I replied that I could not. There were generals waiting on me, I was told, which confused me even more, and I asked what the hell all of this about?

"Don't you know?" came the reply, and I admitted that I did not. I was reminded of the extraordinary work that I had done in Korea in community relations, and for the advance of the US-ROK strategic alliance. This amazed me. Extraordinary work, I'm thinking? As far as I was concerned, all that I did was what I had always done. I just interacted with my local colleagues as I was inclined to do wherever I went. I did what I like to do, which is drink beer and eat good food and hang out in good company. How does that translate into a major effort in support of the United States' strategic alliances? They agreed to postpone the ceremony to let me go to Colorado with my wife and my daughter, which I thought was pretty amazing. Must have been something real important.

"Bring your wife," the caller went on. "And your daughter, too."

The telephone call was followed up a few days later by an official letter explaining the situation in more detail. I understood then that whatever this was about, it was significant. Still not fully grasping the implication of it, I showed up a few weeks later at the Pentagon, dressed in my fatigues and accompanied by my wife and daughter. We were met and ushered through security and shown into a committee room where nine other awardees and their families were gathered in the company of a number of senior officers, including generals. The liaison officer replied to my query with astonishment.

"You really don't know why you are here?" she asked.

"I have no idea why I am here," I replied. "I'm not in public relations. I am an entomologist!"

"Jason," she said, "I have been working for years to get to this place!"

And then she explained it to me. I had been placed third out of ten soldiers of various ranks selected out of the many thousands of deployments around the world working in support of strategic alliances. I was the not only the only medical officer present, but the only entomologist. One could maybe even say that I was the only entomologist to ever receive this award. The others were mostly signals and various other staff and liaison officers. Amid a great deal of speech-making, pontification, and hand-clapping, many smiles, and as Chantel hopped from one foot to the other, grumbling about all the talking, I stepped up, shook the general's hand and saluted, walking away with a certification. This award, besides the Expert Field Medical Badge, is the one that I am most proud of, and I got it for just doing what I do. I call it my "Roaming Around Award!"

BACK IN KOREA, AS MY TOUR WAS winding down, things began to take a strange turn. I began receiving regular phone calls from Camp Walker in Daegu, from a certain Lt. Peter Price, who was filling the slot that I had occupied during my first deployment. There was to these calls a strangely ingratiating, obsequious tone that did not seem to have any particular purpose, and I did not at the time understand what they were about. He would call frequently and at odd times, to question me about unimportant things or sometimes just to talk with no obvious objective. He seemed to ramble. It was very strange. It was as if he was trying to get under my skin somehow, interrogate or to keep tabs on me for some reason. One day he called while I was on vacation on Jeju Island, and I handed the phone to Beverly, saying, "Here, you talk to the guy."

She took the phone and snapped, "We're on vacation. Just get the hell out of here!"

At the time I did not give it much thought. It certainly never occurred to me that Colonel Small was somehow at the root of it, and even now that I know he was, I still am not sure what the pair of them were trying to do. By then, in any case, my tour was up, and right on schedule, Beverly, Chantel, and I flew out of Korea. I was glad to be out of the country, away from the firehose and the ongoing intrigue and politics of a bureaucratic establishment overcrowded with ambitious people. Within a few weeks, I was back in Maryland with a fresh assignment at the Defense Logistics Agency in Fort Belvoir, Virginia. It would be a few years before I would be back in Korea, and back in the closed world of Ted Small and Peter Price.

I recall when I connected with my dad and talked the whole thing through in the backyard over a sixpack of beer. "Be damn careful," he said to me. "He sounds like a real gnarly bastard."

USUALLY I HAVE VERY good control over my emotions, especially being in the Army. If I am under any stress, I usually take it out in the gym. I've always been a bit of a gym rat, I guess

I still am. This story is one of the rare breaks in my character, as a commander. I had a lieutenant as my executive officer, a second lieutenant. He had just come out of schooling and we know second lieutenants do not understand many things. Matter of fact I was a lieutenant when I slipped into the shit in Korea on my first tour, and that is a great lieutenant joke, and there are lieutenant jokes aplenty.

As a senior officer we should always help and mentor our lieutenants. I did that, and I enjoyed it, especially if they had any promise. Officers take care of other officers and NCOs take care of the enlisted. For the most part, that's how it works. One time an E4 specialist was disrespectful to my lieutenant. The enlisted specialist, who I will call Goodman, was a tall, very well built soldier. He was one of those rare soldiers that was previously an infantry grunt who had switched over to preventive medicine, and so he knew more about the Army than most of my soldiers, even the NCOs. He was very competent in his role as a preventive medicine soldier. He also had a chip on his shoulder, and a bit of a bad attitude. They say attitude is everything, and I believe it.

One day, outside my office, the soldier was trying to gather the soldiers together to go to the motor pool for a task. Goodman told him to his face, "why should I do anything you tell me to do because you don't know shit, you're just a damned second lieutenant?"

I heard this from my office and jumped out of my chair and went into the room. I stood between him and the lieutenant and I looked that guy in the face and I told him, "This is your lieutenant! You do not fuck with him or you're fuckin' with me!" I was in his face, and it was a rare occasion, and it was out of character. I did not like any soldier screwing with my lieutenants. The first sergeant heard and he walked up to me. I told him to take that specialist outside and talk to him about his attitude. I never had any trouble with that specialist again.

THE PALOS VERDES BLUE

Coming back is the thing that enables you to see how all the dots in your life are connected.

ANN PATCHETT

O NE DAY, DURING THEN–SEN. Barak Obama's early presidential campaign, and on a scheduled flight from Los Angeles to Fort Belvoir, Virginia, I found myself seated beside a woman in her early thirties, reading Obama's book *The Audacity of Hope.* As I took my seat, she glanced up at me, and noticing that I was in military uniform, remarked with the kind of lip-curling scorn that causes so many soldiers' hair to rise, "Do you enjoy killing people?"

"I do," I replied with a friendly smile. "Very much so. Sadly, I don't get much chance these days since I am so busy working with different environmental agencies to preserve and protect a particular species of endangered butterfly here in California."

Taken aback, she rearranged her attitude a little bit, closed her book, and placed it on her knee. Now obliged to pursue a conversation, and with evident strain, she smiled and inquired.

I recall once telling my father the same story I told her, the story of the Palos Verdes blue, and his response was, "Give me a can of bug spray and I'll kill them all."

THE DEFENSE LOGISTICS agency is an enormous, multi-faceted bureaucratic machine established during WWII to cope with the massive supply and logistics demand of an enlarged armed service. If a service member can fly it, drive it, wear it or touch it, DLA has got something to do with it. It is headquartered in a huge complex in Fort Belvoir, Virginia, an administrative organ responsible for the smooth running of the largest and most complex military structure the world has ever known. By way of context, in 2003, the DLA performed thirty billion dollars of sales and service, dealing with forty-five thousand daily requisitions. In its various warehouses and storage facilities, located all over the country, the agency stores at any given time more than 5.4 million items of supplies and equipment. This puts it about at number fifty-four in the list of Fortune 500 companies, if it was a company. It is all managed from Fort Belvoir, south of Washington, DC, and it was there that I headed after returning to the United States from Korea.

According to the Defense Visual Information Distribution Service, "Each DLA facility has its own pest management plan that's tailored to address the setting and region." In an introductory article published in the *Army Medical Entomology News* of October 31, 2004, my position was described as staff entomologist, providing, "staff coordination, consultation, and guidance to DLA installations and field activities on all aspects of entomology and pest management, including manpower requirements, operational needs, medical and environmental impact, and procedural matters."

Although, as a career move, this was likely to be a good one, it also had the potential to be routine and uninteresting, and it certainly would have been had I not been placed in charge of a program that would turn out to be any entomologist's dream assignment. This was the matter of the Palos Verdes blue butterfly. This assignment also gave me a voting member status on the Armed Forces Pest Management Board near Washington DC, at the time called the "Bug Board". This is a joint or combined forces panel made up of many committees working on pest management issues in the US armed forces around the world. I got to face time with the best and brightest bug experts.

The Palos Verdes blue is listed as the rarest butterfly in the world and has at times been described as the butterfly that rewrote the Endangered Species Act. The Palos Verdes blue, or *Glaucopsyche lygdamus PalossVerdessensis,* is a small and superficially unremarkable butterfly measuring about an inch from wingtip to wingtip. It was first described in 1977 and noted as endemic to the Palos Verdes Peninsula, which is a tiny acreage of land in Los Angeles County on the southern extremity of the metropolitan area.[1] It was already extremely limited in numbers upon its discovery and acknowledged as threatened by the aggressive march of urban expansion in that area. The Palos Verdes blue is described as locally monophagous, meaning that it is dependent on a single larval food plant. Although it was initially thought that that species was locoweed, or rattlepod (*Astragalus trichopodus lonchus*), it was later established that the common deerweed (*Lotus scoparius*) also served the same function. Both plant species, limited to just a few enclaves within the peninsula, were being eradicated by scraping and land clearance ahead of urban development. By the end of the 1970s,

---

[1] According to the *Journal of Research on the Lepidoptera,* "The taxon was diagnosed as a subspecies of the silvery blue (*Glaucopsyche lygdamus*), a polytypic species comprised of at least ten valid subspecies that are usually found in small closed local colonies across most of North American north of Mexico and extending into easternmost Siberia."

scientists were beginning to sound the alarm that the newly discovered Palos Verdes blue was on the point of extinction.

Notwithstanding its addition to the endangered species list in 1980, which included a mandate to protect its breeding habitat, the pace of urban development continued. In 1982, the city of Rancho Palos Verdes bulldozed what was then the most extensive surviving tract of habitat, which pitched the Palos Verdes blue into such steep decline that soon afterward it was indeed understood to be extinct. An action was brought against the city of Rancho Palos Verdes by the US Fish and Wildlife Service, which claimed that the city administrators were fully aware of the site status of the area and the existence of the butterfly. The city replied that no motion was raised or complaint lodged until the damage was done. The situation was declared a *fait accompli* which, of course, by then it was. The city was subsequently charged by the federal government with violating the Endangered Species Act, but the case was eventually dismissed because a municipality was not a person for the purposes of the law and could not thus be held criminally liable. Directly as a result of this, a Congressional amendment was added to include any entity, private or public, under the terms of the law. So it is that the Palos Verdes is acknowledged as the butterfly that changed the Endangered Species Act. That change in the law, however, did nothing to save it, for by the time it came into effect, the Palos Verdes blue was written off as extinct.

Then an amazing thing happened. In 1994, eleven years after its apparent extinction, a remnant population of some sixty-five individuals was discovered on an underground fuel storage depot in San Pedro, a site owned by the Department of Defense, and administered by the Defense Logistics Agency. The location is on the south slope of the peninsula a few hundred yards west of the I-105, and east of the Rolling Hills Estate. There, while conducting an environmental survey in advance of a Defense Logistics Agency pipeline, UCLA zoologist Rudy Mattoni discovered a small, remnant population. According to Mattoni, quoted in the *New York Times,* "The sun broke through, and there they were." At the time, the population was estimated at no more than sixty-five.

Because the site was a Department of Defense facility, it became the business of the Defense Logistics Agency to facilitate the recovery and long-term survival of the species. The agency and the Military High Command were both swift in appreciating the political value of this event and quick to act upon the opportunity. As my neighbor on the flight from LAX to Washington confirmed, the military is not popular in liberal California, and to soften that hostility, the agency saw value in involving itself in a high-profile conservation effort. Thus, the Defense Logistics Agency, the US Navy and the Department of Defense threw their weight behind the effort to snatch this tiny subspecies from the jaws of extinction.

By the time I joined the agency, the effort was already underway, and in fact, by then, the population was hovering around two to three hundred individuals on a single DLA fuel depot. The Agency was working in combination with a team of partners that included the U.S. Fish and Wildlife Service, University of California, Riverside, the Urban Wildlands Group, Palos Verdes Peninsula Land Conservancy, Moorpark College, America's Teaching Zoo and the Soil Ecology Restoration Group at San Diego State University. There was a whole lot of people involved lets say. In 2005, I attended a White House Conference on Conservation held in St Louis, Missouri, where a member of the Senior Executive Services urged me to take the issue of the Palos Verdes blue very seriously. His words to me, as I recall, were, "Make sure you don't let this blue butterfly die on my watch, or I got your ass!"

I was taken aback, and I told him politely, "No Sir, I won't. I got you're message."

It was a high-level conference intended to highlight the efforts of several federal agencies in conservation work, and members were present, sharing information, handing out leaflets and holding press conferences. I was given a generous budget and a pretty open mandate to do what was necessary to keep the project alive. Mine was more or less a liaison function on behalf of the agency, monitoring what was happening in captive breeding and habitat reclamation, generally signing off on budget requests and running inspections of work underway. I put in my work with the Five Ps by educating myself to the eleventh degree on everything available on the subject. This, in general, was a mountain of academic material and a handful of feel-good press reports that were liberally scattered with my name and quotes from me on progress and status. Everyone was interested in this damn butterfly. It was wonderful, in a way.

My predecessor, he is deceased now, his name was Nelson Powers, had a reputation as a detail-conscious bloodhound who kept abreast of the minutia of the project and demanded consultation on every issue. I am sure the various individuals and agencies involved enjoyed having an easy-going, good ol' boy on board. My attitude to the project was that they were all professionals and my job was just to support them.

"Let's just do it; let's make it happen. Let's get the population up, and let's get it off the installation and onto another site. I've got your back, and just keep me updated." That is what I told the group. One time the site commander of the installation called me into his office. He said, "I know you are doing good with the butterfly, but as you are out an about, could you see about getting rid of those damned homeless off my installation?" There were apparently a lot of homeless that were living on the property at the time. I told him, "yes Sir! I can go take some photos of the, inside their tents and things, and then send them to the police."

So I went into the homeless camp on that defense property and they were out and about, hell, probably at the library. They had an entire tent facility set up. They had grills, and they were reading Shakespeare. I never could understand

Shakespeare. It looked like they were not just surviving but thriving, and thriving well. I sent the photos in and I never heard anything else on that subject again.

It was a prestigious project, and part of my job was to keep the fire burning by feeding it with newsworthy stories and periodic updates. Although the annual Defense Logistics Agency's budget for the project was only about seventy thousand dollars, the fact that the work was going forward on Defense Department land meant it was very much our baby. In all, I took about eight trips from Virginia to Los Angeles, in comfortable accommodations and with a rental car. I made the most of the opportunity. I hung out, explored the city, and ate Korean food. Compared to the boiler-room life on active duty in Korea, it was a breeze. Most importantly, though, it was a situation in which it was very easy to shine.

WHILE AT THE DEFENSE LOGISTICS Agency, I was passed a brief assignment that would, unbeknownst to me at the time, presage a grim chapter of my career. One day, I received a phone call from an administrative assistant to the senior executive of the Defense Logistics Agency, Ella Studer, a high-level civilian administrator who ran a lot of things. My first thought was, "Oh my God, I am in trouble again," but I was not. In fact, I was handed a top-secret brief to investigate certain allegations, made through a whistleblower channel, of various institutional irregularities within the federal policing agency at Fort Belvoir in Virginia.

Just for the sake of context, the DLA Police is a federal agency responsible for security, force protection and anti-terrorism at the DLA Installation Support Headquarters at the Andrew T McNamara Headquarters Complex at Fort Belvoir. The presumed improprieties involved using bomb detection mirrors intended to inspect the undercarriages of incoming vehicles to look up women's skirts, the doctoring of weapons cards to massage weapons training results, and nepotism in terms of favoring friends and family members for promotion.

I queried why I should be chosen for a generic assignment like this, and although the question was not answered directly, I was given to understand that a male was required, since all the details involved were male, and that I was a uniformed member with rank which, in a predominantly civilian agency, was deemed to be important in an issue dealing with other uniformed members. I was available, and I ticked all the boxes, so under a cloak of confidentiality, I was dispatched to get to the bottom of it, under the direct authority of Ella Studer.

In the end, I interviewed a bunch of people, undertook a detailed inspection of various records, and wrote up a report. I enjoyed the assignment because it offered scope for my natural cunning and instinctive sense of ingenuity and character judgment. In the end, however, I was able to come up with nothing conclusive. Word got around when I showed up and began asking questions, and before long, I was fielding phone calls from all kinds of people asking to take me out to lunch and being extra nice to me and   suchlike. I got to interviewing one particular officer on the night shift who seemed particularly evasive, but who also dropped enough general hints at this or that, that I could reasonably guess that he was the one at the bottom of the accusations.

It seemed fairly clear to me that he was pissed off and disgruntled about something, and his recourse was to leak some hazy complaint through an anonymous channel just to stir up the sediment. A large, bureaucratic organization like the Defense Logistics Agency was obligated to investigate any kind of accusation along these lines, in particular if it involved some kind of racist or sexual malfeasance. When I handed in my report, it was acknowledged and filed away with some relief. No one really wants to go down the road of a disciplinary process, and as far as the whistleblower was concerned, an investigation was probably enough satisfaction, and there the matter rested.

This could have been nothing more than a brief diversion from the routine of my day-to-day duties, but it stuck with me as I wrapped up my assignment with the agency. Even though it was quite clearly a shitstorm about nothing at all, it motivated the agency and created a whole lot of discomfort in a lot of people's lives. I am sure those who were disconcerted by it all took comfort from the fact that I was a good ol' boy, same as the Palo Verdes folk. If it gives someone a thrill to look up a woman's skirt with a bomb mirror, then what the hell. I am sure it happens now and again. An investigation usually settles any serious misbehavior, and there is rarely any reason found to take matters further. Still, one disgruntled character in a cubicle somewhere has the power at any time to seriously screw up people's lives. The bureaucratic morass has the potential to be a minefield, and you never know when you are going to get your balls blown off.

In the meantime, at the end of four years, although I enjoyed the work and the environment of the DLA very much, I began to think about a permanent change of station or some other place to move on to. An email from Human Resources Command had been in circulation for some time, requesting interest from an entomologist to serve in Korea, and no one was putting their hand up for it. I was fairly certain by then that I would make lieutenant colonel, and I knew my way around over there pretty good, so after the email circled round a few times, I flagged it and put in an application. By then I had my Community Relations Award of Excellence, which had made a name for me over there, and with a very successful assignment to the DLA, and an excellent Officer Evaluation Report, the omens were all good.

The only possible cloud on the horizon was the fact that Ted Small was still there and still the self-proclaimed expert on US military preventive medicine in South Korea. The word on the street was that, because he had passed the date of his mandatory retirement, he was serving now in the capacity of a civilian contractor. This meant that, while I would be more closely involved with him than I had been on my second tour, he was no longer in uniform and was technically outside of my military chain of command. My job description this time around would be staff entomologist with Eighteenth MEDCOM (Ted Small had served for much of his senior career as chief preventive medicine officer with Eighteenth MEDCOM), which was now overseen by Col. Monica Stewart.

I knew Monica Stewart very slightly from bumping into her when she was a major attached in some capacity to Chipmunk in Maryland. I think our first encounter was in a revolving door, and she came across on first impressions as friendly and approachable. She was a heavy-set woman, pleasant in aspect, and mannish, which is often unavoidable for a woman in military fatigues, and crisply businesslike. I saw her often from then on, and although our professional paths did not cross, we remained on friendly and collegial terms. The idea of being supervised by her did not seem problematic.

I was excited by the prospect of coming home to Korea. The work would be staff officer's work, not a command, which was second nature to me by then, so my excitement was mainly to eat authentic *kimchi*, drink in the richness of Korean culture, and perhaps even move on from there to an assignment in Thailand, Japan, or Hawaii. We wound up our affairs in Virginia, and with excitement and a sense of homecoming, Beverly, Chantel and I set off back to north Asia and the familiar and lovely world of South Korea. In hindsight I would have failed my Five Ps. I would never have returned to Korea if I had a hint of what was about to go down.

THIRD TIME A
CHARM

An honest witness does not deceive, but a false witness pours out lies.
PROVERBS 14:5

N JULY, 2008, AS STAFF ENTOMOLOGIST with
Eighteenth MEDCOM, I was invited by the Seoul
American Elementary School to host a reading workshop
as part of the annual summer reading program. My presentation
was titled "Catch the Reading Bug," which turned out to be
memorable and fun, and it worked. The books that I read were
Big Bug Surprise and *I Love You, Stink Bug*. From that day, such
things became a routine part of my life. On the day my daughter
was born, I discovered that I can relate to kids, in my way, that
I like kids, and that they like me. I was still in the giddy phase of
parenthood, and I found community among other parents
sharing that short season of joy. My dad loved kids too, and if
nothing else, he taught me the value of the child in the man. He
found stress relief in the lives and games of children, and so did
I. We lived on base at Itaewon Acres, and the kids came to know
me as the "masked man." I'd get into a Halloween monster mask
and chase them around the neighborhood on my bike. They
would gather in the evening and wait around for the masked

man to show up and then run about screaming and yelling, and I would tear around on my bike making monster noises, and everyone had fun, and then we all went home.

One day I went to the hospital because I had a rash on my chest when I was out collecting insects. So I went to see the dermatologist at the hospital. He happened to live in the same neighborhood of Itaewon Acres, and he looked at me and he said, "Look! That's the masked man, I've finally found him.'

A nurse came running in and said, 'Who is the masked man, he tears around the neighborhood chasing the kinds...maybe we should refer him to mental health?"

FROM THE MOMENT WE TOUCHED DOWN on the tarmac of Incheon International Airport, I had a bad feeling. It was impossible to shake a gnawing and persistent sensation that in some way I was in trouble, and that I had fucked up real bad. It was the same ungrounded feeling of failure that clenched my guts all those years ago as I rode the bus to the CCF. It was nothing that I could put my finger on in the moment, but it was strong, and it was persistent. I shared my unease with Beverly as we unpacked and settled in. "I just know there is going to be some stuff going on here," I told her. "I just know it. I don't know what it is, but I just know it."

In July 2007, I began my assignment with Eighteenth MEDCOM. According to the US Army website, the Eighteenth Medical Command, or MEDCOM, "assumes the role of medical mission command in support of combatant commanders during deployment operations as well as during humanitarian aid and disaster relief operations throughout the Indo-Asian Pacific region."

What that means in layman's terms is preventive medicine on a command level in the Pacific region, with multiple facets and the usual many bureaucratic layers. The unit was first activated in Fort Lee, Virginia, in 1967, as the Eighteenth Medical Brigade, and then reactivated in 1984 in the Republic of Korea, which is where it was when I showed up. However, within just a few months of my attachment, it was scheduled to case its colors and relocate operations to Fort Shafter in Hawaii. I kind of thought I might be going to Hawaii myself. When that happened, I would shift to force health protection with the Sixty-fifth Medical Brigade, subordinate to the Eighth Army, and redesignated in Korea a year earlier. In the meantime, I was assigned to a staff officer position, supervised, at least for the time being, by Col. Monica Stewart.

I do not recall exactly how and when we were reintroduced, but when it happened, it was a friendly and completely routine orientation, exactly as I had experienced with every new command and every new assignment. She welcomed me onto the staff and introduced me to my new colleagues, and for the first few weeks or so, everything went along fine.

My gut feeling continued that something in this assignment was going to be bad. I could not explain it but I knew something was going to happen. Words did not need to be exchanged to feel. I could sense it form the interaction of people. It was as if they were walking on eggshells or something. Soon enough, I began picking up on rumors that she was crazy or menopausal or some damn thing. In the beginning, I took it with a pinch of salt. Under any kind of female command, some low-level sexism and sexist humor is inevitable. After a while, however, it was impossible not to begin taking it more seriously. Sometimes the talk was that she was a lesbian, that she cruised the base in the early hours on a Harley and dressed in black leather. There was supposed to be a boyfriend in the picture somewhere, but no one had ever seen him. She had a mean and unpredictable temper. Some days she would hand out home-baked cookies with all smiles, and I remember we'd eat right in front of her and say "mmm this is good", and other times she would tear through the department like a tornado. I saw her sometimes driving her car around base, trying to tear off the steering wheel in rage. Maybe she had a touch of bipolar disorder. Seldom did she come into the department before mid-afternoon, and often she could be found alone in her office late at night. That also became rich ground for speculation, because Ted Small was also that way inclined, and sometimes in the small hours their office lights would be on at the same time. Who knows? Stranger things have happened.

Although dealing with challenging personalities is a fact of life in the military, there was something about Monica Stewart that set my gut sense tingling. Maybe it was just because I was so damn certain that some shit was coming down the pipeline that I was suspicious of everyone. There was definitely a technique to dealing with her, but since she usually came in only later in the day, the overlap was mostly pretty limited. I got on with my work, and there were no problems that I could put my finger on. I spoke fairly regularly to my dad, and I told him about it before any real problems started to manifest.

"I seen it all the time," he said to me. "Some people just got nothing else in their lives but work. They live for it. Got nothing else to live for. Sometimes you gotta watch out for those folk. They are little dictators; they see threats everywhere."

He was a businessman, and he had a knack for sizing people up.

"Son, you got a middle-aged woman. She has no man, no husband, and no children. That right there is ninety percent of the issue."

Maybe he was right. I figured that was probably true. She was married to the uniform. A lot of soldiers end up that way, men and women, and by itself, it did not mean anything. Sometimes she could be quite frank and open. Once she said to me, "Can't you see I have no life? The Army is my life." It speaks for itself when an officer retires at the maximum mandatory age limit. However, the fact was that she was due to ship out of Korea in seven or eight months, and I figured that if I could

199

keep my head down and my powder dry until then, I would probably be okay.

Then there was Ted Small. That was really where my gut sense went nuts. He was still in the picture and still the senior fellow of medical entomology in Korea. His was a microworld, a fiefdom slowly built over many years, almost like an academic version of *Apocalypse Now*. It was his fascination, his everything, and most importantly, it had for many, many years been his exclusive turf. Throughout my career, I have seen these little kingdoms form in odd places—it is in the nature of a global bureaucracy—but Ted Small had it real bad.

The KATUSAs posed no threat to him at all, and rotating military personnel were generally in awe of him, and for good reason, because he was both brilliant and internationally respected. He was also a fountain of institutional knowledge just for having been in Korea for so damn long. But he was a researcher, an ivory-tower academic, and I was a staff officer who was an "entomologist" only in the most functional sense of the word. My role was not to fixate on the habits, habitat, and breeding cycle of a mosquito, but to manage and control them and assess their risk to human health. That was my job, and that was as far as I took it. Of course, I was as responsive to him as I would be to any other civilian colleague, but I certainly was not interested in burying my nose in his ass or taking any orders from him.

One day, he approached me at the front desk and asked if I would care to be included in the mailing list on any of his future publications. I declined. I am not sure why. It would not have hurt to have shown some enthusiasm and thanked him, but I did not. I guess I did not see myself as a researcher, nor did I care to work with him, and in fact I was probably even a little bit anti-academic. Maybe he saw that as disrespecting his accomplishments. I don't know. I sure would have if it had been me.

He had a way of ingratiating and smiling that did nothing to hide his fury. Friends have since told me that my email protocols were atrocious, and that surely pissed him off. I could hardly compose a sentence, and I never used spellcheck. I am sure a bit of belching, farting, and ass-scratching happened too. As a PhD and a cultivated man, Ted Small must have found it all very trying. I believe he saw me as an insurgent, maybe some sort of challenge to the *status quo*. If he did, he had no reason to. The focus of my life was not in the office, but on the sports field with Chantel and her team, reading to kids in the library, coaching football, riding my bike, or just being at home with the family. That's the deal for a lot of staff assignments overseas. You put in your hours, and you enjoy the ride. Whatever might have been the metrics, and however it all came to pass, my gut sense began to tingle whenever Doctor Small was around.

"Watch your back, Jake," my father warned me, "because that's where it's gonna come from."

Then, in July of 2007, good news came through the pipeline. The Human Resource Command promotion list was published, and my name was on it. In a few months I would be confirmed as a lieutenant-colonel. These promotions were wonderful because I still thought of myself as Private Pike, but now I was an officer, a senior officer. It was huge because it strengthened my position and gave me hope that I would get the better of myself and stay out of trouble. I kept my mind focused on my family, did my job, and involved myself in the community.

THE FAMILY MOVED into a house in the residential quarter of the garrison known as Itaewon Acres. It was a tight community of American and allied service families, all isolated somewhat from the outside world. Chantel was enrolled in first grade, and as parents, Beverly and I involved ourselves in school life and the garrison community. Beverly was an outgoing and popular personality in an environment where officers' wives are often integral to the careers of their husbands. I was the "masked man" and she was the "popcorn lady," because she was known for making real good buttered popcorn, and the kids liked that. I coached basketball and soccer, and together we were recognized by the community with various honorary diplomas and certificates. One time we were nominated as volunteer family of the year and we sat down with three-star and four-star generals. She was a good mother and a good wife, and I am pretty sure that without her support, what eventually went down would have gone down a whole lot sooner.

In mid-April 2008, a week or so before she was due to be transferred out, Colonel Stewart visited me in my office for verbal counseling. The encounter was brief, no more than ten minutes, and it was concerned ostensibly with my Officer Evaluation Report. I was made to understand that my evaluation would not be good following numerous minor complaints about the quality of my work. These complaints originated from more than one "unnamed source" within the department. The name of Capt. Peter Price was dropped, and my mind shot back to Fort Belvoir, and that night-shift officer leaking anonymous accusations and stirring things up. Now my gut sense was really roaring.

Then, at some point, the conversation pivoted around to my family and its well-being, and in particular my daughter. This was followed by a very carefully worded query about the frequency of my visits to the Seoul American Elementary School, and what I did there. I admitted I did regularly visit the school, sometimes for coaching, or community outreach, but mainly to eat lunch with Chantel and her friends. I coached soccer and basketball, taught a class on insect diversity to the Yongsan Garrison Cub Scouts, and helped a few of them gain their Public Health Merit Badge—and yes, I was the "masked man."

She turned to the window and seemed to ruminate on these details for a while. Then she turned back, looked past me, and remarked with apparently casual sincerity: "You know, you might be good with the front office, but when they hear about your problems with young children, I predict things will not be quite so good."

I could not believe what I had just heard. I stared hard at her, but she would not make eye contact. A feeling overcame me that I had never felt before. I am sure my face turned red with anger, and my hands began shaking. I told myself to keep cool, or I swear I could have killed her right there. I fought to hold my composure.

"Anyone can check my record," I replied stiffly.

"You know," she went on, as if she hadn't heard, "this sort of behavior will need to be investigated. You know that, right? I'll have to present your case to the board when it meets at the end of April, and what do I tell them? That you are just strange? That you are crazy?"

"Yes," I replied. "Why don't you just tell them I am crazy?"

"I can't do that."

"Then I don't know what else I can tell you."

With that, and with a tight smile, she excused herself and walked out of my office.

In that moment, the penny dropped. I sat down at my desk and looked out of the window. In my conversations with my father, he said simply, "Keep a cool head, son, just a keep a cool head. Remember, Jake, these high-ranking people did not get to their rank without knowing how to dodge a land mine—or bury a land mine."

I had stepped on a damned land mine. I developed an attack of diarrhea, and my anger and distress were so acute that I later admitted myself into the 121st General Hospital and was treated for an anxiety attack. My mind returned to a conversation with Ed Evans—who warned me to watch my six o'clock—and other officers who hinted in different ways that Ted Small could be a scheming, ruthless bastard at times. I remembered also my father telling me, "Watch your back, son, because that is where it will come from."

WHEN AN OFFICER ACHIEVES SENIOR RANK, he or she becomes very difficult to get rid of. To really grab the attention of the powers that be, some horrendous and wicked charge or accusation is demanded. An example could be sexism or toxic leadership or deviant types of behavior. However, the value lies not in a provable point, but in the accusation itself. The cherished legal notion of innocent until proven guilty does not have much bearing on administrative law. The civilian courts figured out a long time ago that military justice is best left to the military, because different rules apply. A good example would be a platoon leader who makes a bad decision under fire and gets someone hurt. It is not feasible for relatives to then to hire a lawyer and sue that platoon leader because he made a bad decision under fire and little Johnny got killed. This typically remains the case until every avenue of the military appeal process has been exhausted. As a consequence, all but a very small percentage of military criminal and disciplinary issues are handled in house.

Under administrative law, the standard of proof required is a *preponderance* of the evidence. Thus, if an individual falls victim to a false allegation and then replies that he or she is innocent, the chain of command is faced with a problem. Who do they believe? The accuser or the accused? And if there is more than one accuser, it becomes even more complicated. When accusations are made, accusations that are impossible to prove or disprove, and rumors begin to circulate, the question becomes how much time and resource does the chain of command want to invest in getting to the bottom of it? Potentially, a commander can convene a board of inquiry under the administration of a neutral officer to investigate the situation if he or she deems it necessary, or desirable. That is kind of how it went down in Fort Belvoir. If it is swept under the carpet and an accuser is unhappy, he or she has the option to write to their congressperson, which means that the Army will be obligated to investigate the issue again. If there is genuine substance to a charge, it will be dealt with through the Code of Military Justice. If not, the accusation will just linger like a turd on your plate, creating an unholy stink that will eventually be smelled all the way up the chain of command.

The power, therefore, lies in the accusation.

There are three hot-button issues always guaranteed to grab attention: racism, sexism, and sexual impropriety or deviancy, in particular anything involving children. Rumors began circulating almost immediately that I was a pedophile and, worse still, that I was somehow guilty of interfering with my daughter. Chantel was healthy and in good spirits, doing well at school and happy, which a ten-minute conversation with her teachers and counselors would confirm. That meant nothing in the face of the rumor mill. The whole business was so confusing and ugly that I was ready to quit the Army right then, and then do some serious physical damage to Colonel Stewart and Ted Small and, if I could track his ass down, Peter Price, too. I was ready to kill.

It surprised me how my emotions swung so wildly during this period, from rage to depression to anxiety. I felt mad, sad, and guilty at different times, or all at the same time. My guilt confused me because I was guilty of not a damned thing except being a good father. Mad because it had happened, sad because it had happened, and guilty because it had happened. I felt guilt mostly for the effect that it had on Beverly, who also had to live with the bullshit, and Chantel. Beverly took a stoic, level-headed and pragmatic view, advising me just to step out and keep doing the same stuff and let it blow over. My dad thought it possible that Monica Stewart had suffered something in her own childhood that made her sensitive to accusations of sexual abuse against children. His advice was also just to face the wind and keep moving forward. That was easy to say. One day, the community gathered for a five-mile charity run, and I noticed a couple of kids struggling to get on their bikes, and I walked over to help. An officer in my chain of command hurried over and yelled, "Hey, keep away from my kids."

A lot of civilians reading this might ask why the hell not just quit and move on? In the military that is not so easy, particularly if you have a unique specialty. Trust me, I did think about getting out, and I almost transferred to another branch. After so many years, and with benefits and pensions, it is impractical just to give it all up and walk away. The military is a hierarchy, and change on that level requires a written request and all manner of bureaucratic hurdles, and in the end, reflects badly on your record. Beverly did not want me to quit. She had a level head. She just said "You're doing good!" Besides that, I had been indoctrinated with a never-quit mentality, and I was not about to change. Beverly and Chantel were at peace with it, so at least two thirds of the family was in a good place.

This was in layman's terms an executive level body slam. They were working the system to their advantage to body slam the Pike.

A week or so after that initial counseling session, I was invited into Colonel Stewart's office to be interviewed over my Officer Evaluation Report, and the matter of my low competence and poor performance. She seemed to find it very difficult, tearing up a few times as she read through the litany of my deficiencies. I was struck by the feeling that she was doing all of this this against her will. Everything was referenced in the language of "I heard." Someone told her, she said, that I had volunteered for Korea to avoid active service in the Middle East.

Ted Small once remarked that I was illiterate and dilatory and vague in verbal communication, which I would agree with . All the while, rumors of my sexual proclivity for children were added to and embellished by somebody, kept on the boil, and given context and detail by the day. The name Peter Price from time to time emerged from the swamp. There was nothing concrete or specific, just the low-level pinpricks of accusation and criticism that were the preamble to a poor assessment. In the end, I was served up a very poor Officer Evaluation Report, the only one that was ever filed while I was on active duty.

Then, in April 2008, Col. Monica Stewart received her orders, boarded a plane for Hawaii and was gone. Ted Small, however, remained, and he was quite openly irritated that I had not been transferred to Hawaii with the unit. She was replaced by Lt. Col. Mitchell Meyers, who brought with him a breath of sanity and a return to the comfortable *status quo* of male command. When apprised of the situation, he said little but clearly understood what a shitstorm the whole thing had been. He spoke to Colonel Stewart at an exchange of command and later warned me that even though she was heading to Hawaii, she was still dangerous. Either way, with Monica Stewart out of the picture, rumors of child sexual abuse began to dissipate. It is the nature of South Korea that personnel are frequently rotated, so it did not take very long for anyone who might have been influenced against me to leave and be replaced. For a while, life returned to normal.

IN APRIL 2009, a year after Colonel Stewart's departure, I was called into the office of the commander of Eighteenth MEDCOM, Col. Jeffrey Clark, ostensibly to be briefed by representatives of Military Intelligence and the Criminal Investigation Division on the situation that I was facing. I had no idea what this could mean, and I approached the command office on the top of Dragon Hill with a sense of deep anxiety. Knocking on the door, I was invited in and presented to a shabbily dressed and corpulent fifty-something man who introduced himself as Chris McCormick. He was affable and friendly and looked me directly in the eye as he shook my hand. My gut sense was in overdrive. What the fuck is all this about, I was thinking?

Although I expected the discussion to center on the child abuse issue, this time it did not. Instead, in a very roundabout way, I was interrogated about my ongoing relationship with Major Park, who was by then retired, Vietnamese friends of Beverly and a few other people outside the garrison with whom I regularly mixed and socialized. Someone had been surveilling me and knew my movements and relationships. I was told that information had been received that I was passing on military intelligence to a foreign source. I was advised of my rights and told that I should consult a lawyer. This time I was not so much shocked as enraged. I had been on the investigating side of exactly this kind of issue, and I knew how the game was played.

"I haven't done a damned thing," I retorted, this time almost laughing. "This is all bullshit."

And it was. Another vague but wicked accusation, through formal channels, serious enough in implication to prompt an investigation, but ultimately unprovable. On that note, Chris McCormick wrapped up the interview, and placing his hand on my shoulder as I walked out the door, he said quietly, "Try not to let this bother you."

Try not to let this bother you? Hell, that was a tall order.

My mind was racing as I walked down a fluorescent-lit corridor and out into the cool morning. A week or so earlier, a pretty damn strange thing happened that did not make sense at the time but sure made sense now. I was walking out of the 121st General Hospital in Yongsan one morning when the inspector general of the 18th MEDCOM, his name was Colonel Geoff

Faux, passed me walking the other way. We greeted one another, and in passing he remarked, "Hey, Jason, don't forget to put your CAC into your computer when you log in today." A CAC is a Common Access Card, which is a general security pass for cyber access. At the time I thought that was a very strange thing to say because doing it was standard doctrine.

A few hours later, Ted Small came rushing into my office with the news that a malaria case had been detected at the hospital and we needed to get there quickly. This was wildly out of character, and he was in a hell of a hurry, agitating as I shut down my computer and pulled out my CAC card, and I wondered what the hell was going on. Now the penny dropped, and I figured they were trying to get into my computer. Then that computer crashed, and when the IT folks came and checked it out, they could not figure out why, and everything on the computer was gone.

Years later, after my retirement, I ran into Chris McCormick at Fort Sam Houston in San Antonio. "What the hell was all that about at Yongsan?" I asked him, and he smiled.

"I'm glad it all worked out for you," he said. "We have to do our job when we get information. I'm glad everything worked out."

A month after that interview, an email appeared in my inbox from Human Resources Command. It reads exactly as follows:

"Good morning from HRC, and I hope all is well. As you know or may not know, you are currently on the OTSG Accepted List and in an unauthorized position. Therefore, we [HRC] are going to reassign you to the Eighth Army ESO (Executive Science Officer) billet this August (2009)—current officer [Maj. Lindquist] is scheduled to PCS this September to attend the CCC (Captain's Career Course). Your experience and knowledge of PM operations within Korea make you an excellent choice for this position and will be a career-enhancing assignment. I spoke to both Col. Logan and Col. Jones, and they support the move to have you fill this position. Maj. Lindquist is currently filling this billet, and he will be able to provide you with additional information on what the position entails."

CLEARLY, THE SMELL HAD FOUND its way to DC. The news came completely out of the blue, not only to me but to all of my supervisors and commanders. It was not coordinated in the chain of command. Typically, a transfer along these lines does not occur without preamble and consultation. I guess the investigations and revolving accusations had become so burdensome to the chain of command that they made the decision simply to transfer me. My dad called it "passing the trash." I can guess that when the news reached him, Ted Small picked up the phone and dialed Peter Price's number, and the two congratulated one another on a job well done. For me it was a step up the ladder, filling the boots of an environmental science officer, in a bigger pond with bigger fish. I am sure those behind the transfer would have preferred that I be dishonorably discharged, but second prize is better than nothing. I was out of his hair and banished from his world. He was happy, and things quieted down, at least for a while.

Over the holiday season of 2009, I was invited to my old Preventive Medicine office Christmas party, and there I ran into the man himself. I wandered over and greeted him, and as we exchanged pleasantries, I remarked casually that I was so enjoying life in the Eighth Army that I was considering extending my time, which was bullshit. His eyes narrowed, his jaw clamped, and he regarded me for a few seconds before spinning on his heels and walking away. The next day was a Saturday, and, to my surprise, I received a telephone call from Capt. Peter Price. After all the usual friendly banter, which still rang as hollow as bamboo, he began talking about the idea of forming an entomology council to bring together everyone involved in the field in South Korea under the Armed Forces Pest management Board, or the "Bug Board", to bring everyone involved in South Korea under a single entity.

Who calls on a Saturday morning to talk about forming a professional club, I was thinking? On the following Monday, a barrage of emails hit the department, all of which I ignored, and I attended none of the proposed meetings. Years later, I wrote to Peter Price inquiring about the progress of the committee under the Bug Board and received no reply. Clearly it was no more than an effort, as Winston Churchill once said, to keep your friends close, but your enemies closer.

Once or twice after that, I asked Peter Price out to lunch or dinner, but he never accepted. There is an old Asian saying: "Never trust a man who will not eat or drink with you."

In the meantime, in February 2010, I was invited to attend the Annual Tri-Service Entomology Conference, held at its usual place, at the Jacksonville Air Naval Base in Florida. This was a gathering of entomologists from the three main branches of the uniformed services and was as much a social as a professional gathering. I invited my parents and they drove down from South Carolina for it. At a pre-dinner cocktail party, I tried to introduce my father to Ted Small. He had his back to us as we approached, and as he wrapped up a conversation, I greeted him. He turned and saw my father and me, and without saying a word, he hurried off.

Later, over dinner, Dad and I got to talking about taking him out. He and I had spoken regularly as the issue played out, and because of it, we had grown much closer. It was very concerning for him and the stress that it placed on me affected him too. Fred Pike was also involved in the conversation, and between him and my father, both accustomed to settling matters with their fists, kicking the shit out of Ted Small was both logical and justified. This conversation carried over into the next few days and was firmed up with details of times, places, and weapons. The intention was just to beat the crap out of him and hurt him severely. Dad was right behind me on it, and ready to do what needed to be done.

By the end of the conference, however, I had changed my mind. It was just too risky. It seemed to me that if Ted Small had been able to damage my life so badly on fabricated information, what could he do if I gave him solid grounds for a criminal complaint? In the end, we called it off. As Dad said to me, "If you wrestle with a pig, you both get dirty, except the pig likes it."

I talked to my dad much during this conference. "I never seen so many ass-kissing politicians in one place!" he said. He was intrigued by a particular Air Force entomologist, a colonel, who walked with a cane. "Damn son, look at him, they need to cashier his ass out. He can't even walk. In my day they'd cashier you out if you was broke like him."

THE MORAL OF THIS STORY is that the military establishment, in particular the bureaucratic branches, has the potential to be a minefield, and every officer at one time or other steps on a mine. I suppose, in hindsight, I stepped on a few too many mines. It was also, maybe more importantly, a failure of the Five Ps. My gut instinct told me at the very beginning that I had made a mistake, and that gut instinct turned out to be right. "Pre-Planning Prevents Piss Poor Performance." Taking this "Third Time a Charm" assignment in Korea was the biggest mistake of my life. In hindsight I screwed up a lot of things professionally and personally, but I was not going to be quite so unaware going into the future. This would not be the last time that I would find myself in that minefield, but it would be the last time that I would walk in unaware and unprotected.

INTO
AFGHANISTAN

He will wipe away every tear from their eyes, and death shall be no more,
neither shall there be mourning, nor crying, nor pain anymore, for the
former things have passed away.
REVELATION 21:4

TYPICALLY, DURING AN EVENT LIKE THE Tri-Service Conference, Human Resource Command will take the opportunity to offer career counseling and advice to officers in transition. I had about four months remaining of my deployment to South Korea, and I was anxious to get some good intel on what might be in the pipeline for me. I was invited to attend, and one afternoon I made my way into a meeting room where I was met by Maj. Winico Martinez and Col. Scott Gordon, the latter at the time the Army's top bug man. Both of these men were top-flight officers in their field, with experience in this and other commands, and fully on top of their assignments. Kind of like water-walkers in a way. After the customary greeting and salutations, I seated myself at a vinyl-topped table in the expectation of some solid guidance and possibly a few deployment options. For a full three minutes, they sat opposite and looked at me without saying a word. It was the damnedest thing. Eventually, I broke the silence.

"Y'all got anything for me?"

They just sat and looked at me and said nothing. For a while, I thought maybe this was some kind of interrogation technique related to the security investigation, but then it occurred to me that so much shit must have been stirred up lately around the name of Lieutenant Colonel Pike that there was nothing safe to say and no safe place to assign me. It was the strangest damned situation I have ever been in. The minutes ticked by in awkward silence.

"Have y'all got nothing to tell me?" I eventually asked.

Silence.

"Can you y'all respond to goodbye?"

Silence.

I stood up and wished them a good day and left the room. I was pissed and insulted. Returning to Korea, I worked through the last few months of my assignment with a bad feeling that more shit was on its way. Then, a few weeks before we were due to ship out, word came through the pipeline that I would be heading back to "Chipmunk". It was not the best news, and in some ways it was a step back, but the understanding was that this time I would be in a supervisory role, which was, I guess, in a small way, a career advance. We packed up, and with a circuitous travel facility, spent four nights in Hawaii at the Armed Forces Recreation Center at Hale Koa, before making landfall on the mainland. There I received a courtesy telephone call from an ex-colleague, Tom Burroughs, who was keeping my seat warm in Aberdeen.

"Just want to let you know," he said, "word has come through that they've got you pegged to go to Afghanistan as a commander."

I thought to myself, "Well I'll be damned!"

WE DECIDED TO SETTLE for the duration in Lorton, Virginia, close to our rental house, with a view to me commuting a few times a month to the Chipmunk in Aberdeen. I knew I would probably be more involved in preparing for overseas deployment than working as a departmental bureaucrat, so it made sense. An interesting side story is that word got out that I was sleeping in the back of my truck in the Walmart parking lot on the few nights a week that I was required to be at the Aberdeen Proving Ground. Tom Burroughs, my supervisor, called me into his office and said, "Hey Jason, we don't need a lieutenant colonel in the Army getting killed or mugged sleeping in his truck. Please get a rental or a hotel."

A co-worker once even invited me to bunk down at his place during the week. I eventually found a cheap rental on Craigslist. I put out an add saying a poor soldier needs a place to sleep a few nights a week, and it was very cheap.

I had mixed feelings about Afghanistan. In Korea, Beverly, Chantel, and I had been given the opportunity to bond as a family in a family-orientated environment. Afghanistan was not that. The decision, therefore, to leave my wife and daughter for a year was not easily taken. Many soldiers on deployment to a war zone suffer that anxiety. On the other hand, it was an opportunity, not only to recover from a very bruising few years in Korea, but also probably the only chance I would get to serve in a war zone, and if I was going to make full colonel, it would be on the back of something like this. It was just a second chance at redemption.

A couple of things happened in the weeks before I got proactive in preparing for deployment that are probably worth reporting. In any kind of permanent change of station, or when a soldier enters a different unit, there is a period that we call "in-process," which is just the grunt work of getting settled in. One of the many formalities is picking up a gate pass to get in and a security pass to enter the department. It is secret, but not top-secret, and even if you have some mark on your record, like my DUI, you usually will get the clearances you need so long as you are up front and tell the truth. I had no problem at all getting my security clearance, and I recall one morning as I was sitting in my cubicle with my feet on the desk reading something when Tom Burroughs walked in.

"Hey, how's in-process going?" he asked.

"Fine," I replied. "Everything's doing pretty good. No problems."

"Did you go through security?"

"I did."

"Did you get your security badge?"

I nodded in the affirmative.

"Well, let me see it," he said.

I pulled out my red security badge and showed it to him. He looked at it and stood for a moment scratching his head before he turned and walked away.

"Oh my God!" I thought to myself. That was proof that rumor and innuendo were still circulating through the hierarchy. Tom Burroughs was more tied into the grapevine than I was, since he was a regular attendee of many meetings of the "Bug Board." He'd probably heard somewhere that Jason Pike is in some sort of security investigation and figured that I would never get clearance. A little later he came back and told me in a friendly and collegial way that I was not pegged to take over the supervisory position in the department—that would remain his—but that I would return to the role of projects officer.

It is hard to understand sometimes how all these things are figured out. Although I was disappointed, it did offer me plenty of time and opportunity to max out on the Five Ps as I prepped for Afghanistan. I trusted Tom because I had known him for a long time. If he told me something I believed it. Tom Burroughs supported me by making no real demands as I set about getting to grips with what would be the most challenging phase of my career. It is a generally understood fact that the most difficult part of deploying a unit to a war zone is in getting it there. Once a unit lands in-country, it's just a matter of getting on with the job. The US military bureaucratic machine is as exhausting as it is exacting, and just getting a unit of thirteen men and women through the hoops and past the mandatory training is an exercise in detail and endurance.

Then, in October 2010, while attending a conference of the "Bug Board," held at Walter Reid Army Institute of Research in Silver Springs Maryland, I ran into Capt. Peter Price. He intercepted me with the same gushing and ass-kissing approach that he had used less than a year earlier to try and sink me. He had heard of my deployment to Afghanistan, and clearly he sensed an opportunity.

"Man,, hey man, you gotta take me as your executive officer!" he said. "Can you do that? Can you do that for me?"

He was literally begging me, on the sidelines of the "Bug Board", but this time I knew better. My guts were tingling big time.

I could hardly find the words. There, at a damn Bug Board meeting, he had the balls to do that? I almost took him outside and beat the shit out of him. I wanted to so bad, and I very nearly did. I really think he was purposefully trying to agitate me to do something like that. Remembering all the good advice I had ever had from my father, I turned and walked away. I had maxed out already on the Five Ps, put in a whole lot of preplanning for the deployment, and laid out a strategy for coordinating training. I was on top of my game. This was my moment, and would it be worth ending it all right there just because of him?

THE UNIT THAT I WAS TAKING INTO THE FIELD was the 452nd Medical Detachment, a reserve unit out of Perrine, Florida. I arrived in Aberdeen Proving Ground, Maryland, out of Korea on the 4th of July weekend of 2010, on the advice that I would be leaving for Afghanistan in January or February 2011, seven months down the road.

The 452nd was a small, preventive medicine unit of about thirteen soldiers, and assigned as my executive officer was an Army Reserve officer from Puerto Rico whose name was Capt. José Vasquez. Most of the unit members were from around Miami, so it was not unusual to have folk who were not fluent in English. The Army Reserve is a different animal from the regular Army and the National Guard. While a Guard unit typically comprises men of a single district or location—so integrated, they often say, that they are almost inbred—a Reserve unit is drawn from widely dispersed sources and, in general, the soldiers are less cohesive and certainly less disciplined.

Captain Vasquez, although he was an engineer with the Veterans Administration, had no grasp of English at all. He had twenty years as an Army Reserve, ten years as enlisted and ten years as an officer. There was bad blood between us from the outset because he had assumed that he would command the unit in Afghanistan, and the appearance ahead of him of an active service PROFIS with the rank of lieutenant colonel really pissed him off.

The unit gathered at Fort McCoy in Wisconsin, where there were probably upwards of one thousand Reserve soldiers from various commands preparing for deployment to Afghanistan. One night, Captain Vasquez led a few members of the unit to the local bars in a government vehicle to drink. They took along a designated driver, and they hid the vehicle, but they were spotted, and the tag number reported back to the base. They were intercepted at the gate in the early hours, and I was sent for to deal with them. For the first time in my career, I gave out an honest-to-goodness ass-chewing, which did nothing but deepen the animus between Captain Vasquez and me. These were not combat soldiers but Medical Department personnel in the reserves, and for the next few days, I took all kinds of crap from my fellow officers. "Lieutenant Colonel Pike, sir," ran the typical bullshit, "you gonna be able to handle those soldiers over there in Afghanistan, sir?"

I felt very embarrassed by all of this. Out of a thousand soldiers that were training at Forty McCoy, Wisconsin, we were only thirteen, and we were looked down on as the fuck-ups!

But the good news is that I knew I had a piece of gold somewhere in the cards. Among those soldiers was Malisha Palmer, who I remembered from El Salvador as a go-getting young corporal from Alabama. That hard-charging redhead seemed like a gift from God!

She was a sergeant first class with a superb instinct for leadership and a low tolerance for bullshit, and, as they say, an officer is only as good as his first sergeant. Captain Vasquez was sulking and working to rule, and I had no appetite to deal with him. I felt pretty confident that I could ace this deployment if I could avoid being dragged down into the weeds by a dilatory and uncooperative executive officer. I did try at the last minute to slot in a replacement, but it was too late. This was likely to be the climax of my career, and if I fucked it up it would be the defining fuck-up. After Korea, I was pretty alert to the enemy within, and Captain Vasquez had all the characteristics of a disruptive and problematic team member. As my dad would say, "You could put his brains in a hummingbird's ass, and it would fly backward."

It turned out that Malisha Palmer was suffering from some sort of degenerative spinal disease and was handed orders to take medical leave, which completely threw a wrench in the gears. There was no time to train up a replacement. She could deploy only with a special waiver, and I pleaded with her—I told her that she was the best thing that ever happened to me, and I'd be up shit creek if she left—and she agreed under certain conditions to sign a waiver request. She certainly did not need to come, since she already had a combat patch, but I told her

219

she had to or I would be toast. I could not picture handling the deployment without reliable and competent support from a good NCO. What I needed was a bloodhound for the minor details to cover my disability. I was pretty sure that without her I would drown in that damn firehose. We applied for a waiver, and it was granted. She told me she would only do it if she was first sergeant, and I told her no doubt she was first sergeant.

The unit assembled at Fort McCoy in Wisconsin, where there were hundreds of Reserve soldiers from various commands preparing for deployment to Afghanistan. Training at Fort McCoy included firearms drill and hand-to-hand combat to prepare a soldier, any soldier, for the eventuality of having to fight. We were not a combat unit, but every soldier, no matter who, had to have that capability. An interesting aspect of this training came with the *Defense Occupational Environmental Health Readiness System* (DOEHRS). DOEHRS is an archival system developed by the Chipmunk, or the Center for Health Promotion and Preventive Medicine in Maryland, in response to problems thrown up by the Gulf War Syndrome. I can recall that the conversation in those days surrounding Gulf War Syndrome was what the hell was it and what was causing it. "Where is the data?" was the question most frequently asked, and from that, a system of recording health data coming out of war zones, and everywhere US military personnel were deployed, was developed. If in a future conflict, little Johnny comes home from war with a rash, and even more so if a whole bunch of soldiers come home with symptoms, then there is a database on hand to map and determine what was taking place at any given time. Nothing resembling Gulf War Syndrome ever came out of the Afghanistan war, with the possible exception of burn pits—sites where the general trash of the base was burned—and the possibility that soldiers downwind suffered some symptoms as a consequence of breathing that shit in.

While I was at the Chipmunk, the DOEHRS was still under development. It was driven mostly by the work of a cadre of committed civilians who were eager to get it into the hands of as many medical units as possible. There were civilian technocrats available to train units, and true to the Five Ps, I jumped on that pretty quickly. I coordinated a lot of civilians to come down from Maryland to train my soldiers on how to use the system. It was just a question of getting onto the webpage and filling out data on any kind of sampling results, mapping, and general reporting. It was all entered into a central archive that could be referenced in any future situation where liability was claimed or challenged. I drummed it into my people that it was not just about sampling, making recommendations, and enforcing. It was also about contributing to the advance of knowledge and the prevention or proof of future issues like Gulf War Syndrome. It was also pretty cool to think that there would be a permanent record of all the work we did in one year in Afghanistan. At that time, I was one of very few, if any, commanders in Afghanistan, or anywhere, making serious and consistent use of the system, and I like to think my team was part of that pioneering effort. It is also worth mentioning that we trained other preventive medicine personnel in Afghanistan on the proper and effective use of the system.

The DOEHRS system is an example of the kind of training that the unit underwent at Fort McCoy before a brief visit to Fort McChord in Washington State. We had so much training it is unbelievable really. There, more detailed practical training and validation took place. We were tested by preventive medicine officers to confirm that we were good. There was also an exercise to weed out the lame, crazy or lazy – somehow we made it out of that one. We also picked up weapons and signed out kits, and at last the finish line was in sight.

Then, one evening, while I was home in Virginia, my brother Denny called to let me know that Dad had been admitted to the emergency room at Mary Black Campus Hospital with a suspected urinary tract infection. In the beginning, it did not really seem that serious, but as the days passed, it became clear that it was. I was due to visit Fort Jackson, South Carolina, on the Friday for a meeting of commanders of the 44th Medical Brigade who were preparing to deploy to Afghanistan. I took off on the Thursday afternoon and drove up to Spartanburg.

BY EARLY JANUARY 2011, IT WAS BECOMING clear that my dad was dying. The family gathered at his bedside. The intimate moments that had passed between him and me, the difficult conversations and the stories told and retold, were over. His mind was wandering, and his grasp of the moment was taken away. Throughout the months of my ordeal in Korea, and during the preamble to Afghanistan, he and I had talked almost daily. There was nothing more now that required explanation or affirmation. His boy was a man, his journey was approaching its climax, and he was dying. He understood where the road from here led. He did not want to delay it, to place the burden of expense on the family, or to present himself as a weakened and dying man. He was ready to move on, and it was time.

Beside him stood my mother, his wife of fifty years, along with his children and grandchildren. My mother wrung her hands and faltered on the threshold. In the end, she asked me to do it, and that seemed both right and natural. I asked him if he was ready to see Jesus, and if so, then to raise his right hand. He raised his right hand, and the switch was turned. When taken off that ventilator, Dennis Earl Pike did not remain in this world for very long. With his passing was extinguished the breath of an extraordinary life.

"We had a good run, me and ol' Zekey-Boy," Fred mused sadly when the news reached him. "We had a good run. Lot of fun together, had a lot of fights, goddamn. You got acquaintances, and you got friends. There's a big-ass difference.

'ol Zekey-Boy was my friend. We'd go to war for one another. Done that a couple of times."

In the days that followed, I was calm and accepting. The practicalities absorbed all our energies. It was not until the funeral, when I looked around and saw a large assemblage of people, many that I did not even know, that my grief overwhelmed me. Stories were told and reminiscences shared, and when it came to my turn, I abandoned my prepared speech and unleashed a stream of consciousness, cussing and crying, maybe not really making much sense, as that terrible weight of grief finally settled on me.

Afterward, when the family parted ways, I felt a crippling sense of anxiety. I asked myself if I was fit to take a unit of soldiers into a war zone. A deep pain had settled in my chest, and I was pretty sure that I was having a heart attack. We climbed into my truck and pulled an all-nighter to Fort Belvoir, and there I checked myself into the medical facility. Tests were run and no problems were discovered, so I checked myself out and went home. I found myself behaving with uncharacteristic aggression towards anyone, even on the phone, telling anyone who gave me the slightest irritation or resistance to go fuck themselves, or worse. It was abnormal for me. I spoke to Fred and told him that I did not feel that I could do this. How could I accept a command in a war zone in the state of mind that I was in? I had to resign my command. It was the only responsible thing to do.

He smiled, and asked, "What would ol' Picky boy say to you if he was here? What would he want you to do?"

It was a question that did not really need an answer. I discovered that the elliptical trainer at the gym helped me process my grief. I would get onto that machine and think through the good, the bad and the ugly. I cried on it, got angry on it, and laughed on it. If you saw me on that machine you would think me crazy as hell. That left-right-left process helped me much, ordering my thoughts through a rhythmic and repetitive motion. Over a few weeks, I processed my grief that way, dealt with my anxieties, and then strapped on my boots and made ready to ship out to Afghanistan. I was ready. My only anxiety now lay in leaving Chantel and Beverly for a full year. Since my marriage, and since Chantel's birth, they had been with me through all the highs and the lows. This would be not only my first combat tour, but my first extended period away from them. I was trained for war, but I was not trained for the grief of my father's passing.

AFGHANISTAN

Before you are a leader, success is all about growing yourself. When you become a leader, success is all about growing others.
JACK WELCH

O N A COLD MORNING IN EARLY MARCH 2011, the 452nd Medical Detachment boarded a crowded Air Force C–17 and lifted off from SeaTac International Airport. After a brief layover in Baltimore, which gave me the opportunity to say goodbye to Beverly and Chantel, we took off again to touch down seventeen hours later at the US Transit Center at Manas Airport in northern Kyrgyzstan. Manas Air Base is a significant transfer complex, with soldiers coming and going at all hours from Afghanistan in a massive and bewildering logistical operation. I was amazed at the twenty-four-hour operation, not just the United States, but many other countries coming and going to support their own operations in Afghanistan.

Pretty soon we were processed out, remaining for just a few days before reembarking for a flight over the western Himalayas to land a few hours later at Kandahar Air Base. Almost immediately, we were alerted to the fact that we had arrived in a war zone by a brief mortar and rocket attack.

Although it came as a shock to us tenderfeet, it was greeted by the old-timers at the base as just a routine irritation. Everyone took cover in a bunker and waited for the all-clear before the business of the complex resumed.

A few days were spent in Kandahar dealing with the usual bullshit-laden military bureaucracy before we were airborne again, this time heading west to the Herat Province and the westernmost major US air base at Shindand. Flying in, my initial and overwhelming impression was of brown. The brown landscape—bleak, uniform, and unfeatured—reminded me a little bit of the high deserts of the United States. The base complex of Shindand was also brown; people were dressed in brown, and their skin was tinted a strange yellow color from the dust that was ever present under a constant wind. When I went home on leave in November 2011, Chantel called me *Oompa Loompa* after the dark-skinned dwarves featured in Willy Wonka's Chocolate Factory. There were frequent *shamals*, or spontaneous dust storms, that came out of nowhere, obscuring the sun and getting grit into every damn thing, including hair, clothes, and more. Then you had these waves of dust storms that came through. I recall describing these *shamals* in a roughly scripted oral testimony taken upon my return:

THEY CALL THEM *SHAMAL* EVENTS. Well, a sandstorm. I think you've seen pictures where you have this huge, dark cloud that comes over you. It's just a storm with lots of sand. It's sort of like a blackout. It blocks off the sun, and it's even difficult to walk around in. You sort of just embed down and survive the sandstorm. It's like a wave of wind that occurs every five seconds and it is about sixty miles per hour. It shakes the tents. We were in these Alaskan tents, and we had these bunks, and it would just shake the entire tent. The worst part of the *shamal* is it starts out slow and gets faster and faster, peaking

226

around midnight and subsiding slowly until it dies off at about 3 a.m. If you are outside at all, you are gonna have lots of sand coming up against your legs, whipping against you. You need to be covered up on the legs, definitely covered up. That occurred every day from May to October as a normal weather event. There weren't a lot of things that could survive that. They had roaming dogs out there. I remember walking out to go use the bathroom, and there were these wild dogs just walking around.

THE ONLY VARIATION ON BROWN was the blue sky and an occasional Afghan tribesman crossing the shimmering landscape with a herd of skinny goats. It amazed me that those damn goats could find anything to eat out there. It was a forbidding and inhospitable landscape, its human habitations gathered in low clusters of earthen construction, as brown and featureless as the world around them. They were separated from us by a windswept no man's land, a double chain-link fence, and lines of fortification beyond which we did not venture, and into which they were invited only to work. There was no social interaction, no bars or restaurants, nothing but the sterile routine of military life isolated by hundreds of miles of desert and surrounded by a remote and unfriendly society living in the tenth century.

At a general elevation of above three thousand feet, and with an average humidity of twenty percent, what was known then as Regional Command West lay above the mosquito belt and was not in any real way subject to insect-borne diseases. The issue, therefore, was primarily sanitation in what was a sprawling and vastly expanded Soviet-era airbase, with a handful of scattered satellite bases and combat installations embedded in the surrounding country. We were not required to travel anywhere overland, which minimized the danger and associated stress, but moved between the various camps by helicopter.

These were either military Black Hawks or contracted helicopters that were similar.

The town of Shindand is really nothing more than a shattered remnant of an ancient frontier post on the central Asian steppes, a waypoint along the old Silk Road. It is about fifty miles east of the border with Iran and perhaps two hundred miles northwest of Kandahar. The nearest significant city is Herat, capital of Herat Province, within which lies Shindand District. Beyond the precincts of armed camps and bases, it was Taliban country, and by the time we landed, the war had arrived at a point of unspoken stalemate. Before deployment, we were given a basic history lesson on Afghanistan, the fabled "graveyard of empires," a medieval society of tribal complexion that had proved itself ungovernable to generations of outside rulers. The British occupied Afghanistan twice, first in 1829 and again in 1878, in both instances as part of a complex interplay between British India and Imperial Russia, and on both occasions, it proved to be a disaster. The epic retreat from Kabul in 1842 claimed the lives of upwards of twelve thousand British troops and civilians in what remains arguably the worst defeat in British military history. In 1979, the Soviet Union invaded Afghanistan and quickly came to regret it, getting bogged down and only extricating itself in 1989. In 2001, it was our turn.

The hidden message to us, as the latest major power to get embroiled in Afghanistan, was that this was a war without end, without goals and without any real hope of long-term success. Beyond the wire and the revetments lay a bleak landscape containing almost nothing recognizable to a Western soldier, or an American consumer. I would not go so far as to say that we felt that we were wasting our time, but we were certainly under no illusion that we were doing any good or changing the world in any way for the better. My advice to my soldiers was simply to do their job well for the sake of their comrades and nation and to go home with a good evaluation and a combat patch. On a more practical level, my advice was to use their time wisely and save their money while they had no opportunity to spend it. Although a few of my soldiers expressed regret that they would not be kicking in doors with the infantry, we got on with the job at hand and counted down the days.

WHENEVER I AM ASKED, "What is military preventive medicine?" my answer is usually that it looks a lot like your own local public health department. The mantra of a field preventive medicine unit is to "break the chain of disease transmission." The 452nd Medical Detachment, and the field of preventive medicine in general, has a long tradition in the United States Armed Forces. Work in the field typically involves the inspection of facilities and the submission of recommendations that are then either passed up the chain of command or brought to the attention of local commanders, who then implement those recommendations themselves or bring in contractors. The aim of this work is to ensure the highest possible standards of sanitation and hygiene to prevent the localized spread of disease. This is no different from the work of a health inspector in commercial catering back home. The targets of inspections tend to be everyday threats such as water quality, food service sanitation, air quality, soils, culturally endemic diseases, entomology, vector surveillance, and general sanitation in areas where soldiers eat, sleep, and play.

Most of my work was done just getting to Afghanistan. On arrival my soldiers knew what to do, and they really needed no assistance. I used to joke with my First Sergeant Malisha Palmer that she could do my job easily, and she would reply that she really could not. I held the rank, and, of course, the authority, but in practical terms a monkey could do my job, because I had done so much coordination and training before I even got to Afghanistan. The goal of a commander is to have

229

his or her unit so well trained that they have nothing to do. That is the Jesus level. It is never going to happen, but that is the goal.

The work was routine, moving between camps by helicopter, and similar in many respects to my previous medical detachments, with the main differences being that this time it was in a combat zone. Teams were assigned sectors and locations and traveled by air to undertake inspections. Insect-borne diseases were almost nonexistent, and by the time we arrived in-theater, the various protocols of camp sanitation and hygiene had been long established, so it was simply a case of ensuring compliance and drawing attention to areas that required attention. In a remote and inaccessible region of a remote and inaccessible country, it was mainly water quality and general base-site assessments that occupied our time. We would input these base-site assessments into the DOERS system. Much of the work was also in instruction and education—keeping soldiers alert to the risks and aware of potential problems and giving them the necessary tools. A simple example would be ensuring that soldiers sleep a certain distance from one another to limit the spread of colds, flu, and other respiratory infections. To make sure that the toilet facilities are a certain distance away from where the soldiers eat or sleep.

The 452nd Medical Detachment had under its purview about seven thousand personnel, including Coalition forces and civilians scattered across nineteen camps within our area of operations. Only one site, Bala Murghab, or BMG, was found to be conspicuously lacking in sanitation and hygiene. BMG was a typical remote fighting base, located in the high mountains close to the border of Turkmenistan, in a kind of no man's land, known to its rotating garrison as the "land of the forgotten soldier." It lay under almost constant mortar and rifle fire from adjacent Taliban positions and was only practically accessible by air. It was supplied by regular airdrops and could be cut off from the outside world for long periods during the winter. Although there are numerous epic sagas of war told about BMG, and the operations to secure and retain it, it was a grim and filthy place. Portable toilets were rarely swapped out and were all overflowing and fly-ridden, with garbage at absolute capacity. It was so remote and inaccessible, and so dangerous and overcrowded, that just keeping up with basic hygiene and sanitation was almost impossible. We visited and took pictures of it and pushed it aggressively up the chain of command, eventually landing a report on a high-level desk in Bagram. It took a robust intervention to get contractors in there to clean it up and implement basic protocols, but once we were successful, word got around and we rarely suffered from a lack of help and cooperation. The cleanup of BMG was an aggressive intervention, and a real feather in our cap.

We were not a combat unit, we were combat service support, so the only action we saw was the periodic mortar and rocket attacks that were less frequent in Shindand than in Kandahar, and generally seen as less a threat than an inconvenience. Usually they were Chinese mortars, and typically they came in between dusk and late evening, I would say between five and nine o'clock, maybe ten o'clock. They were timed by a crude delay system, which involved a water bottle tied to a stick with a pinprick hole that slowly drained the water. At a certain point, the device was triggered and fired in a very general direction. Mostly they landed on the airfield, and only once can I recall that the dining hall was hit and set on fire. No one was ever hurt that I can remember. One morning, I was walking back from the mess hall to my office when a Humvee patrolling the perimeter fence was completely destroyed by an IED. It was a hellish explosion, and the vehicle was destroyed, and everyone in it was killed. I do recall that the plume of dust went way up into the air.

Like most field commanders, I had two computers in my office. The first was on a NIPER, or *Nonsecure Internet Protocol Router* network, and the second on a SIPER, or *Secret Internet*

Protocol Router. All secret or sensitive information came through over the SIPER. One morning, information was circulated on SIPER that a suicide bomber had infiltrated the base. The first line of defense against an attack like that was the dogs, and as I stepped out of my tent with my Beretta M9 locked and loaded, I looked around and noticed that the dogs and their handlers were on high alert. I took a walk around, saying nothing to alert the soldiers, searching for something that might look like a suicide bomber, but I found nothing. I was locked and loaded an prepared to kill. A little later it was reported that he had left the base and blown himself up at another installation closer to Herat.

Day-to-day life was routine-driven and predictable, with nothing much to do other than work, work out, walk around the base and watch Netflix. On a normal day, I would be out of bed at around four-thirty or five o'clock in the morning, have coffee, check my inbox to make sure there was no crisis to deal with, check my phones, and briefly check in with headquarters. I might do a video call with my daughter or my wife, check on regular email, personal email, drink more coffee, work out, eat breakfast, and then come back to my desk to deal with my everyday administrative activities. Once or twice, I did go out with some of my soldiers on a camp inspection, but pretty quickly, I figured out that was a waste of my time. They knew what to do. They had great enlisted leadership. One time I visited a camp and was stuck out in no man's land for about three weeks due to weather. I cannot overemphasize the importance of a commander remaining at all times in contact with his unit by a reliable system of communications. It was just not practical or necessary for me to be absent and incommunicado, out wandering around base camps in the remote countryside.

An interesting fact worth reporting is that during my time in Afghanistan, I lost ten pounds, despite eating more than I ever had as an adult or a teenager. I ate not only all the regular helpings but, uncharacteristically for me, I got into pies, cakes, peanut butter, and chocolate. My friend and previous supervisor, Lt. Col. Mitchell Myers, a public health doctor then serving in Thailand, would regularly send me Thai tobacco. I would often sit outside in the evenings smoking that tobacco and watching all the unmanned aerial aircraft going in and out. I checked my cholesterol while I was over there and it was off the chart!

First Sergeant Palmer and I worked very closely together, and as I had sensed from the very beginning, she was my guardian angel. Once a week, I briefed my higher headquarters on our status and how we were doing through a satellite linkup that rarely if ever worked. Telephone and video communications were notoriously unreliable. Typically, when contact was made, the message was simply, "All is well," and that was that. Any additional orders or extra guidance came in by email, which did work. My supervisor was in the Marine Corps base at Camp Dwyer in the Helmand Province. An Army chaplain based in Shindand created a sort of cigar club where many folks would get together and talk about the Bible and smoke cigars. He had a poster put up around camp that said "come smoke cigars and talk about religion". I found it quite unique that a high-ranking officer was promoting a nicotine product on post by way of religion, but I am attracted to that type of thing, and I became a regular, developing a taste for cigars that remains with me.

One thing I vividly recall was the day counts. Stepping off the aircraft at Kandahar, I heard the comment, "I've got twenty days." That meant twenty days until the end of a tour. There was a hierarchy that I am sure every soldier in every foreign deployment is a part of. The longer you have on your ticket, the lower down that pecking order you are. With three hundred days to go, I felt pretty inadequate, but I felt much better with my Oompa Loompa complexion and twitching edginess when it came to my turn to say, "I've got twenty days."

There were, of course, many twists and angles to this routine. One was, "I got one hundred days and a shit!" The typical reply was, "No! You done shit, so that is one hundred and one days."

One time while I was in Kandahar, a soldier tried to salute me, but I took off, and then came back later and said to him, "Don't ever salute me in combat, because I want to get home alive!"

Our training is never to identify senior officers in war, for the simple reason that snipers are always on the lookout for high-value targets. It is unusual in a war zone for the formality of saluting to be mandatory. His response was, "That is command policy in Kandahar." And he was correct.

I said, "I don't care about command policy; my damn policy is to stay alive, so do not salute me!"

THE ONLY SERIOUS ISSUE TO disturb the smooth, professional function of the unit was disciplinary. Having conducted an investigation in Virginia, and been the subject of an investigation in Korea, I now found myself dealing with exactly the same type of issue from the top down. Captain Vasquez, aggravated at being passed over for command, refused to accept the fact and adopted a policy of undermining the unit and being subversive. When that did not stir up a reaction (we just bypassed him), he fell back on just making himself as disagreeable as possible. At the onset of the deployment, I dispatched him to Camp Stone in western Herat, to get him away from the unit, where he was assisted by Sgt. Yira Rodriguez. While life at Shindand was ordered and routine, with Sgt. First Class Malisha Palmer running a tight and efficient ship, from Camp Stone came a steady stream of communications indicating that all was not well up there.

I have seen toxic leadership. Toxic leadership is a reality. The military establishment has a specific doctrine when defining and dealing with a toxic command environment. Army Doctrine Publication 6-22, *Army Leadership and the Profession*, deals with this specific aspect of military leadership, defining the characteristics of toxic leadership under several bullet points. It does somewhat stand to reason that, with such a complex system of a chain of command with strictly defined hierarchies, leadership abuses and excesses will surface often. I have seen them often in my thirty-one years. It horrifies me. Leadership is a subtle art. It is partly learned and part instinct, and the difference between regular and irregular forces is often defined by the quality of leadership. In a regular, constituted army, where discipline is unquestioning, poor leadership can survive and endure for the duration of a bad commander's career. As I mentioned earlier, senior officers are often very difficult to get rid of. In an irregular force, the Taliban, for example, where fighters are villagers and tribesmen united by a common cause, leadership is anointed by common consent, and that consent can be withdrawn at the moment that a commander loses the confidence and respect of his detachment. Not so the Armed Forces of the United States.

Chapter 8-49 of *Army Leadership and the Profession* has this to say on the subject of abusive leadership, "Abusive behaviors—includes behaviors that involve a leader exceeding the boundaries of their authority by being abusive, cruel, or degrading others. These behaviors are contrary to what is required for the moral, ethical, and legal discharge of their duty. Specific examples include, but are not limited to, bullying, berating others for mistakes, creating conflict, ridiculing others because of the authority held, domineering, showing little or no respect to others, insulting or belittling individuals, condescending or talking down to others, or retaliating for perceived slights or disagreements."

Although my experience in Korea was certainly an example of toxic leadership in precisely this context, it was subtly planned, and with a specific objective in mind. That scenario was characterized by the efforts of one man, through his circle of influence, to discredit and remove me, an officer. Ted Small was an intelligent, accomplished and devious character who made very effective use of the system. In Afghanistan, I watched the same blunt instrument of leadership abuse, as defined above, play out between my S.Sgt. Yira Rodriguez and Capt. José Vasquez, who had to date been such a royal pain in the ass.

His assumption that he was in line to command the detachment was derailed when an active-service PROFIS officer was seconded in ahead of him. He had probably acted on that assumption and put the word out, and so it could only have been a humiliation for him to be passed over. He made this fact known to me, and I asked him what the hell I was supposed to do? Did he expect me, a lieutenant colonel, active service and two ranks ahead of him, to act as *his* executive officer? He had been in uniform for twenty-years and could speak and write no English. I used a Google translate app to do the best I could. Discipline in the Army Reserve is less rigid than in the regular ranks, and so although he could not show overt indiscipline, he could very easily make life difficult, and he did.

Yira Rodriguez was an excellent staff sergeant, dedicated, hard-working, and diligent. She was of Cuban origin, and Captain Vasquez was Puerto Rican, and although I had no idea at the time, traditionally among Latin American immigrant communities there has been friction between these two. Cubans are seen as industrious and upwardly mobile, while Puerto Ricans tend to be more laid back and easygoing. I don't know if this factored into it in any way, but Captain Vasquez seemed to dislike Sergeant Rodriguez, who was loyal to me, and immediately targeted her for an onslaught of petty antagonism. Once again, the same old formula played out. Accusations were vague and difficult to substantiate, centering on perceived racism, favoritism, and insubordination. Inevitably, he was kept out of the loop, not out of any direct effort to provoke him, but just because it was easier not to have to deal with him.

My leadership style was to trust the chain of command and allow NCOs to do their job with a minimum of interference. I had done the Five Ps and my soldiers knew what to do. They were all professionals; their training had been done, and once in the field, I expected them to do their jobs with as little counseling and direction as possible. I felt that it was better, as these petty issues began to crop up between them, to just let them work it out themselves rather than impose a Big Brother solution from above. This is usually a workable system in the field of preventive medicine. Preventive medicine is a procedure-driven, administrative discipline that does not often demand the kind of forward leadership necessary in a combat unit. Although I became aware of the antagonism and victimization of Staff Sergeant Rodriguez, there was not very much in the short term that I could do about it. Naturally, I suffered uncomfortable flashbacks to my own experience in Korea, and because of that I felt an instinctive empathy towards her, and I was absolutely on her side. I counseled him numerous times, sometimes speaking bluntly and sternly, but none of it seemed to have any effect. In the end, over five written counseling reports were signed by him and filed. I felt that I was talking to a rock! I did the very best that I could under the circumstances.

On July 23, 2011, Sergeant Rodriguez telephoned into the control room at Shindand in evident distress, pleading with Sergeant First Class Palmer and me to come to Camp Stone to address a serious problem. The following day we flew to Camp Stone and found that all was indeed not well. After a two-and half-hour meeting with Captain Vasquez and Staff Sergeant Rodriguez, I concluded that Vasquez was a very troubled character and easily identifiable as the source of the problem. What follows is an abridged version of the notes I took that day.

CPT [CAPTAIN] VASQUEZ and I had a 2.5-hour conversation today, and at times it was heated, one may find a few interesting notes not captured in my counseling.

1. **Investigations:** He is threatening an IG [Army Inspector General] complaint against me, and when asked I why he said, "It is personal," and I responded, "Go ahead." Additionally, he is threatening an EO [Equal Opportunity] complaint against CSM [Command Sergeant Major] Motes due to comment about "horrific grammar" in a previous email and he feels offended by a comment made by CSM Motes. I explained to him that we are leaders in war, and my intent is to keep our eyes on our soldiers and the mission. He then said, "After all this is over," by which I believe he means after the deployment, he will initiate the complaints/investigations. I have reason to believe he would begin work while here in Afghanistan and then find his contacts in Florida to get them processed.

2. CPT Vasquez enjoys speaking about a past IG complaint where a particular SFC [sergeant first class] in Puerto Rico said his wife was dumb in an email, and this he states was the primary reason why the IG investigation was successful. He talks about going to Puerto Rico and finding that SFC and kicking the crap out of him on the street. When he talks of this IG complaint, he speaks in a tone that appears pleasing. I hear different parts of this same IG complaint in our casual conversations each time I talk to CPT Vasquez either at Camp Stone, Mobilization site, or other events.

3. He has self-referred himself to CST (Combat Stress Control) since May 11 and does state he has issues emotionally. He said it is "you guys' fault." I assume HQ 452nd Medical Detachment, Shindand. He showed me a prescription of Ambien prescribed at a later date. The first I heard he self-referred himself was in June and not May. In June, after the firearms incident, a CST

238

provider called me (apparently he discharged a firearm accidentally) Now I learn the firearms incident was an incident and not an investigation. CPT Vasquez says he has been in Combat Stress since May 11, which is news to me. I was of the understanding given by a CST provider that it was June. I praised him for this and asked him to continue.

4. He provided me past OERs [Officer Evaluation Reports] and his resume that he wants me to read. This I assumed was an attempt to shed light on his record as a good soldier since in the very recent past. COL Darnauer has provided some substantive information in a 16 September 2011 memorandum that questions his behavior as possibly destructive to a soldier and in fact I concur with the memorandum. Not adhering to the chain of command was discussed and the importance of using a chain of command.

5. SSG Packer came as well to Shindand to pick up some cold-weather gear, where we learned he brings his breakfast into the office just like SSG Rodriguez did, and it is not a problem with CPT Vasquez. This adds to inconsistencies in CPT Vasquez's stories about personal grievances with his subordinates and continues me to question his honesty.

6. **Wine in the room.** He denies knowing about wine in the room of SSG Rodriguez until SSG Packer found it during the inventory.

7. **OCONUS travel**. He denies traveling to Jamaica on R&R travel.

FOR MOST OF OUR DISCUSSION, I tried to shed light on the core issue, which is his mental health, in my opinion. NCO Evaluation Reports, Memorandum of Reprimand, MFRs, and other problems are just symptoms coming out of a core issue, and I praised him for going to CST, Combat Stress Control, and encouraged him to stay with it. I explained the common denominator of events without going into detail in each event to point light to the core area. CPT Vasquez attempts to fight off each problem, as it is someone else's problem. I told him the common denominator is you. I do not believe he understands my counseling about core problem areas, as he is in a self-survival mode of reacting to "he-said, she-said" or "he-wrote, she-wrote" battle areas while not making an effort to understand the overall issue. My conclusion is that CPT Vasquez is a very troubled soldier.

In the end, I pulled the entire detachment out of Camp Stone on the logic that it was winter. The region served by Camp Stone had become mostly inaccessible, and everything necessary to prepare for the next unit to move in was in place. Captain Vasquez was shipped out early on medical grounds with the award of a less-than-best military commendation. That seemed to put an end to it, and when an Inspector General's complaint was submitted, it had to do with racism. I was briefly interviewed by a member of the IG's staff, at the same rank as I, and I rejected all and any accusations of racism. That was the last I heard of it. I did not even have to sign a form. The word that came back through the grapevine was that Vasquez battled with alcohol for a few years and was eventually processed out with the rank of major.

I guess this story has a few morals. The first is that authority can be a tool or a weapon, it just depends on the circumstances and the nature of the man or woman in command. Toxic leadership and the abuse of authority is a fact of life in the uniformed services, in just the same way as it is in any large bureaucracy—civil, military, or corporate. In the military, however, the effect of it can be devastating and much more difficult to deal with. Sgt. Yira Rodriguez was not in a position to simply walk off the job, and mid-ranking and senior officers can be very difficult to indict and get rid of. While Captain Vasquez would have been removed from an executive position if he had been in business or the civil service, in the Army, his behavior was noted but overlooked, and his promotion went ahead as scheduled. The emphasis lies on command leadership in any situation to deal with such a state of affairs, and I think, bearing in mind that I had seen the phenomenon from both sides, I had a better handle on it than most. In the end, the issue was handled with a minimum of institutional fallout or recrimination. I signed off on Sergeant Rodriguez's package to become a Second Lieutenant, and I am very proud of this!

In Kandahar, as we were preparing to ship out, a large ceremony was held in a hangar where ranks of servicemen and women were awarded the Bronze Star for their service in Afghanistan. The Bronze Star Medal is typically awarded for heroic service, meritorious achievement, or meritorious service in a combat zone and is not an automatic award for simply serving in a war zone. A Bronze Star was pinned on my chest as an award for command in a time of war, and I recommended that Sgt. Malisha Palmer be similarly awarded, and she was.

WINDING DOWN

There is no real ending. It's just the place where you stop the story.
FRANK HERBERT

I HAD EVERY REASON TO BELIEVE AS I returned to the United States after a successful tour in Afghanistan that I would be promoted to full colonel. My Officer Evaluation Report was the best I had ever filed. At the top of the report sheet, before any other comments are made, three tick-boxes determine standards of performance and recommendations for promotion. They typically are: "Unsatisfactory performance, do not promote"; "Satisfactory performance, promote"; and "Outstanding performance, must promote." The box ticked on my OER was the last of these. In addition, in the various comments, it was remarked, "Promote immediately. LTC Pike has the absolute potential to serve the Army Medical Department as a COL. He should be placed in another command position of even greater responsibility. Select for resident Senior Service College."

Strangely, there was a big part of me that did not want to go down that road. In so many ways I was done with the Army after Afghanistan. It was the Korean investigation fiasco, then my ad's death and then Afghanistan. It was a one, two, three punch in a short amount of time. Just not quitting was a huge accomplishment. Promotion to full colonel would require an ongoing commitment to serve in the Army and I was not sure that I wanted to do that. Afghanistan was a ringing endorsement of the Five Ps. The net result of that was a flawless execution over there. Every member of my team, with one notable exception, had performed well, and the results were acknowledged and remarked upon. It was the climactic moment of my career, and a damned good time to quit. I now found the Human Resources Command, those folks in Washington, DC, much easier to deal with. That ol' turd on my plate had been flushed away, and the stink was gone. I had redeemed myself. It is an unwritten rule that when you come out of a war zone, they offer you a handshake and the thumbs up on a sweet assignment.

SHIPPING OUT OF AFGHANISTAN was a lot like shipping in, except it was much easier because everybody wanted to get the hell out of there. We were laid over briefly in Kandahar before flying out to Manas and on to the US airbase at Royal Air Force Mildenhall in England. There I drank my first beer in a good long while. From England, we flew directly to Dallas, where we were met by a reception party organized to welcome the troops home. They were screaming and yelling and waving flags and making us all feel like rock stars. That is Texas for you. From there, I caught a scheduled flight to Washington-Baltimore, where I was reunited with Beverly and Chantel. I felt very happy. I felt so sharp and strong. I could have picked up Chantel and took her all the way back home with my backpack on. I used up some leave that I had stacked up and we took a quick vacation to the Dominican Republic, after which I faced the question of where to go from here.

In the short term, I was placed back in Aberdeen Proving Ground, Maryland, the Chipmunk, under the supervision of Tom Burroughs with the choice to either stay there or take up a position on offer in Germany. Germany was a three-year assignment, and I had it in mind to cut that back to two years and retire. We took a family vote, and both the girls voted to go to Germany—Beverly for the travel opportunity and Chantel because Beverly wanted to go. I had never been to Europe (except briefly to Italy in the National Guard), and it was an opportunity. I would not be serving in the capacity of an entomologist as much as an environmental science officer, which was a step up for me personally and a move in a different and interesting direction. I accepted the assignment and in the fall of 2012 began making preparations.

Something interesting is the fact that, even though I shared my plans with no one, I received two or three emails from the CIA—authentic and verifiable communications—inviting me to join the organization. I thought that was pretty strange. I guess they have spooks combing emails to identify retiring officers, and then they throw out the net to try and bring in men and women with training and skills.

A number of my peers, including Tom Burroughs, expressed surprise that I was given an assignment in Germany. I guess that my work in Afghanistan was noted. The BMG operation, coordinated on the ground by Sgt. Yira Rodriguez, was an achievement within the context of the Medical Department, and I think as it made its way up the chain of command it certainly was noticed. It is tough to conceptualize just how bad the situation was up there, with soldiers living in filth, portable toilets overflowing with shit and toilet paper and a burn pit piled high with trash. It was a cesspool, and getting it in order was a logistical achievement that was probably seen as a feather in all of our caps. It also would have reflected very well on higher command, and they like that sort of thing.

In August 2012, my orders came through, and within a couple of weeks, we were in transitional accommodation in Landstuhl, looking around for a place to rent. Landstuhl is a sprawling facility, the headquarters of US military medical services in Germany and the location of the main US military hospital. It is situated just outside the Ramstein Air Base, which is the main US military installation in the country. We found a place in a small village nestled in the surrounding hill country, and after settling Chantel in the Landstuhl Base middle school, we established ourselves and made ourselves comfortable for the duration.

My role, once again, was in staff capacity (chief of risk management, US Army Public Health Command, Region–Europe). This was a different name for the old Chipmunk. I was supervising a group of officers whose job it was to map and monitor sites and locations related to US military activity, mostly to keep up an ongoing database and fortify the military and the government against any future environmental liabilities. It was a different environment from Korea for the reason that life was less encircled by the base and more open to general travel and exploration. Schools and social institutions were definitely part of base life, but it was common for officers to live off base, and since English is widely spoken, it is easy to integrate and get involved in local life, society, and culture. Landstuhl is located close to the borders of France and Austria, so we were able to regularly visit both for skiing in the winter and hiking and sightseeing in the summer.

Col. Mitch Meyers showed up on a separate assignment soon after we arrived, and since we had become close friends after events in Korea, our families teamed up and got in some travel. We visited Israel and different parts of Europe, as well as Britain and Ireland, once spending a week in Prague, where an interesting thing happened.

Chantel and I went on a Segway tour of the city, and I noticed a small and corpulent man who seemed to be taking an unusual interest in us. I was pretty sure he had identified me as a US serviceman and would try to make some sort of approach. I told Chantel he would probably try to engage her in conversation and ask about me, who I was, and where I worked. Sure enough, he did. She was then, as she still is, a confident and forthright girl, and she was old enough to bullshit, and she did. I am not sure who he was or what he was interested in, besides generally mining for information for whatever reason. It does happen. Officers arriving in Europe are usually given a security brief warning us about those kinds of encounters, and probably I should have taken Chantel into the security office to report the encounter, but I did not.

And that was how the final two years of my military career were spent. I was pretty much done. In the spring of 2014, I was awarded the Legion of Merit which, according to my commendation, was for "Exceptionally meritorious conduct in various positions of great responsibility during the period 1 October 2004 to 30 September 2014." It so happened that Sgt. Malisha Palmer, friend and colleague in two deployments, was also stationed at Landstuhl, and between her and my senior supervisor, a ceremony was organized to honor the occasion. That is the award that means the most to me, even more than my Bronze Star, and was a fitting way to wrap up a thirty-one-year active service career in the US Army. In May 2014, while I was on transitional leave, and we were back in San Antonio looking for a house and planning life post-military life, I received a phone call from my brother Denny that I had been anticipating for some time.

My mother, having survived brain and lung cancer, was now dying of pancreatic cancer. She needed twenty-four-hour care, and my brother asked me if I would come up from Texas and help with the task. I did. The experience of watching my mother die was less emotional and traumatic than it had been watching my father. I felt a strange sense of peace as she was going through chemotherapy sessions, and dying. She was living in the house in Boiling Springs that she had shared with my father before he died. Her condition was terminal; she knew it, and we knew it, and so her treatment was palliative and without any expectation of recovery. I recall her then, as always, displaying an iron will. She was tough. As a family, we discussed an assisted-living environment and toured a few facilities, but in the end, we decided to bring home-care in. With typical exactitude, she fired all her home-care professionals – at that time I though I might get fired too – until we decided to bring in Diane Cole, who had overseen and handled my father's end of life.

I recall finding peace in the moment. I camped out in the spare room of the house and found that I slept more deeply and more restfully there than I had for very long time. My mother was a woman with whom I had always had a challenging relationship, without the easy camaraderie and common ground that I had always enjoyed with my father. While I would not say that the divide was completely bridged, we did settle on common ground, and when it ended, it ended well. On 17 October 2014, at the age of seventy-six, she crossed the mortal horizon. Her memorial was not as widely celebrated as my father. It was in the end a quiet, intimate, and private affair.

CONCLUSION

Compound interest is the eighth wonder of the world. He who understands
it, earns it ... he who doesn't ... pays it!
ALBERT EINSTEIN

I N LATE 2020, AS THE FIRST WAVES OF COVID–19
were beginning to make a serious impact, like just about
everybody else, I found myself sitting at home in San
Antonio, Texas, without a whole lot to do. At about the same
time, a new administration took office under the leadership of
President Joe Biden, which prompted a liberalization of controls
at the southern border, and an immediate rush of illegal migrants
and asylum seekers attempting to cross into the United States.
This created an immediate and double-layered health crisis at the
border, in particular in regard to the tens of thousands of
unaccompanied minors. The issue very quickly emerged as a hot
political potato, and suddenly the Centers for Disease Control
and Prevention, the CDC, became the busiest agency across the
spectrum of US administrative departments.

Initially, I volunteered to return to the Army under my
current rank of lieutenant colonel to support the Covid effort
within the Army, but I think there were probably just too many
retired senior officers doing the same, and I was not invited to

do so. However, hundreds of positions with the CDC opened up on the USA Jobs website, in particular calling for members of the military with preventive medicine and public health background and experience. It seemed like an obvious segue from military to civilian service, and doing the Five Ps, I got all my papers and resume together and fired out a massive email blast to every damn advertisement out there. I think I even applied to be a police officer in Greenland.

Although most of these applications, ninety-five plus percent, were ignored, and some were failed, a few bullets hit the target, and on the principle that beggars can't be choosers, I ran with the first solid offer I got. It was a two-year temporary position as a public health analyst, and it turned out to be telework. Hell, everyone was doing telework at that time. I figured that I could stay at home, crunch numbers, and draw money, and initially, that is what I did.

I was kind of surprised that the CDC was not more of a natural progression from one federal agency into another, but the question I was asked often was who did I know? And that's how you get in. It is not so much what you know as who you know. As it turns out, I did not know many people, and to compensate for that, I just went with the machine gun blast approach. In the same way as the CIA trawled the military for likely retiring officers to recruit, I figured the federal health agencies would be the same, but I guess not.

However, when you are in, you are in, and the really interesting stuff began to happen as things commenced to get crazy at the border. The job on the southern border came up in March 2021. The idea of working with children appealed to me in a significant way, and I jumped on it. I applied for it maybe five or six times and kept getting the runaround, until finally, maybe because of my sheer persistence, I got it. I guess because of the heavy political overtones to the situation and the fact that the southern border is kind of an open political sore pretty much all the time, the layers of procedure and process necessary to gain clearance was damned incredible. It took months for various clearances to run through the system, particularly criminal screening for any type of past malfeasance of any kind with kids. There was a zero-defect requirement, as it should be, and I wondered a few times as things were delayed if shit was still circulating through the system about what went down in Korea. In the end I was cleared and headed down to Fort Bliss in El Paso, Texas.

The kids coming in were mostly from central America—El Salvador, Guatemala, and Nicaragua—and being pushed up a pipeline run by *coyotes*, who are people smugglers, and dumped on the southern border to qualify as unaccompanied minors. The screening and processing operation took place, and at the time of writing was still taking place, in a compound within the Fort Bliss complex, surrounded by a forty-foot wall and run like a military encampment. A rotating, twenty-four-hour staff of about four thousand people ran the operation, with the numbers of kids varying from about a minimum of two hundred to a probable maximum of two or three thousand. Typically, they arrive on base on a big, air-conditioned bus to be disembarked at an in-processing center. There they are photographed and given IDs before being Covid tested, health screened, and admitted. They given mandatory shots against flu, measles, mumps, and rubella, and a Covid shot if they wanted one (a lot of them did have Covid), and any health care that they need. I found that most of them were malnourished to some degree, smaller in stature than most American kids, and often with lice and intestinal parasites. They would then be assigned to dormitories—females and males segregated—and processed through case management. The goal is to get them out to a family member or a sponsor in the United States. Case management is a huge logistical, number-crunching operation that deals with tens of thousands, maybe hundreds of thousands of cases at any one time.

I though often about my dad as I was working this assignment with the children. I know that he would not have been able to stand watching the kids coming across the border in this way. This was kind of like his life. He was an orphan and he was barefoot and had been mistreated growing up. I broke down and I cried and could not sleep one night because of the memories of my father. It was about the kids, but it was also about my dad as well.

After they are in-processed, their day-to-day existence is just like any other kid's. They get up; they have breakfast; they do classes and have entertainment. Their freedom is limited because they are contained in a complex, and they are watched over twenty-four hours a day. If they have to get up in the night and go to the toilet, someone has to go with them and keep an eye on them. They are mostly if not all Spanish-speaking, and there are Spanish-speaking people around all the time. There was no real opportunity to hang out with them, get out on the field and kick a ball around, and I think if I had tried, I would have been shut down quicker than a heartbeat and on the bus back to San Antonio. It is kind of a shame, but that's how the operation was run. It is basically a number-crunching operation, run tighter than the military, with briefings and stats and a whole lot of desk work. Not that different to a day on base in Afghanistan, and it even looked like Afghanistan, although the standard of hygiene and cleanliness were exceptional.

The moral of this quick and concluding story is just that life after retirement as a medical officer with the US Army is rich with possibilities. There is no higher standard of trained personnel out there for the front-line roles of disease prevention and public health that those who passed through the military. The Centers for Disease Control and Prevention is just one of many agencies and organizations that take on this role, and they are always on the lookout for people with the expertise, discipline and organizational experience offered by the military.

AFTER A FEW YEARS OF MILITARY RETIREMENT, and having worked the Five Ps, and all the indoctrination heaped onto me by my father—compound interest and all—I established a well-rounded and healthy investment portfolio. I owe my career to the military, all my training and most of my education, and now it is time to give back. One of the recipient organizations that I am currently involved with is Upstate Warrior Solution, a nonprofit out of Greenville, South Carolina, whose mission is to provide help to veterans of all stripes, including Reserve members, to access all the many and various benefits that are available. In exchange for this support, a room at a new transitional center is to be dedicated and named after my father, and his Navy and Marine Corps medal displayed. Other similar organizations include the Wounded Warrior Project, a very well-known body providing help and assistance to injured and disabled veterans; Canyon Heroes, an organization that uses water rafting and other water sports as a healing mechanism for disabled veterans; Reel Thanx, which uses sport fishing as a method of contact, association, and healing—and there are others. In 2022, I was a sponsor and a participant of the Disabled American Veterans Association–hosted Disabled American Veterans National Winter Sports Clinic in Aspen, Colorado.

I have donated to my alma mater, Spartanburg Methodist College and Clemson University, and one of my interests is in the evolving idea of integrating a veteran stories project to create a historical archive, overcoming what is almost an institutional reluctance to credit veterans with their experiences, to revitalize traditions of storytelling, and to provide some catharsis for old soldiers in relating the tales and anecdotes of their service. To support that, all the proceeds from the publication of this book will go to these causes.

Made in United States
Orlando, FL
20 August 2023

36272991R00153